Air Fryer Meal Prep

800 Healthy Make-Ahead Meals and Freezer Recipes for Your Busy Family: A Cookbook

Jennifer Newman

Text Copyright © Jennifer Newman

All rights reserved. No part of this guide may be reproduced in any form without permission in writing from the publisher except in the case of brief quotations embodied in critical articles or reviews.

Legal & Disclaimer

The information contained in this book and its contents is not designed to replace or take the place of any form of medical or professional advice; and is not meant to replace the need for independent medical, financial, legal or other professional advice or services, as may be required. The content and information in this book has been provided for educational and entertainment purposes only.

The content and information contained in this book has been compiled from sources deemed reliable, and it is accurate to the best of the Author's knowledge, information and belief. However, the Author cannot guarantee its accuracy and validity and cannot be held liable for any errors and/or omissions. Further, changes are periodically made to this book as and when needed. Where appropriate and/or necessary, you must consult a professional (including but not limited to your doctor, attorney, financial advisor or such other professional advisor) before using any of the suggested remedies, techniques, or information in this book.

Upon using the contents and information contained in this book, you agree to hold harmless the Author from and against any damages, costs, and expenses, including any legal fees potentially resulting from the application of any of the information provided by this book. This disclaimer applies to any loss, damages or injury caused by the use and application, whether directly or indirectly, of any advice or information presented, whether for breach of contract, tort, negligence, personal injury, criminal intent, or under any other cause of action.

You agree to accept all risks of using the information presented inside this book.

You agree that by continuing to read this book, where appropriate and/or necessary, you shall consult a professional (including but not limited to your doctor, attorney, or financial advisor or such other advisor as needed) before using any of the suggested remedies, techniques, or information in this book.

Contents

Part 1: Air Fryer Cookbook

Introduction	6
Chapter 1	
Air Fryer Basics	7
Chapter 2	
Breakfast, Snack and Appetizers Recipes	9
Chapter 3	
Meat (Pork, Beef and Lamb) Recipes	66
Chapter 3	
Poultry Recipes	95
Chapter 4	
Seafood Recipes	117
Chapter 5	
Vegetable Recipes	124
Chapter 6	
Dinner Recipes	162
Conclusion	188

PART-II The Complete Air Fryer Cookbook

Introduction	*190*
1-Anti-Odor/Anti-Grease Filters	*193*
Chapter 1	
Breakfast Recipes	*195*
Chapter 2	
Snacks and Appetizers	*209*
Chapter 3	
Seafood and Fish recipes	*225*
Chapter 4	
Poultry	*256*
Chapter 5	
Beef, Pork, Lamb Recipes	*279*
Chapter 6	
Vegan and Vegetarian Recipes	*302*
Chapter 7	
Desserts	*348*
Conclusion	*398*

PART-I

Air Fryer Cookbook for Beginners

Instant, Healthy, Delicious Recipes

To Fry, Roast, Grill and Bake.

Jennifer Newman

Introduction

An Air Fryer is an appliance that mainly uses a hot air system distributed through fans to cook food. This is how the air fryer works; although it depends on the model, it may vary slightly.

Oil-free fryers help you prepare food more healthily thanks to the fact that they fry through hot air. In a way, these fryers are similar to a miniature oven, cooking food with lots of hot air circulating at high speed. These fryers are known in two forms, oilless fryers or air fryers.

Perhaps you may come to think that oil-free fryers are similar and straightforward devices among all the models that exist. However, when you go to buy an oil-free fryer, it is essential that you take into account some aspects, which differentiate an oil-free fryer from another to make it easier for you to choose the fryer that best suits your needs.

There many benefits when using an air fryer. They are easy to use and clean. They do not cause odor because the air or steam they expel is infinitely less than that of conventional fryers, and of course, the lower consumption of fat and cholesterol in the food must be noted.

In this book, you will find many aspects to consider when it comes to an air fryer. Also, we are going to give you the best tips to choose the best air fryer. And finally, you will find information to clean the air fryer and 200 amazingly easy recipes for fast & healthy meals that anyone can cook.

Enjoy it!

Chapter 1

Air Fryer Basics

Since air fryers appeared, there has been much speculation about their use and guarantees, so the first thing I will clarify for you is what an air fryer is.

If the term Air Fryer sounds like much hot air, your speculations are exactly correct! A better Taurus air fryer is simply a revolutionized kitchen appliance for cooking food through the circulation of superheated air. It is a new Philips invention that offers healthy and tasty food with less oil.

Deep fryers use Rapid Air technology to cook any food that would otherwise soak it in fat. This new technology works by circulating air at high degrees to fry foods such as fish, potatoes, cakes, chicken, etc.

It is necessary to mention that air fryers are very easy to use, so if you have not had a fryer before, you will learn to use it without significant problems. Usually, you only have to follow a few simple steps to get the fryer up and running and cook your favorite dishes in a much healthier way than with a traditional deep fryer.

How to Use it?

The first thing you may be wondering is how is it possible to fry without oil. And it is a half-truth because although oil is necessary to fry, the amount used for cooking is small.

Therefore, it must be clarified that the name "without oil" that it receives is not entirely real, since it is necessary a little. And its operation for cooking food consists mainly of the circulation of hot air at high speed.

Their use could not be more straightforward. It could be said that they are like a miniature oven and much healthier than cooking with much oil.

An air fryer combines several different cooking methods in one conventional appliance.

- An electrical coil suspended above food provides radiant heating, just like a heater. This dry heat penetrates the food and heats it internally.
- Meanwhile, a fan placed above the coil creates a stream of superheated air that flows around and under the food. This is convection heating, a cooking method often found in commercial ovens.
- The action of frying turns the small amount of oil that is used into a fine mist that coats the food while it circulates. This action mimics the effect of a traditional deep fryer.
- As the hot air flows in, the food's moisture creates the steam needed to finish the cooking process.

Advantages of Air Fryers

- There is no mess.
- It is possible to reduce 85% of fat in food.
- You will cook without fumes or odors in the kitchen or on clothes.
- You will save on oil since this type of fryers work without oil, although, as I mentioned before, you can add a teaspoon.
- They do not cause splashing when used.
- They are easier to clean.

Cooking tips

1. To get golden fries quickly and saving several calories, it is convenient to cook them in two stages at different temperatures, first at 660°F and then at 750°F.
2. 2In the case of chicken wings, crispiness results when the skin is covered with baking powder before frying. (As an additional tip, you should know that the baking powder expands with the heat and forms bubbles around the chicken, achieving the crunchy effect.)
3. For the healthiest, veggies are a hit in the air fryer, especially squash, eggplant, and brussels sprouts that finish tender on the inside and crisp on the outside.

Chapter 2

Breakfast, Snack and Appetizers Recipes

Hemp Seed Porridge

Servings: 3

Preparation time: 10 min

Cook time: 15 minutes

Ingredients

- 2 tbsp of flax seeds
- 4 tbsp of hemp seeds
- 1 tbsp butter
- ¼ tsp salt
- 1 tsp of Stevia
- ½ ground ginger

Steps to Cook

1. Place the flax seeds and hemp seeds in a bowl that fits in the basket of the air fryer. Sprinkle the seeds with the salt and ground ginger. Next, combine the almond milk and Stevia. Stir the liquid and pour it into the seed mixture.
2. After this, add the butter
3. Preheat the air fryer to 370^0F and cook the porridge hemp seeds for 15 minutes. Stir carefully after 10 minutes of cooking. When the time is up, remove the porridge from the hem of the fryer basket pan and chill for 3 minutes.

Nutritional Information:

- Calories: 106
- Carbohydrates: 4.2g
- Fat: 18.2g
- Protein: 5.1g

Scrambled Eggs With Streaky Bacon

Servings: 4

Preparation time: 10 min

Cook time: 10 minutes

Ingredients

- 6 oz. Bacon
- 4 eggs
- 5 tbsp heavy cream
- 1 tsp of butter
- 1 tsp of paprika
- ½ tsp of nutmeg
- 1 tsp of salt
- 1 tsp ground black pepper

Steps to Cook

1. Chop the bacon into small pieces and sprinkle with salt. Stir the bacon gently and strain it into the air fryer basket. Cook the chopped bacon in the fryer preheated to 360°F for 5 minutes.
2. Meanwhile, beat the eggs in the bowl and beat well.
3. Sprinkle the beaten egg mixture with the paprika, nutmeg, and ground black pepper.
4. Gently beat the egg mixture.
5. When the time is up, spoon the butter into the chopped bacon and pour in the egg mixture.
6. Add the heavy cream and cook for 2 minutes.
7. Stir the mixture with the help of the spatula until you get the scrambled eggs and cook the dish for another 3 minutes.

Nutritional Information:

- Calories: 387
- Carbohydrates: 2.3g
- Fat: 32.1g
- Protein: 21g

Hash Breakfast

Servings: 4

Preparation time: 8 min

Cook time: 8 minutes

Ingredients

- 1 zucchini
- 7 oz cooked bacon
- 4 oz cheddar cheese
- 2 tbsp of butter
- 1 tsp of salt
- 1 tsp ground black pepper
- 1 tsp of paprika
- 1 tsp of ground thyme

Steps to Cook

1. Chop the zucchini into small cubes and sprinkle with the salt, ground black pepper, paprika, coriander, and ground thyme.
2. Preheat the air fryer to $400°F$ and the butter in the air fryer basket tray.
3. Melt it and add the zucchini cubes
4. Cook the zucchini for 5 minutes.
5. Meanwhile, mash the cheddar cheese
6. When the time is up, shake the zucchini cubes carefully and add the cooked bacon
7. Sprinkle the zucchini mixture with the grated cheese and cook for 3 more minutes.

Nutritional Information:

- Calories: 445
- Carbohydrates: 3.5g
- Fat: 36.1g
- Protein: 26.3g

Green Cheddar Soufflé

Servings: 4

Preparation time: 10 min

Cook time: 8 minutes

Ingredients

- 5 oz. Cheddar cheese
- 3 eggs
- 4 tbsp heavy cream
- 1 tbsp chives
- 1 tbsp of dill
- 1 tsp parsley
- ½ tsp ground thyme

Steps to Cook

1. Break the eggs into the bowl and beat them carefully.
2. Add heavy cream and beat for 10 more seconds.
3. Add chives, dill, parsley, and ground thyme.
4. Sprinkle the egg mixture with the grated cheese and stir
5. Transfer the egg mixture into 4 ramekins and place the ramekins in the basket of the air fryer.
6. Preheat the air fryer to 390°F and cook the souffle for 8 minutes.

Nutritional Information:

- Calories: 244
- Carbohydrates: 1.7g
- Fat: 20.6g
- Protein: 13.5g

Bacon Chocolate Chip Cookies

Servings: 6

Preparation time: 15 min

Cook time: 10 minutes

Ingredients

- 1 egg
- 4 oz. Cooked bacon
- 1 cup of almond flour
- ½ tsp of baking soda
- 1 tbsp apple cider vinegar
- 3 tbsp of butter
- 4 tbsp heavy cream
- 1 tsp dried oregano

Steps to Cook

1. Beat the egg in the bowl and beat it
2. Chop the cooked bacon into small cubes and add it to the beaten egg. Then sprinkle the mixture with the baking soda and apple cider vinegar.
3. Add the heavy cream and dried oregano.
4. Add the butter and almond flour and mix well.
5. When the dough is smooth and runny, the dough is cooked.
6. Preheat the air fryer to 400°F.
7. Pour batter into muffin cups.
8. When the air fryer is preheated, place the muffin shapes in the air fryer basket and cook for 10 minutes. When the time is up, and the muffins are made, remove them from the air fryer.

Nutritional Information:

- Calories: 226
- Carbohydrates: 1.8g
- Fat: 20.5g
- Protein: 10g

Egg Omelette

Servings: 6

Preparation time: 10 min

Cook time: 15 minutes

Ingredients

- 6 eggs
- 1/3 cup heavy cream
- 1 tomato
- ½ onion
- 1 tbsp of butter
- 1 tsp of salt
- 1 tbsp of dried oregano
- 6 oz Parmesan
- 1 tsp of chili

Steps to Cook

1. Beat the eggs in the basket tray of the air fryer.
2. Chop the tomato and cut the onion
3. Add the vegetables to the egg mixture
4. Pour the heavy cream
5. Sprinkle the liquid mixture with butter, salt, dried oregano, and chili.
6. Then crumble the Parmesan cheese and add it to the mixture as well.
7. Sprinkle the mixture with the silicone spatula.
8. Preheat the air fryer to 375^0F and cook the frittata for 15 minutes.

Nutritional Information:

- Calories: 202
- Carbohydrates: 3.4g
- Fat: 15g
- Protein: 15.1g

Chicken Liver Pâté

Servings: 7

Preparation time: 10 min

Cook time: 10 minutes

Ingredients

- 1 lb. Chicken liver
- 1 tsp of salt
- 4 tbsp of butter
- 1 cup of water
- 1 tsp ground black pepper
- 1 onion
- ½ tsp dried coriander

Steps to Cook

1. Chop the chicken liver roughly and place it on the tray of the air fryer basket. Peel the onion and dice it. Pour the water into the air fryer basket pan and add the chopped onion.
2. Preheat the air fryer to 360°F and cook the chicken liver for 10 minutes. When the time is up, strain the chicken liver mixture to discard from the liquid.
3. Transfer chicken liver mixture to a blender.
4. Add the butter, ground black pepper, and dried cilantro. Mix the mixture until you get the texture of the pate.
5. Then transfer the liverwurst into the container and serve immediately or store in the fridge.

Nutritional Information:

- Calories: 173
- Carbohydrates: 2.2g
- Fat: 10.8g
- Protein: 16.1g

Roasted Cherry Tomatoes

Servings: 2-4

Preparation time: 5 min

Cook time: 15 minutes

Ingredients

- ½ lb. cherry tomatoes
- 2 teaspoons of Provencal spices/herbs
- 1 clove garlic, minced
- 2 tbsp of olive oil
- 1 tbsp of Modena balsamic oil
- Salt to taste

Steps to Cook

1. Cut the cherry tomatoes in half.
2. Season them with Provencal spices, minced garlic, salt, olive oil, and balsamic.
3. Place the tomatoes in the deep fryer without oil (using the tray-accessory) and leave them to cook for 15 minutes at $350°F$. Enjoy!

Nutritional Information

- Calories: 30
- Carbohydrates: 6.6g
- Fat: 0.5g
- Protein: 1.5g
- Sugar: 4.8g
- Cholesterol: 0mg

Bread Of Cassava Fluor

Servings: 7

Preparation time: 10 min

Cook time: 35 minutes

Ingredients

- 1 cup of cassava
- 1 cup of brown sugar
- 2 tbsp flour
- 1 tsp ground cinnamon
- 1 egg
- ¼ cup oil
- 1 tbsp butter
- ½ tbsp baking powder
- 2 tbsp of refined sugar
- ½ cup milk
- ½ cup of cottage cheese
- guava strips to taste

Steps to Cook

1. Separate the yolk from the white.
2. Beat the egg white, sweetened with refined sugar, and reserve. Line the bottom of the pan with curd and layer with guava strips.
3. Beat the remaining ingredients in a blender or mixer (except yeast).
4. Add the yeast and mix.
5. Add the egg white and mix it with a spoon.
6. Pour into a greased or nonstick round skillet that will fit in the air fryer.
7. With the air fry already preheated for 5 minutes, put it for 35 minutes at a temperature between 320°F and 350°F. After cooling, turn the plate onto a plate and serve.

Nutritional Information:

- Calories: 75.4
- Carbohydrates: 12.3g
- Fat: 2g
- Protein: 1.9g

Avocado Stuffed With Cheese

Servings: 1-2

Preparation time: 5 min

Cook time: 10 minutes

Ingredients

- 1 avocado
- 4 cherry tomatoes
- 1.7 oz, feta cheese
- 1 chive
- 1 clove garlic
- fresh thyme to taste
- fresh basil to taste
- Salt to taste
- olive oil to taste
- lemon juice to taste

Steps to Cook

1. Dice the tomatoes and feta cheese.
2. Chop the garlic, chives, and thyme well.
3. Mix all the ingredients well and add a tablespoon of olive oil.
4. Cut the avocado in half and remove the pip.
5. Next, we will season the avocado with lemon juice on top,
6. The avocado holes that the pip has left, we will fill with the mixture of tomato, cheese, and spices that we had made at the beginning
7. (If you want, you can also add diced ham or bacon.)
8. Put the two stuffed avocado halves into the Air Fryer (without preheating) and leave to cook for 10 minutes at 350°F.

Nutritional Information

- Calories: 160
- Carbohydrates: 5.8g
- Fat: 14.7g
- Protein: 2g
- Sugar: 0.7g
- Cholesterol: 0mg

Gluten-Free Bread

Servings: 4

Preparation time: 10 min

Cook time: 35 minutes

Ingredients

- 1 egg
- ½ tbsp of oil
- 2 tbsp of milk or water
- 1 tbsp oatmeal
- 1 tbsp chickpea or coconut flour
- 1 tbsp of sweet powder
- 1 tsp baking powder
- a pinch of salt
- Oil for greasing

Steps to Cook

1. In a small bowl, break the egg and beat slightly.
2. Add all the other ingredients, leaving the yeast last.
3. Grease a bowl that fits the basket of the air fryer.
4. Pour in the bread dough and smooth out with a spatula.
5. Bring that to the air fryer previously preheated at 360°F for 30 minutes or until the base is golden brown and the batter has risen.
6. Turn the bread over and leave it until the other side is also golden, always keeping the bowl covered.

Nutritional Information:

- Calories: 120
- Carbohydrates: 17g
- Fat: 6g
- Protein: 3g

French Toast With Ham And Egg

Servings: 1

Preparation time: 5 min

Cook time: 8 minutes

Ingredients

- 1 toast
- 1 egg
- Grated cheese)
- Dices of ham
- Margarine
- Salt
- Pepper

Steps to Cook

1. Crush the inside of the toast with a teaspoon (leaving a frame of 1-2 cm).
2. On the edge that you have left, spread margarine and sprinkle grated cheese on top (only on the frame!) Crush the cheese a little so that it does not fall when putting it later in the basket of the fryer without oil.
3. Then put an egg on the toast and season it to taste with a little salt and pepper. Finally, add some diced ham to the egg white.
4. Preheat the fryer to 360°F and then carefully insert the toast into the basket of the Air fryer. Let cook for 8 minutes at 360°F and ... ready!

Nutritional Information:

- Calories: 199
- Carbohydrates: 14
- Fat: 12g

- Protein: 8.8g
- Sugar: 1.8g
- Cholesterol: 195mg

Whole Wheat Bread

Servings: 2

Preparation time: 10 min

Cook time: 35 minutes

Ingredients

- 2 eggs
- 2 tbsp of water
- 1 tbsp oatmeal
- 2 tbsp whole wheat flour
- 1 pinch of salt
- 1 tsp chia
- 1 tsp baking powder
- Oil for greasing

Steps to Cook

1. In a small bowl, break the eggs and beat slightly.
2. Add water, flour, salt, and chia.
3. Add the yeast and mix.
4. Lightly grease a bow that fits the basket of the air fryer.
5. Pour the batter and spread with a spatula.
6. Cover the bowl and cook at 360^0F for 30 minutes or until the bread rises and turns brown.
7. Turn the bread over and keeping the bowl covered, cook until the other side is also golden.

Nutritional Information:

- Calories: 81
- Carbohydrates: 14g
- Fat: 1.1g
- Protein: 4g

Pizza Balls

Servings: 2

Preparation time: 5 min

Cook time: 15 minutes

Ingredients

- Pizza dough (purchased or homemade)
- Crushed tomato
- Tuna
- cheese
- 3 tbsp of butter
- 1 tbsp of oregano
- 2 cloves of garlic

Steps to Cook

1. Roll out the pizza dough and cut it into squares. A little crushed tomato, cheese, and tuna are placed on each piece.
2. Once the ingredients are added, close the pizza pieces until they form a ball.
3. Finally, we varnish the balls with a little warm butter (to which we have previously added a little oregano and minced garlic). Then we put the balls in the air fryer (without preheating) at $360°F$ for 15 minutes ... and voila!

Nutritional Information:

- Calories: 350
- Carbohydrates: 30g
- Fat: 21g
- Protein: 10g
- Sugar: 8g
- Cholesterol: 160mg

Sandwich

Servings: 1

Preparation time: 5 min

Cook time: 20 minutes

Ingredients

- 2 slices of bread
- Tomato to taste
- cheese to taste
- pepper to taste
- a little tomato sauce

Steps to Cook

1. Add the tomato sauce on one side of each slice of bread. Add the tomato, cheese, pepper between the two pieces of bread, and fix it with a toothpick so that the ingredients of the sandwich do not move.
2. We put the sandwich in the air fryer (previously preheated) for 12 minutes at 340°F ... and voila!
3. You will find a sandwich with crispy toast on the outside and creamy on the inside.

Nutritional Information:

- Calories: 155
- Carbohydrates: 28g
- Fat: 1.9g
- Protein: 6.2g
- Sugar: 3.4g
- Cholesterol: 0mg

Vegan Bread

Servings: 2

Preparation time: 10 min

Cook time: 35 minutes

Ingredients

- 1 cup of warm water
- 1 ½ tsp salt
- 1 tbsp of olive oil
- 2 cups of wheat flour
- 1 cup whole wheat flour (or cornmeal)
- 2 tsp dry organic yeast
- 1 tbsp brown sugar
- August grains to decorate

Steps to Cook

1. In a bowl, mix ¼ cup of water, organic yeast, and brown sugar. Let stand for 10 minutes. Reserve.
2. In another bowl, mix the dry ingredients, add the liquids, and the reserved yeast. Mix everything to form a homogeneous dough. Knead the dough well.
3. Cover the dough and rest in a warm place for 1 hour or until doubled in size.
4. Set the Air Fryer for 5 minutes at 360°F to preheat.
5. Divide the dough into two parts. With the fryer turned off, put the bread in the basket. Let it rest there for 10 minutes.
6. Then set the Air fryer to 10 minutes at 360°F to bake until needed. They come out beautiful and golden!

Nutritional Information:

- Calories: 118.9
- Carbohydrates: 20.5g
- Fat: 3.5g
- Protein: 3.6g

French Fried Potatoes

Servings: 4

Preparation time: 5 min

Cook time: 20 minutes

Ingredients

- 1 lb. of potatoes
- 2 tsp of olive oil
- Salt & spices

Steps to Cook

1. Set the fryer temperature to 390°F.
2. Set the timer to 20 minutes.
3. Put the potatoes in the fryer. The capacity of the Rapid Air system allows the potatoes to be cooked as they come from the freezer or refrigerator.
4. Do not forget to stir the potatoes from time to time to get even cooking.
5. Add salt to enjoy this delicious and healthy dish

Nutritional Information:

- Calories: 192
- Carbohydrates: 23g
- Fat: 9g
- Protein: 2g
- Sugar: 0.9g
- Cholesterol: 300mg

Sweet Potato Ball

Servings: 2-4

Preparation time: 10 min

Cook time: 20 minutes

Ingredients

- 1 lb of boiled, peeled, and crushed sweet potatoes.
- 1 ¼ cup powdered sweet tea
- ¾ cup sour tea
- ½ cup of water
- ¼ cup of olive oil tea
- 1 tbsp of chia
- ½ tbsp of salt

Steps to Cook

1. Mix all the ingredients and mix until you get a homogeneous mass.
2. Take small portions and make balls, place on a baking sheet, and bake in the Air Fryer at 400°F for about 20 minutes.
3. Serve immediately.

Nutritional Information:

- Calories: 72
- Carbohydrates: 12.48g
- Fat: 1.53g
- Protein: 1.97g

Onion Rings

Servings: 8

Preparation time: 10 min

Cook time: 10-12 minutes

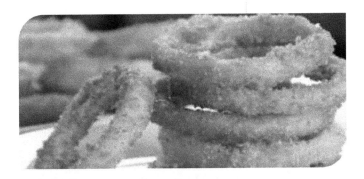

Ingredients

- 1 large red onion
- 2 cups all-purpose flour
- 6 eggs
- 2 ½ cups breadcrumbs

Steps to Cook

For the onion rings:

- Peel and cut the onion into thick slices (approx. 2 centimeters thick), then separate them into rings.
- Place the flour, beaten eggs in another bowl, and breadcrumbs in the last bowl in one float bowls. Well-cooked and the mixture of chickpea flour, vinegar and water have linked the ingredients.

To bread:

- For EVERY dip ring and cape in this order: Egg mix
- Flour mix
- Egg mix (this is the second time in the egg)
- Flour mix (this is the second time in flour)
- Egg mix (this is the third time in the egg).
- Finally, in the bread crumbs (press to cover well
- Place ALL the coated onion rings on a metal baking sheet and put them in the freezer for at least 30 minutes.

NOTE: You can do this up to a week in advance.

Cooking in the Air Fryer:

- Preheat fryer to 375°F
- place the breaded onion rings in a single layer in the air fryer basket and cover with a little spray oil
- Fry for about 10-12 minutes.

- Onion rings are ready when tender, golden brown, and crisp.

Nutritional Information:

- Calories: 192
- Carbohydrates: 23g
- Fat: 9g

- Protein: 2g
- Sugar: 0.9g
- Cholesterol: 300mg

Flat Bread

Servings: 2-4

Preparation time: 10 min

Cook time: 30 minutes

Ingredients

- ¼ cup of warm water
- 1 tbsp of olive oil
- ½ tsp salt
- ½ tbsp baking powder
- 1 to 2 cups Flour for knitting

Steps to Cook

1. Mix the water with the oil, the salt, and the yeast and gradually add the flour until it comes off your hands. Work the dough on a floured surface just until smooth. Let stand for 15 minutes covered with a cloth.
2. Cut in equal parts and give it the shape you want. The more refined it is, the crunchier it will be after grilling.
3. Place on a baking sheet and bake in the Air Fryer at 400°F for about 30 minutes

Nutritional Information:

- Calories: 72
- Carbohydrates: 12.48g
- Fat: 1.53g
- Protein: 1.97g

Onion Bread

Servings: 2-4

Preparation time: 10 min

Cook time: 30 minutes

Ingredients

- 1 cup of white wheat flour
- ½ cup whole wheat flour
- 1 tbsp of vegetable oil
- 1 tsp salt
- 2 tsp baking powder
- ½ cup of warm water
- ¼ cup green onions, chopped
- ¼ tsp black pepper (optional)

Steps to Cook

1. In a bowl, add the flour, salt, and yeast, mixing well. Add the water gradually, alternating with the oil. Add the ingredients well until you get a smooth and uniform dough. If using black pepper, add last. If desired, you can use other spices or dried herbs of your choice. Add the chopped green onions and mix well with the batter. Reserve.
2. Grease a medium bowl and preheat the air fryer at 360°F for 5 minutes.
3. Place the dough in the greased bowl, cover, and bake for about 10 minutes. After this time, turn the dough over and let it bake on the other side.

Nutritional Information:

- Calories: 161
- Carbohydrates: 27g
- Fat: 3g
- Protein: 4g

Golden Tacos

Servings: 1-2

Preparation time: 5 min

Cook time: 5 minutes

Ingredients

- ½ lb. chicken breast
- Tortillas to taste
- Cream to taste
- Lettuce to taste
- Avocado to taste
- Tomatoes to taste
- Grated cheese to taste
- Tabasco to taste
- Salt to taste
- Olive oil to taste

Steps to Cook

1. Salt the chicken breast. Cut the chicken breast and cook in the air fryer (without preheating) at 350°F for 16 minutes.
2. Once the chicken breast is cooked, crush the meat into small pieces with your hands.
3. Fill the tortillas with the chicken meat that you have minced and roll until they are well closed.
4. To brown the tacos nicely, varnish the outside of the tortillas with a little olive oil. Next, introduce the dowels in the air fryer at 390°F for 6 minutes.
5. To finish, decorate the tacos with cream, chopped salad, tomato pieces, avocado, and grated cheese ... and ready to eat!

Nutritional Information

- Calories: 19
- Carbohydrates: 4g
- Fat: 1g
- Protein: 1g
- Sugar: 0.5g
- Cholesterol: 30mg

Tornado Potatoes

Servings: 2-4

Preparation time: 5 min

Cook time: 20-25 minutes

Ingredients

- 4 small potatoes
- ½ tsp of salt
- ½ tsp of pepper
- 1 tsp of garlic powder
- 1 tsp of paprika
- 1 tsp grated Parmesan cheese
- Olive oil
- Wooden skewers

Steps to Cook

1. Enter the skewer in each potato until it comes out to the other side.
2. With one hand, place the sharp knife diagonally on one end of the potato until the knife touches wood, while with the other hand, turn the potato in the opposite direction. In this, cut all the potatoes in the form of a good spiral.
3. Once finished, we stretch the potato along the skewer. Then we will give a few strokes of olive oil on the spirals.
4. On a separate plate, mix salt, pepper, paprika, garlic powder, and striped Parmesan cheese.
5. Next, we will sprinkle the potatoes with the spice mixture, using a teaspoon.
6. Cut the ends of the skewer; in case the skewers are longer than the fryer basket and introduce the potato skewers in the fryer.
7. Let cook at 320°F for 20-25 minutes.

Nutritional Information:

- Calories: 180
- Carbohydrates: 22g
- Fat: 7g
- Protein: 8g

Hash Pancake

Servings: 7

Preparation time: 7 min

Cook time: 9 minutes

Ingredients

- 1 tsp of baking soda
- 1 tbsp of apple cider vinegar
- 1 tsp salt
- 1 tsp ground ginger
- 1 cup of coconut flour
- 5 tbsp of butter
- 1 egg.
- ¼ cup of heavy cream

Steps to Cook

1. Combine the baking soda, salt, ground ginger, and flour in the bowl.
2. Next, Take the separate bowl and break the egg there. Add the butter and heavy cream.
3. Use the hand mixer and mix the liquid mixture well.
4. Next, combine the dry mix and the liquid mix and stir until smooth.
5. Preheat the air fryer to $400°F$.
6. Next, pour the pancake mix into the basket pan of the air fryer—Cook the pancake hash for 4 minutes.
7. After this, stir the pancake hash well and continue to cook for 5 more minutes.

Nutritional Information:

- Calories: 178
- Fat: 13.3g
- carbohydrates: 10.7g
- Protein: 4.4g

Slices Of Meatloaf

Servings: 6

Preparation time: 10 min

Cook time: 20 minutes

Ingredients

- 8 oz ground pork
- 7 oz. of ground beef
- 1 onion
- 1 egg
- 1 tbsp of almond flour
- 1 tsp of chives
- 1 tsp salt
- 1 tsp cayenne pepper
- 1 tbsp of dried oregano.
- 1 tsp of butter
- 1 tsp of olive oil

Steps to Cook

1. Beat the egg in the large bowl. Add the ground beef and ground pork. After this, add the almond flour, chives, salt, cayenne pepper, dried oregano, and butter. Peel the onion and dice it. Place the chopped onion into the ground beef mixture.
2. Use your hands to make the meatloaf mixture homogeneous.
3. Preheat the air fryer to 350°F.
4. Make the meatloaf shape from the ground beef mixture.
5. Sprinkle the fryer basket with the olive oil inside, and over the meatloaf there.
6. Cook the meatloaf for 20 minutes.

Nutritional Information:

- Calories: 176
- Carbohydrates: 3.4g
- fat: 2.2g
- Protein: 22.2g

Apple Chips

Servings: 1-2

Preparation time: 5 min

Cook time: 45 minutes

Ingredients

- 1 Apple
- 2 tbsp of water
- juice of half a lemon

Steps to Cook

1. You just have to remove the center of the apple to remove the seeds. Cut the apples into thin slices and mix them with two tablespoons of water and the juice of half a lemon. The apple slices are then allowed to dry while the air fryer/air fryer is preheated to 180°F.
2. To get some dried apple rings, we will cook the apples for 60 minutes at 185°F. If we prefer crispy apple chips, we leave them in the Air fryer for another 45 minutes.

Nutritional Information:

- Calories: 16
- Carbohydrates: 4.2g
- Fat: 0g
- Protein: 0.1g
- Sugar: 3.7g
- Cholesterol: 0mg

Bacon Burger

Servings: 2

Preparation time: 10 min

Cook time: 8 minutes

Ingredients

- ½ tomato
- ½ cucumber
- ½ onion
- 8 oz. of ground beef
- 4 oz. of cooked bacon
- 1 egg
- 1 tsp of butter
- 2 oz. Lettuce leaves
- 1 tsp of ground black pepper
- ½ tsp salt
- 1 tsp of olive oil
- ½ tsp of minced garlic

Steps to Cook

1. Beat the egg in the bowl and add the ground beef.
2. Chop the cooked bacon and add it to the ground beef mixture. After this, add the butter, ground black pepper, salt, and minced garlic.
3. Mix carefully and make the burgers.
4. Preheat the honor to 370⁰F.
5. Drizzle the deep fryer basket with the olive oil inside and place the patties there.
6. Cook the patties for 8 minutes on each side.
7. Meanwhile, finely chop the onion, cucumber, and tomato.
8. Place the tomato, cucumber, and onion on the lettuce leaves.

Nutritional Information:

- Calories: 618
- Carbohydrates: 8.6g
- Fat: 37.4g
- Protein: 59.4g

Potatoes Chips

Servings: 4-6

Preparation time: 20 min

Cook time: 7-10 minutes

Ingredients

- 1/3 lb. of potatoes
- 2 tsp of olive oil
- Salt & spices

Steps to Cook

1. It is essential to leave the thin slices of potatoes 20 minutes in water to lose the starch. Then you have to let them dry well, to be able to put them to cook in the Air Fryer, and they are finally creamy and crispy.
2. In the fryer without oil, introduce a few potatoes at 185^0F for 20 minutes, and well separated to cook well. This way, you get some crispy and delicious homemade chips. Finally, add salt and other spices if you wish (spicy, garlic, pepper ... each to your liking!)

Nutritional Information:

- Calories: 53
- Carbohydrates: 8.4g
- Fat: 1.9g
- Protein: 1.1g
- Sugar: 3.7g
- Cholesterol: 0mg

Patty With Tuna

Servings: 4

Preparation time: 10 min

Cook time: 15 minutes

Ingredients

- Sliced Bread (Without Crust)
- Canned Tuna
- Oregano to taste
- Pepper to taste
- Tomato sauce to taste
- 1 egg

Steps to Cook

1. Prepare the filling. In a bowl or container, add two cans of canned tuna. Add two tablespoons of tomato sauce or fried tomato, also add a little ground pepper and oregano. You can also add if you want some raw or fried onion.
2. Beat an egg well and with a kitchen brush or a spoon, paint the 4 ends of the sliced bread.
3. With your hand or a fork, close the slices, from one corner to another corner.
4. Next, put in the air fryer previously preheated. Cook for 25 minutes at 350°F.

Nutritional Information:

- Calories: 130
- Carbohydrates: 5g
- Fat: 4.9g
- Protein: 15.8g
- Sugar: 0.5g
- Cholesterol: 30.2mg

Flaxseed Porridge

Servings: 4

Preparation time: 5 min

Cook time: 8 minutes

Ingredients

- 2 tbsp of sesame seeds
- 4 tbsp chia seeds
- 1 cup of almond milk
- 3 tbsp flax flour
- 1 tsp of Stevia
- 1 tbsp butter
- ½ tsp of vanilla extract

Steps to Cook

1. Preheat the air fryer to 375°F.
2. Place the sesame seeds, chia seeds, almond milk, flax flour, Stevia, and butter on the tray of the air fryer basket.
3. Add the vanilla extract and cook the porridge for 8 minutes.
4. When the time is up, carefully stirring the porridge and let it rest for 5 minutes.
5. Next, transfer the food into the serving bowls or ramekins.
6. Enjoy!

Nutritional Information:

- Calories: 298
- Carbohydrates: 13.3g
- Fat: 26.7g
- Protein: 6.2g

Omelette With Bacon

Servings: 6

Preparation time: 10 min

Cook time: 13 minutes

Ingredients

- 6 eggs
- ¼ cup of almond milk
- ½ tsp of turmeric
- ½ tsp of salt
- 1 tbsp of dried dill
- 4 oz. of bacon
- 1 tsp butter

Steps to Cook

1. Beat the egg in the bowl of the mixer and add the almond milk.
2. Mix the mixture with the help of the mixer until smooth.
3. Add the turmeric, salt, and dried dill.
4. Then cut the bacon.
5. Preheat the air fryer to 360^0F and place the sliced bacon on the tray of the air fryer basket.
6. Cook the bacon for 5 minutes.
7. After this, turn the bacon on another side and pour the egg mixture over it.
8. Cook the tortilla for 8 more minutes.

Nutritional Information:

- Calories: 619
- Carbohydrates: 1.6g
- Fat: 15.3g
- Protein: 12.9g

Roasted Apple With Yogurt Sauce

Servings: 3

Preparation time: 10 min

Cook time: 15 minutes

Ingredients

- Apples (1 piece per person)
- Cinnamon powder
- Sugar to taste
- Aniseed
- Sugary yogurt or Greek yogurt, etc.
- Vanilla essence to taste
- Honey to taste

Steps to Cook

1. Cut the apple in half with a knife. Leave the skin and remove the seed. Add a little cinnamon powder to the surface of the apple pieces sugar. You can add the sugar 5 minutes before it finishes roasting to caramelize on top.
2. Add the aniseed grain to give it a different touch.
3. Put in the bottom and piece of aluminum foil or silver foil since the apple, when roasted, it will release its juice. Take advantage of this juice to prepare the sauce that you will add to it later.
4. Introduce the apples and set the timer to 10 or 12 minutes at 350°F.

Prepare the yogurt sauce:

5. Pour a plain yogurt into a container; a little of the apple juice you have left in the aluminum foil. A little vanilla essence, although this is optional, and a tablespoon of honey.
6. Mix all ingredients well.

Nutritional Information:

- Calories: 102.6
- Carbohydrates: 25.8g
- Fat: 0.5g
- Protein: 1.6g

Scrambled Egg With Butter

Servings: 4

Preparation time: 10 min

Cook time: 17 minutes

Ingredients

- 4 eggs
- 4 tbsp of butter
- 1 tsp salt

Steps to Cook

1. Cover the basket of the air fryer with the foil and place the eggs there.
2. Next, transfer the basket from the air fryer into the air fryer and cook the eggs for 17 minutes at 320^0F.
3. When the time is up - remove the cooked eggs from the air fryer basket and place them in the cold water to cool.
4. After this, peel the eggs and chop them finely.
5. Then combine the chopped eggs with the butter and add salt.
6. Blend until you get a spread texture.
7. Serve the egg butter with the bread

Nutritional Information:

- Calories: 164
- Carbohydrates: 21.67g
- Fat: 8.5g
- Protein: 3g

Egg Cups With Bacon

Servings: 4

Preparation time: 10 min

Cook time: 15 minutes

Ingredients

- 4 eggs
- 6 oz. Bacon
- ¼ tsp salt
- ½ tsp of dried dill
- ½ tsp of pepper
- 1 tbsp of butter

Steps to Cook

1. Whisk the eggs in the mixing bowl
2. Then add the salt, dried dill, and pepper. Mix the egg mixture carefully with the help of the hand mixer
3. Then spread 4 ramekins with the butter
4. Cut the bacon and put it in the prepared ramequins in the form of cups
5. Then pour the egg mixture into the middle of each ramekin with bacon
6. Set the air fryer to 360°F
7. Put the ramequins in the fryer and close it.
8. Cook the dish for 15 minutes
9. When the time is up, you will get slightly crispy bacon and tender egg mixture
10. Remove the egg cups in the fryer and serve.

Nutritional Information:

- Calories: 319
- Carbohydrates: 1.2g
- Fat: 25.1g
- Protein: 21.4g

Coconut Empanadas

Servings: 4

Preparation time: 20 min

Cook time: 15-20 min

Ingredients

For the filling:
- 2 cups of milk
- ½ cup grated sweetened coconut
- 1/3 cup sugar
- 3 tbsp cornstarch
- 1 pinch of salt
- 3 egg yolks
- 1 tsp coconut extract (optional)

For the empanada dough:
- 2 ¼ cups flour
- 1 pinch of salt
- 2/3 cup vegetable shortening
- 4-6 tbsp of ice water
- ½ cup of sugar

Steps to Cook

1. P For the filling: In a medium saucepan, heat the milk with the grated coconut over medium-low heat until it starts to boil. Remove from the heat and let it cool until it is at room temperature.
2. In a blender or food processor, blend the milk and coconut mixture. Add the sugar, cornstarch, a pinch of salt, and the egg yolks. Blend until everything is well incorporated.
3. Pour the mixture into the saucepan and heat over medium heat, continually stirring until the mixture thickens, about 5 to 8 minutes. Remove from heat and add the coconut extract; let it cool.
4. For the empanada dough: In a large bowl, combine the flour with the pinch of salt. Add the vegetable shortening. Add the water, one tablespoon at a time, until the dough forms a ball.
5. Preheat the air fryer to 350°F.
6. Divide the dough into 2 parts. Roll each piece of dough out onto a floured surface until 1/4-inch thick. Cut the dough into 4- to 6-inch circles. Place 2-3 tbsp of coconut filling in the center of each dough circle. Fold the dough in half and seal the edges well.

7. Arrange the empanadas on a lightly greased baking sheet. Bake the empanadas for 15 to 20 minutes or until the empanadas are lightly golden brown.
8. Sprinkle the patties with sugar. Enjoy with a cup of coffee with milk.

Nutritional Information:

- Calories: 270
- Carbohydrates: 13.3g
- Fat: 24.6g
- Protein: 5.7g

Baked Avocado With Egg

Servings: 2

Preparation time: 8 min

Cook time: 15 minutes

Ingredients

- 1 avocado
- ¼ tsp turmeric
- ¼ tsp black pepper
- ¼ tsp salt
- 2 eggs
- 1 tsp butter
- ¼ tsp flax seeds

Steps to Cook

1. Take the deep bowl and combine the turmeric, ground black pepper, salt, and flaxseed. Shake gently to make it homogeneous.
2. After this, cut the avocado into 2 pairs.
3. Whisk the eggs in separate bowls
4. Sprinkle the eggs with the spice mixture
5. Gently lay the eggs in the avocado halves.
6. Put the avocados in the air fryer.
7. Put in the preheated air fryer at 355°F and close it.
8. Cook the dish for 15 minutes.

Nutritional Information:

- Calories: 288
- Carbohydrates: 9.4g
- Fat: 26g
- Protein: 7.6g
- Sugar: 5g
- Cholesterol: 300mg

Hash With Ham

Servings: 3

Preparation time: 10 min

Cook time: 10 minutes

Ingredients

- 5 oz. *Parmesan*
- 10 oz. Ham
- 1 tsp of butter
- ½ onion
- 1 tsp ground black pepper
- 1 egg
- 1 tsp of pepper

Steps to Cook

1. Shred the Parmesan cheese
2. Cut the ham into the small strips
3. Peel the onion and dice it.
4. Beat the egg in the bowl and beat with the hand
5. Add the ham strips, butter, diced onion, and butter
6. Sprinkle the mixture with the ground black pepper and paprika. Mix
7. Preheat air fryer to 350°F
8. Transfer the ham mixture to 3 ramekins and sprinkle with the grated Parmesan cheese.
9. Place in the air fryer and cook for 10 minutes

Nutritional Information:

- Calories: 372
- Carbohydrates: 8g
- Fat: 23.7g
- Protein: 33.2g

Egg Tortilla With Mushroom

Servings: 9

Preparation time: 10 min

Cook time: 12 minutes

Ingredients

- 1 tbsp of flax seeds
- 7 eggs
- ½ cup of cream cheese
- 4 oz of mushrooms
- 1 tsp of olive oil
- 1 tsp of ground black pepper
- ½ tsp of paprika
- ¼ tsp of salt

Steps to Cook

1. Cut the mushrooms and sprinkle them with the salt, paprika, and ground black pepper.
2. Preheat the air fryer to 400^0F.
3. Spray the inside of the air fryer basket pan with olive oil and place the sliced mushrooms there.
4. Cook the mushrooms for 3 minutes.
5. Stir carefully after 2 minutes of cooking.
6. Meanwhile, beat the eggs in the bowl.
7. Add the cream cheese and flax seeds.
8. Mix the egg mixture carefully until smooth.
9. Next, pour the tortilla mix into the air fryer basket pan over the mushrooms.
10. Gently stir the tortilla and cook for another 7 minutes.

Nutritional Information:

- Calories: 106
- Carbohydrates: 1.5g
- Fat: 8.7g
- Protein: 5.9g

Breakfast Cloud Eggs

Servings: 2

Preparation time: 8 min

Cook time: 4 minutes

Ingredients

- 2 eggs
- 1 tsp of butter

Steps to Cook

1. Separate the eggs into the egg whites and the egg yolks
2. Then beat the egg whites with the help of a mixer until you get firm white peaks.
3. Spread basket tray on air fryer with handle
4. Preheat air fryer to 3000F
5. Make the medium clouds of the whitewash peaks in the basket tray of the prepared air fryer.
6. Place the tray in the basket in the air fryer and cook the cloud eggs for 2 minutes.
7. After this, remove the basket in the air fryer, place the egg yolks in the center of each egg cloud and return the basket to the air fryer.
8. Cook the dish for 2 minutes
9. After this, remove the cooked dish from the basket and serve

Nutritional Information:

- Calories: 80
- Carbohydrates: 0.3g
- Fat: 6.3g
- Protein: 5.6g

Breakfast Cloud Eggs

Servings: 4

Preparation time: 15 min

Cook time: 10 minutes

Ingredients

- 1 tbsp of dried dill
- 1 egg
- 1 tsp salt
- 10 oz. Cauliflower
- 1 tsp of olive oil
- 1 tsp of parsley
- ½ tsp of ground white pepper)

Steps to Cook

1. Wash the cauliflower carefully and cut it into small pieces. Put in the blender and mix well.
2. Beat the egg in the cauliflower mixture and continue mixing for 1 more minute.
3. Transfer the mixed cauliflower mixture into the bowl. Sprinkle with salt, dried dill, almond flour, parsley, and ground white pepper.
4. Mix carefully with the help of the spoon
5. Preheat air fryer to 355^0F
6. Sprinkle the air fryer basket tray with the olive oil
7. Make fritters from the cauliflower mixture and put them in the basket tray of the air fryer.
8. Close the air fryer and cook the fritters elsewhere and cook for 7 more minutes.
9. When the fritters are cooked, serve them hot.

Nutritional Information

- Calories: 54
- Carbohydrates: 4.8g
- Fat: 3.1g
- Protein: 3.3g

Western-Style Omelette

Servings: 4

Preparation time: 10 min

Cook time: 10 minutes

Ingredients

- 1 green pepper
- ½ onion
- 5 eggs
- 3 tbsp of cream cheese.
- 1 tsp of olive oil
- 1 tsp of dried coriander
- 1 tsp dried oregano
- 1 tsp of butter
- 3 oz parmesan, grated

Steps to Cook

1. Beat the eggs in the bowl and beat well.
2. Sprinkle with the cream cheese, dried cilantro, and dried oregano. Add the grated Parmesan and butter and mix in the egg mixture.
3. Preheat the air fryer to 360°F.
4. Pour the egg mixture into the air fryer basket tray and place it in the air fryer—Cook the tortilla for 10 minutes. Chop the green pepper and chop the onion. Pour the olive oil into the pan and preheat it well. Add the chopped green pepper and roast it for 3 minutes over medium heat. Add the diced onion and cook the onion for 5 more minutes. Stir the vegetables frequently. Remove the cooked tortilla from the basket tray of the air fryer and place it on the plate. Add the roasted vegetables and serve

Nutritional Information:

- Calories: 204
- Carbohydrates: 4.3g
- Fat: 14.9g
- Protein: 14.8g

Bread With Tomato-Mozzarella Toast

Servings: 2-4

Preparation time: 25 min

Cook time: 45 minutes

Ingredients

- Baguette/bread
- 7 cherry tomatoes
- 1 mozzarella
- 1 chive
- 1 clove garlic
- Basil to taste
- Olive oil to taste
- Salt to taste

Steps to Cook

1. Dice all the ingredients and mix with a splash of olive oil.
2. Cut a baguette into slices and cover with the rest of the ingredients. Let it cook in the fryer without oil (Air fryer) for 6 minutes at 390°F (without preheating).
3. You can also use bread rolls instead of the loaf of bread.

Nutritional Information:

- Calories: 228
- Carbohydrates: 15g
- Fat: 15g
- Protein: 9g
- Sugar: 2.2g
- Cholesterol: 28mg

Chicken and Cheddar Cheese Sandwich

Servings: 2

Preparation time: 10 min

Cook time: 10 minutes

Ingredients

- 2 slices of cheddar cheese
- 6 oz of ground chicken
- 1 tsp of tomato puree
- 1 tsp cayenne pepper
- 1 egg
- ½ tsp of salt
- 1 tbsp of dried dill
- ½ tsp of olive oil
- 2 lettuce leaves

Steps to Cook

1. Combine ground chicken with cayenne pepper and salt. Add the dried dill and stir. Then beat the egg into the ground chicken mixture and stir well with the help of the spoon.
2. Make two medium patties from the ground chicken mixture.
3. Preheat the air fryer to 380°F.
4. Drizzle the fryer basket pan with the olive oil and place the ground chicken patties there.
5. Cook the chicken patties for 10 minutes. Turn the
6. patties to the other side after 6 minutes of cooking.
7. When the time is up, transfer the cooked chicken patties onto the lettuce leaves.
8. Sprinkle with tomato puree and top with cheddar slices

Nutritional Information:

- Calories: 324
- Carbohydrates: 2.3g
- Fat: 19.2g
- Protein: 34.8g

Meat And Egg Patties Roll

Servings: 6

Preparation time: 15 min

Cook time: 8 minutes

Ingredients

- ½ cup almond flour
- ¼ cup of water
- 1 tsp salt
- 1 egg
- 7 oz. Ground beef
- 1 tsp paprika
- 1 tsp ground black pepper
- 1 tsp olive oil

Steps to Cook

1. Preheat the water (bring it to a boil)
2. Combine the almond would with the salt and stir.
3. Add the boiling water and beat carefully until the mixture is homogeneous. Knead the dough and smooth
4. Leave the dough. Meanwhile, combine ground beef with paprika and ground black pepper.
5. Mix the mixture and transfer it to the pan.
6. Roast the meat mixture for 5 minutes over medium heat. Stir frequently.
7. After this, beat the egg in the meat mixture and stir.
8. Cook the ground beef mixture for 4 more minutes.
9. Roll up the dough and cut it into the 6 squares.
10. Put the ground beef mixture in each box.
11. Roll the squares to make the dough sticks
12. Sprinkle the dough sticks with the olive oil
13. Place the prepared dough sticks in the basket on the air fryer.
14. Preheat the air fryer to 3500F and put the egg meat rolls there.

Nutritional Information:

- Calories: 150
- Carbohydrates: 2.5g
- Fat: 9.6g
- Protein: 13g

Beef Sandwich

Servings: 2

Preparation time: 11 min

Cook time: 16 minutes

Ingredients

- 6 oz of ground beef
- ½ pitted avocado
- ½ tomato
- ½ tsp of chili flakes
- 1/3 tsp of salt
- ½ tsp ground black pepper
- 1 tsp of olive oil
- 1 tsp of flax seeds
- 4 lettuce leaves

Steps to Cook

1. Combine the minced meat with the chili flakes and salt. Add the flax seeds and stir the meat mixture with the help of a fork.
2. Preheat the air fryer to 370^0F.
3. Pour the olive oil into the basket tray of the air fryer.
4. Make two patties from the beef mixture and place them on the basket tray of the air fryer.
5. Cook the burgers for 8 minutes on each side.
6. Meanwhile, cut the tomato and avocado.
7. Separate the ingredients into 2 slices.
8. Place the avocado and tomato on two lettuce leaves.
9. Next, add the cooked minced beef patties.
10. Serve sandwiches only hot

Nutritional Information:

- Calories: 292
- Carbohydrates: 5.9g
- Fat: 17.9g
- Protein: 27.2g

Quiche Of Spinach And Cheese

Servings: 6

Preparation time: 15 min

Cook time: 21 minutes

Ingredients

- ½ cup of almond flour
- 4 tbsp of water, boiled
- 1 tsp salt
- 1 cup of spinach
- ¼ cup of cream cheese
- ½ onion
- 1 tsp of ground black pepper
- 3 eggs
- 6 oz cheddar cheese, grated
- 1 tsp of olive oil

Steps to Cook

1. Combine the water with the almond flour and add salt. Mix the mixture and knead the soft, non-sticky dough. Next, spray the basket pan of the air fryer with the olive oil inside.
2. Set the air fryer to 375°F and preheat.
3. Roll up the dough and place it on the tray of the crust-shaped air fryer basket. Place the air fryer basket tray in the deep fryer and cook for 5 minutes.
4. Meanwhile, chop the spinach and combine it with the cream cheese and ground black pepper.
5. Slice the onion and add it to the spinach mixture. Stir gently. Beat the eggs in the bowl and beat them.
6. When the time is up, and the quiche crust is cooked - transfer the spinach filling into it.
7. Sprinkle the filling with the grated cheese and pour in the beaten eggs.
8. Set the air fryer to 350°F and cook the quiche for 7 minutes. Reduce the heat to 300°F and cook the quiche for 9 more minutes. Let the cooked quiche cool well and cut it into pieces

Nutritional Information:

- Calories: 248
- Carbohydrates: 4.1g
- Fat: 20.2g
- Protein: 12.8g

Roasted Padron Peppers

Servings: 2

Preparation time: 5 min

Cook time: 10 minutes

Ingredients

- Padron peppers
- Olive oil
- Fat salt

Steps to Cook

1. Mix the peppers with 1-2 tablespoons of olive oil and put them to "fry" in the air fryer at 390°F (without preheating) for 10 minutes.
2. After 5 minutes, open the fryer and stir the peppers. In the end, you just have to pour coarse salt on the peppers and voila!

Nutritional Information:

- Calories: 31
- Carbohydrates: 6g
- Fat: 0.3g
- Protein: 1g
- Sugar: 4.2g
- Cholesterol: 0mg

Keto Egg Roll

Servings: 4

Preparation time: 10 min

Cook time: 8 minutes

Ingredients

- 6 tbsp coconut flour
- ½ tbsp salt
- 1 tsp paprika
- 1 tsp butter
- 4 eggs
- 1 tsp chives
- 1 tbsp olive oil
- 2 tbsp boiled water, hot

Steps to Cook

1. Put the coconut flour in the bowl. Add salt and boiling water. Mix and knead the soft dough
2. After this, let the dough rest. Meanwhile, break the eggs into the bowl. Add the chives and paprika.
3. Whisk with the help of the hand
4. Then put the butter in the pan and preheat well
5. Pour the egg mixture into the melted butter in a pancake. Then cook the egg pancake for 1 minute on each side. Remove the cooked egg pancake and cut it. Roll the prepared dough and cut it into 4 squares. Put the chopped eggs in the dough squares and roll them in the shape of the sticks. Brush the egg rolls with the olive oil.
6. Preheat air fryer to 355°F. Place the egg rolls in the air fryer—Cook for 8 minutes.

Nutritional Information:

- Calories: 148
- Carbohydrates: 8.2g
- Fat: 10g
- Protein: 7.1g

Baked Chicken Sausages

Servings: 6

Preparation time: 15 min

Cook time: 12 minutes

Ingredients

- 7 oz. Ground chicken
- 7 oz. Ground pork
- 1 tsp minced garlic
- 1 tsp salt
- ½ tsp nutmeg
- 1 tsp olive oil
- 1 tbsp almond flour
- 1 egg
- 1 tsp chili flakes
- 1 tsp ground coriander

Steps to Cook

1. Combine ground chicken and ground pork in a bowl
2. Whisk the egg into the mixture
3. Then mix with the help of the spoon.
4. After this, sprinkle the meat mixture with the minced garlic, salt, nutmeg, almond flour, chili flakes, and ground coriander.
5. Mix to make the smooth texture of ground beef.
6. Preheat the air fryer to 360^0F
7. Make the medium sausages to the ground beef mixture
8. Drizzle the basket tray of the air fryer with the olive oil inside.
9. Place the prepared sausages in the basket of the air fryer and place it in the air fryer.
10. Cook the sausages for 6 minutes on each side.

Nutritional Information:

- Calories: 156
- Carbohydrates: 1.3g
- Fat: 7.5g
- Protein: 20.2g

Blackberry Muffins

Servings: 5

Preparation time: 15 min

Cook time: 10 minutes

Ingredients

- 1 tsp of apple cider vinegar
- 1 cup of almond flour
- 4 tbsp of butter
- 6 tbsp of almond milk
- 1 tsp of baking soda
- 3 oz blackberry
- ½ tsp of salt
- 3 tsp of Stevia
- 1 tsp of vanilla extract

Steps to Cook

1. Put the almond flour in the mixing bowl
2. Add the baking soda, salt, Stevia, and vanilla extract.
3. Add the butter, almond milk, and apple cider vinegar
4. Break the berries gently and add them to the almond flour mixture.
5. Stir carefully with the help of the fork until the dough is homogeneous.
6. Leave the cupcake mixture in the warm place for 5 minutes.
7. Preheat air fryer to 400°F. Prepare the cupcake shapes. Next, pour the dough into the cupcake shapes. Fill half of each cupcake shape.
8. When the air fryer is preheated, place the cupcake forms with the filling in the basket on the air fryer. Close the air fryer. Cook the muffins for 10 minutes.

Nutritional Information:

- Calories: 165
- Carbohydrates: 4g
- Fat: 16.4g
- Protein: 2g

Soufflé Omelette

Servings: 2

Preparation time: 8 min

Cook time: 8 minutes

Ingredients

- 2 eggs
- 2 tbsp of dried parsley
- 1 tbsp heavy cream
- ¼ tsp ground chili
- ¼ tsp salt

Steps to Cook

1. Preheat the air fryer to 391°F
2. Break the eggs into the bowl and add the heavy cream
3. Whisk mixture carefully until the smooth liquid texture is obtained
4. Sprinkle the egg mixture with the dried parsley, ground chili, and salt.
5. Mix with the help of the spoon
6. Lugo take 2 ramekins and pour the souffle in it.
7. Place the ramequins in the fryer basket and cook for 8 minutes.

Nutritional Information:

- Calories: 116
- Carbohydrates: 0.9g
- Fat: 9.9g
- Protein: 5.9g

Buffalo-Style Cauliflower

Servings: 5

Preparation time: 10 min

Cook time: 15 minutes

Ingredients

- 8 oz. Cauliflower
- 6 tbsp of almond flour
- 1 tsp chili
- 1 tsp cayenne pepper
- 1 tsp ground black pepper
- 1 tomato
- 1 tsp minced garlic
- ½ tsp salt
- 1 tsp of olive oil

Steps to Cook

1. Wash the cauliflower carefully and separate it into the medium foil
2. Sprinkle the cauliflower flowers with the salt
3. Chop the tomato approximately and transfer it. Mix the mixture.
4. Preheat air fryer to $350°F$
5. Generously sprinkle cauliflower florets in almond flour
6. Place the coated cauliflower florets in the fryer basket and cook for 15 minutes, stirring the cauliflower flowers every 4 minutes.

Nutritional Information:

- Calories: 217
- Carbohydrates: 10.8g
- Fat: 17.9g
- Protein: 8.4g

Cheese Tots

Servings: 5

Preparation time: 12 min

Cook time: 3 minutes

Ingredients

- 1 egg
- ½ cup almond flour
- ½ cup coconut flakes
- 1 tsp thyme
- 1 tsp of ground black pepper
- 1 tsp of paprika

Steps to Cook

1. Beat the egg in the bowl and beat it
2. Combine coconut flour with thyme, ground black pepper, and paprika. Stir carefully.
3. Sprinkle mozzarella balls with coconut flakes
4. Transfer the balls to the beaten egg mixture
5. Cover them in the almond flour mixture
6. Put mozzarella balls in the freezer for 5 minutes.
7. Preheat air fryer to 400^0F
8. Put the frozen cheese balls in the preheated air fryer and cook for 3 minutes.

Nutritional Information:

- Calories: 166
- Carbohydrates: 2.8g
- Fat: 12.8g
- Protein. 9.5g

Chicken Sausage Balls

Servings: 5

Preparation time: 10 min

Cook time: 8 minutes

Ingredients

- 8 oz. Ground chicken
- 1 egg white
- 1 tbsp dried parsley
- ½ tsp salt
- ½ ground black pepper
- 2 tbsp almond flour
- 1 tsp olive oil
- 1 tsp paprika

Steps to Cook

1. Beat the egg white and combine it with the ground chicken
2. Sprinkle chicken mixture with dried parsley and salt
3. Add the ground black pepper and paprika
4. Stir the dough carefully using the spoon
5. Wet your hands and make the small balls of the ground chicken mixture
6. Sprinkle each sausage ball with the almond flour.
7. Preheat air fryer to 380°F
8. Drizzle the basket tray of the air fryer with the olive oil inside and place the sausage balls there.
9. Cook for 8 minutes on each side until golden.

Nutritional Information:

- Calories: 180
- Carbohydrates: 2.9g
- Fat: 11.8g
- Protein: 16.3g

Tofu Scramble

Servings: 5

Preparation time: 15 min

Cook time: 20 minutes

Ingredients

- 10 oz. Tofu cheese
- 2 eggs
- 1 tsp chives
- 1 tbsp apple cider vinegar
- ½ tsp salt
- 1 tsp ground white pepper
- ¼ tsp ground coriander

Steps to Cook

1. Crumble the tofu cheese and sprinkle with the apple cider vinegar, salt, ground white pepper, and ground coriander. Mix and leave for 10 minutes to marinate
2. Preheat air fryer to 370°F
3. Transfer the marinated grated tofu cheese to the basket tray of the air fryer and cook the cheese for 13 minutes.
4. Meanwhile, beat the eggs in the bowl.
5. When the cheese is done cooking, pour the egg mixture into the grated tofu cheese and stir with the help of the spatula well.
6. When the eggs start to firm, place in the air fryer and cook for an additional 7 minutes.

Nutritional Information:

- Calories: 109
- Carbohydrates: 2.9g
- Fat: 6.7g
- Protein: 11.2g

Chapter 3

Meat (Pork, Beef and Lamb) Recipes

Roasted Pork Ribs

Servings: 5

Preparation time: 30 min

Cook time: 30 minutes

Ingredients

- 1 tbsp of apple cider vinegar
- 1 tsp cayenne pepper
- 1 tsp minced garlic
- 1 tsp of mustard
- 1 tsp chili flakes
- 16 oz pork ribs
- 1 tsp sesame oil
- 1 tsp salt
- 1 tbsp of paprika

Steps to Cook

1. Chop the pork ribs more or less. Then sprinkle the pork ribs with cayenne pepper, apple cider vinegar, minced garlic, mustard, and chili flakes.
2. Then, add the sesame oil and salt. Add the paprika and mix in the pork ribs. Leave in the fridge for 20 minutes. After this, preheat the air fryer to 360°F.
3. Transfer the pork ribs into the basket of the air fryer and cook for 15 minutes.
4. After this, turn the pork ribs to the other side and cook the meat for 15 more minutes.

Nutritional Information:

- Calories: 350
- Carbohydrates: 0.2g
- Fat: 31.4g
- Protein: 15.5g

Roasted Pork Sticks

Servings: 4

Preparation time: 15 min

Cook time: 10 minutes

Ingredients

- 1 tsp dried basil
- 1 tsp of nutmeg
- 1 tsp oregano
- 1 tsp apple cider vinegar
- 1 tsp of paprika
- 10 oz. Pork fillet
- ½ tsp of salt
- 1 tbsp olive oil
- 5 oz parmesan, grated

Steps to Cook

1. Cut pork steak into thick strips
2. Combine ground ginger, nutmeg, oregano, paprika, and salt in a shallow bowl, stir.
3. Sprinkle the pork strips with the spice mixture.
4. Sprinkle the meat with the apple cider vinegar
5. Preheat air fryer to 380^0F
6. Sprinkle the basket of the air fryer with the olive oil inside and place the pork strips (sticks) there.
7. Cook for 5 minutes. Turn the pork sticks to the other side and cook for 4 more minutes.

Nutritional Information:

- Calories: 315
- Carbohydrates: 2.2g
- Fat: 20.4g
- Protein: 31.3g

Pork Rinds

Servings: 8

Preparation time: 10 min

Cook time: 7 minutes

Ingredients

- 1 lb pork rinds
- 1 tsp of olive oil
- ½ tsp of salt
- 1 tsp chili flakes
- ½ tsp of ground black pepper

Steps to Cook

1. Preheat the air fryer to 365°F.
2. Drizzle the basket tray of the air fryer with the olive oil inside.
3. Next, place the pork rinds in the basket tray of the air fryer.
4. Sprinkle the pork rinds with the salt, chili flakes, and ground black pepper.
5. Mix gently.
6. After this, cook the pork rinds for 7 minutes.
7. When the time is up, gently shake the pork rinds.
8. Transfer the plate to the large container and let it cool for 1 to 2 minutes

Nutritional Information:

- Calories: 239
- Carbohydrates: 0.1g
- Fat: 20.8g
- Protein: 36.5g

Beef Stew

Servings: 6

Preparation time: 15 min

Cook time: 23 minutes

Ingredients

- 10 oz short ribs of beef
- 1 cup of chicken broth
- 1 clove garlic
- ½ onion
- 1 carrot
- 1 potato
- 4 oz green peas
- ¼ tsp of salt
- 1 tsp turmeric
- 1 green pepper
- 2 tsp butter
- ½ tsp of chili flakes
- 4 oz. kale

Steps to Cook

1. Preheat the air fryer to 360°F. Place the butter in the air fryer basket pan. Add the short ribs of beef.
2. Sprinkle the short ribs with the salt, turmeric, and chili flakes—Cook the short ribs of veal for 15 minutes.
3. Remove the seeds from the green pepper and slice it. Cut the carrot and potato, slice.
4. Slice the kale and slice the onion. When the time is up, pour the chicken broth over the short ribs of beef. Add the chopped green bell pepper and diced onion, the carrot, and the potato. Sprinkle the mixture with the green peas.
5. Peel the garlic clove and add it to the mixture as well. Mix with the wooden spatula.
6. Next, chop up the kale and add it to the stew mixture. Stir the stew mixture one more time and cook it at 360°F for an additional 8 minutes.

Nutritional Information:

- Calories: 144
- Carbohydrates: 7g
- Fat: 5.8g
- Protein: 15.7g

Rib Steak With Cayenne Pepper

Servings: 2

Preparation time: 10 min

Cook time: 13 minutes

Ingredients

- 1 lb. rib steak
- 1 tsp salt
- 1 tsp cayenne pepper
- ½ tsp of chili flakes
- 2 tbsp cream
- 1 tsp of olive oil
- 1 tsp lemongrass
- 1 tbsp butter
- 1 tsp garlic powder

Steps to Cook

1. Preheat the air fryer to 360°F. Take the shallow bowl and combine the cayenne pepper, salt, chili flakes, lemongrass, and garlic powder. Stir the spices gently. Then sprinkle the rib steak with the spice mixture. Melt the butter and combine it with cream and olive oil.
2. Coat the mixture.
3. Pour the rotated mixture into the air fryer basket pan.
4. Cook the steak for 13 minutes. Do not stir the steak during cooking.
5. Serve the steak. You can cut the steak if you like

Nutritional Information:

- Calories: 708
- Carbohydrates: 2.3g
- Fat: 59g
- Protein: 40.4g

Roasted Slices Bacon

Servings: 4
Preparation time: 15 min
Cook time: 10 minutes

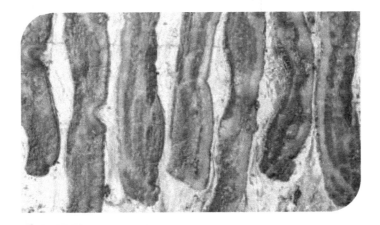

Ingredients

- 8 oz. Bacon
- ½ tsp dried oregano
- ½ tsp salt
- ½ tsp ground black pepper
- ½ tsp ground thyme
- 4 oz. Cheddar cheese

Steps to Cook

1. Cut the bacon and rub it with the dried oregano, salt, ground black pepper, and ground thyme on each side.
2. Leave the bacon for 2 to 3 minutes to soak the spices
3. Preheat air fryer to 3600F
4. Place the sliced bacon on the shelf of the air fryer and cook for 5 minutes.
5. Turn the sliced bacon to the other side and cook for 5 more minutes.
6. Shred the cheddar cheese. When the bacon is cooked, sprinkle with the grated cheese and cook for an additional 30 seconds.

Nutritional Information:

- Calories: 423
- Carbohydrates: 1.5
- Fat: 33.1g
- Protein: 28.1

Roasted Pork Chops

Servings: 3

Preparation time: 10 min

Cook time: 11 minutes

Ingredients

- 1 tsp peppercorns
- 1 tsp kosher salt
- 1 tsp minced garlic
- ½ tsp of dried rosemary
- 1 tbsp butter
- 13 oz pork chops

Steps to Cook

1. Rub the pork chops with the dried rosemary, minced garlic, and kosher salt.
2. Next, preheat the air fryer to 365°F.
3. Put the butter and peppercorns in the basket tray of the air fryer. Melt the butter.
4. Then place the prepared pork chops in the melted butter.
5. Cook the pork chops for 6 minutes.
6. Then turn the pork chops on another side.
7. Cook the pork chops for 5 more minutes.
8. When the meat is cooked - pat it dry with the help of the paper towel.
9. Serve immediately

Nutritional Information:

- Calories: 431
- Carbohydrates: 0.9g
- Fat: 34.4g
- Protein: 27.8g

Stuffed Beef Heart

Servings: 4

Preparation time: 15 min

Cook time: 20 minutes

Ingredients

- 1 lb beef heart
- 1 white onion
- ½ cup of fresh spinach
- 1 tsp salt
- 1 tsp ground black pepper
- 3 cups of chicken broth
- 1 tsp of butter

Steps to Cook

1. Prepare the beef heart for cooking: remove all the fat from it. Then peel the onion and dice it.
2. Chop the fresh spinach. Combine the diced onion, fresh spinach, and butter. Stir. After this, cut the heart of the beef and fill it with the spinach and onion mixture.
3. Preheat the air fryer to 400°F.
4. Pour the chicken broth into the air fryer basket tray.
5. Then sprinkle the prepared stuffed veal heart with the salt and ground black pepper. Put the prepared veal heart in the deep fryer and cook for 20 minutes.
6. When time is up - remove the cooked heart from the air fryer and slice. Next, Sprinkle the air fryer slices with the remaining liquid from the air fryer.

Nutritional Information:

- Calories: 216
- Carbohydrates: 3.8g
- Fat: 6.8g
- Protein: 33.3g

Roasted Pulled Pork

Servings: 4

Preparation time: 15 min

Cook time: 20 minutes

Ingredients

- 1 tbsp chili flakes
- 1 tsp black pepper
- ½ tsp of paprika
- 1 tsp cayenne pepper
- 1/3 cup of cream
- 1 tsp kosher salt
- 1 lb pork tenderloin
- 1 tsp ground thyme
- 4 cups of chicken broth
- 1 tsp of butter

Steps to Cook

1. Pour the chicken broth into the air fryer basket tray.
2. Add the pork fillet and sprinkle the mixture with the chili flakes, ground black pepper, paprika, cayenne pepper, and kosher salt.
3. Preheat the fryer to 370°F and cook the meat for 20 minutes.
4. After this, strain the liquid and grind the meat with the help of 2 forks. Then add the butter and cream and mix—Cook the pulled pork for 4 more minutes at 360°F.
5. When the pulled pork is cooked, let it cool briefly.

Nutritional Information:

- Calories: 198
- Carbohydrates: 2.3g
- Fat: 6.8g
- Protein: 30.7g

BBQ Beef Jerky

Servings: 6

Preparation time: 25 min

Cook time: 2h 30 minutes

Ingredients

- 14 oz beef flank steak
- 1 tsp of chili
- 3 tbsp apple cider vinegar
- 1 tsp black pepper
- 1 tsp onion powder
- 1 tsp garlic powder
- ¼ tsp of liquid smoke

Steps to Cook

1. Cut the steak into medium pieces and then beat each piece of sliced beef. Take the bowl and combine the apple cider vinegar, ground black pepper, onion powder, garlic powder, and liquid smoke. Beat gently with the help of the fork.
2. Then transfer to the beaten pieces of beef into the prepared mixture and stir well.
3. Leave the meat from 10 minutes to 8 hours to marinate.
4. Next, place the marinated pieces of meat on the shelf of the air fryer.
5. Cook the beef for 2 h 30 minutes at 150°F.
6. When beef is cooked - transfer to a serving plate.

Nutritional Information:

- Calories: 129
- Carbohydrates: 1.1g
- Fat: 4.1g
- Protein: 20.2g

Popcorn Pork

Servings: 4

Preparation time: 20 min

Cook time: 21 minutes

Ingredients

- 1 lb. pork tenderloin
- 2 eggs
- 1 tsp of butter
- ¼ cup of almond flour
- 1 tsp kosher salt
- 1 tsp of paprika
- 1 tsp ground coriander
- ½ tsp of lemon zest

Steps to Cook

1. Chop the pork tenderloin into large cubes. Then sprinkle the pork cubes with the kosher salt, bell pepper, ground coriander, and lemon zest. Gently mix the meat. Break the egg into the bowl and beat it. Sprinkle the meat cubes with the egg mixture.
2. Coat each pork cube in the almond flour.
3. Preheat the air fryer to 365°F.
4. Put the butter in the basket pan of the air fryer and then put the pork bites there.
5. Cook the pork bites for 14 minutes.
6. Turn the pork bites to another side after 7 minutes of cooking.

Nutritional Information:

- Calories: 142
- Carbohydrates: 0.9g
- Fat: 5.4g
- Protein: 21.9g

Cheddar Stuffed Pork Meatballs

Servings: 6

Preparation time: 15 min

Cook time: 8 minutes

Ingredients

- 1 lb ground pork
- 5 oz. cheddar cheese
- 1 tbsp dried oregano
- 1 large egg
- ½ tsp of salt
- 1 tsp of paprika
- 1 tbs butter
- ½ tsp of nutmeg
- 1 tsp minced garlic
- ½ tsp of ground ginger

Steps to Cook

1. Break the egg into the bowl and beat it. Then sprinkle the beaten egg with the salt, paprika, nutmeg, and ground ginger. Stir gently and add the ground pork. After this, add the dried oregano and minced garlic. Mix the mixture with the spoon.
2. When you get the meat of homogeneous strength - make 6 medium balls.
3. Cut the cheddar cheese into 6 medium cubes.
4. Fill the pork meatballs with the cheese cubes.
5. Preheat the air fryer to 365°F.
6. Place the butter in the air fryer basket pan and melt.
7. Then put the pork meatballs and cook for 8 minutes.
8. Stir the meatballs once after 4 minutes of cooking.

Nutritional Information:

- Calories: 295
- Carbohydrates: 3g
- Fat: 20.6g
- Protein: 23g

Crispy English Bacon

Servings: 4

Preparation time: 7 min

Cook time: 10 minutes

Ingredients

- ½ tsp of ground thyme
- ½ tsp of ground coriander
- ¼ tsp of ground black pepper
- ½ tsp of salt
- 1 tsp of cream
- 10 oz Canadian bacon

Steps to Cook

1. Slice the English bacon.
2. Combine the ground thyme, ground coriander, ground black pepper, and salt in the shallow bowl, shake gently. Sprinkle the sliced bacon with the spices from each point side.
3. Preheat the air fryer to 360^0F.
4. Put the prepared sliced bacon in the deep fryer and cook for 5 minutes. Turn the sliced bacon to the other side and cook for 5 additional minutes.
5. When the bacon is cooked and becomes a little crisp - remove the bacon from the air fryer and sprinkle with the cream gently

Nutritional Information:

- Calories: 150
- Carbohydrates: 1.9g
- Fat: 6.7g
- Protein: 19.6g

Beef Strips With Zucchini Spirals

Servings: 8

Preparation time: 15 min

Cook time: 13 minutes

Ingredients

- 1 tsp thyme
- 1 tsp ground black pepper
- 1 tsp salt
- 1 tsp dried dill
- 1 tsp of mustard
- 4 cups of chicken broth
- 2 lbs beef steak
- 1 garlic clove, peeled
- 3 tbsp of butter
- 1 bay leaf

Steps to Cook

1. Cut the beef brisket into strips. Sprinkle the beef strips with the ground black pepper and salt.
2. After this, chop the tomato roughly and transfer it to the blender. Mix well until smooth.
3. Spray the basket pan of the air fryer with the olive oil inside and place the meat strips—Cook for 9 minutes at $365°F$. Stir the beef strips carefully after 4 minutes of cooking.
4. Meanwhile, wash the zucchini carefully and make the spirals of the vegetables with the help of the spiralizer. When it is time to cook the meat - add the zucchini spirals over the meat. Sprinkle with the tomato puree, water, and Italian spices.
5. Cook the dish for 4 more minutes at $360°F$.
6. When the time is up and in cooked dishes, stir gently with the help of the wooden spatula

Nutritional Information:

- Calories: 226
- Carbohydrates: 35.25g
- Fat: 5.3g
- Protein: 12g

Slices Of Veal Parmesan

Servings: 9

Preparation time: 15 mi

Cook time: 11 minutes

Ingredients

- 12 oz. beef brisket
- 1 tsp kosher salt
- 7 oz. Parmesan, sliced
- 1 white onion
- 1 tsp turmeric
- 1 tsp dried oregano
- 2 tsp butter

Steps to Cook

1. Cut the beef brisket into 4 slices. Sprinkle each piece of meat with the turmeric and dried oregano. Next, spread the air fryer basket pan with the butter.
2. Put the meat slices there. Peel the white onion and cut it. Layer the sliced onion over the beef slices. Next, make the layer of Parmesan cheese.
3. Preheat the air fryer to 365°F.
4. Cook the beef slices for 25 minutes. When the time is up, and the beef slices are cooked - let the dish cool slightly to make the cheese a bit solid

Nutritional Information:

- Calories: 348
- Carbohydrates: 5g
- Fat: 18g
- Protein: 42.1g

Beef With Broccoli

Servings: 4

Preparation time: 10 min

Cook time: 13 minutes

Ingredients

- 6 oz. broccoli
- 10 oz. beef brisket
- 1 white onion
- 1 tsp of paprika
- 1/3 cup of water
- 1 tsp canola oil
- 1 tsp of butter
- 1 tbsp of flax seeds
- ½ tsp of chili flakes

Steps to Cook

1. Cut the veal brisket into the medium. Next, Sprinkle the veal pieces with the paprika and chili flakes. Mix the meat with the help of your hands.
2. Next, preheat the air fryer to 360°F.
3. Spray the air fryer basket pan with the canola oil.
4. Put the pieces of beef in the basket tray of the air fryer and cook the meat for 7 minutes.
5. Stir once during cooking. Meanwhile, separate the broccoli into the florets. When the time is up, add the broccoli florets to the air fryer basket tray.
6. Sprinkle the ingredients with the flax seeds and butter. Add water. Cut the onion and also add it to the tray of the air fryer basket. Stir gently. Then cook the dish at 265°F for 6 more minutes.

Nutritional Information:

- Calories: 295
- Carbohydrates: 3g
- Fat: 20.6g
- Protein: 23g

Tenderloin Pork Bites

Servings: 6

Preparation time: 15 min

Cook time: 14 minutes

Ingredients

- 1 lb. of pork
- 6 oz. bacon, sliced
- 1 tsp salt
- 1 tsp turmeric
- ½ tsp of red pepper
- 1 tsp of olive oil
- 1 tbsp of apple cider vinegar

Steps to Cook

1. Cut the pork brisket into the medium bites. Then place the pork bites in the large bowl. Sprinkle the meat with the turmeric, salt, red pepper, and apple cider vinegar. Mix the pork bites carefully and leave for 10 minutes to marinate.
2. Then wrap the pork bites in the sliced bacon. Secure the pork bites with the toothpicks.
3. Preheat the air fryer to 370°F.
4. Place the prepared bacon pork bites on the air fryer pan.
5. Cook the pork trotters for 8 minutes.
6. After this, turn the pork bites on another side. Cook the dish for 6 more minutes.

Nutritional Information:

- Calories: 239
- Carbohydrates: 2.8g
- Fat: 13.7g
- Protein: 26.8g

Garlic Lamb Shank

Servings: 5

Preparation time: 15 min

Cook time: 25 minutes

Ingredients

- 17 oz lamb shanks
- 2 tbsp garlic peeled
- 1 tsp kosher salt
- 1 tbsp dried parsley
- 1 tsp chives
- 1 white onion
- ½ cup of chicken broth
- 1 tsp of butter
- 1 tsp dried rosemary
- 1 tsp of nutmeg
- ½ tsp of ground black pepper

Steps to Cook

1. Chop the garlic more or less. Make the cuts in the lamb shank and fill the stakes with the minced garlic.
2. Then sprinkle the lamb shank with the kosher salt, dried parsley, dried rosemary, nutmeg, and ground black pepper. Gently stir the spices into the lamb shank. Next, place the butter and the chicken broth in the basket tray of the air fryer.
3. Preheat the air fryer to 380°F.
4. Place the diced onion and chives on the air fryer basket tray. Add the lamb shank and cook the meat for 24 minutes. When the lamb shank is cooked - transfer it to the serving plate and sprinkle with the remaining liquid from the cooked meat

Nutritional Information:

- Calories: 205
- Carbohydrates: 3.8g
- Fat: 8.2g
- Protein: 27.2g

Fragrant Pork Tenderloin

Servings: 3

Preparation time: 20 min

Cook time: 15 minutes

Ingredients

- ½ tsp of saffron
- 1 tsp sage
- ½ tsp of ground cinnamon
- 1 tsp garlic powder
- 1 tsp onion powder
- 1 lb. pork tenderloin
- 3 tbsp of butter
- 1 garlic clove, minced
- 1 tbsp of apple cider vinegar

Steps to Cook

1. Combine the saffron, sage, ground cinnamon, garlic powder, and onion powder in the shallow bowl. Then shake the spices gently to make them homogeneous. After this, coat the pork tenderloin in the spice mixture. Rub the pork tenderloin with the crushed garlic and sprinkle the meat with the apple cider vinegar.
2. Leave the pork tenderloin for 10 minutes to marinate.
3. Meanwhile, preheat the air fryer to $320°F$. Place the pork tenderloin on the fryer pan and butter the meat. Cook the pork for 15 minutes. Ready!

Nutritional Information:

- Calories: 328
- Carbohydrates: 2.2g
- Fat: 16.9g
- Protein: 40g

Gravy Pork Chops

Servings: 4

Preparation time: 15 min

Cook time: 17 minutes

Ingredients

- 1 lb. pork chops
- 1 tsp kosher salt
- ½ tsp of ground cinnamon
- 1 tsp white pepper
- 1 cup heavy cream
- 6 oz. white mushrooms
- 1 tbsp butter
- ½ tsp of ground ginger
- 1 tsp ground turmeric
- 1 white onion, minced
- 1 garlic clove minced

Steps to Cook

1. Sprinkle the pork chops with the kosher salt, ground cinnamon, ground white pepper, and ground turmeric.
2. Preheat the air fryer to 375 degrees Fahrenheit.
3. Pour the heavy cream into the air fryer basket tray.
4. Then cut the white mushrooms and add them to the heavy cream. After this, add the butter, ground ginger, minced onion, and minced garlic.
5. Cook the sauce for 5 minutes. Then stir in the cream sauce and add the pork chops. Cook the pork chops at 400°F for 12 minutes.
6. When the time is up, gently stir the pork chops and transfer to the serving plates.

Nutritional Information:

- Calories: 518
- Carbohydrates: 6.2g
- Fat: 42.2g
- Protein: 28g

Chili Lamb Chops

Servings: 6

Preparation time: 20 min

Cook time: 10 minutes

Ingredients

- 21 oz. lamb chops
- 1 tsp of chili
- ½ tsp of chili flakes
- 1 tsp onion powder
- 1 tsp garlic powder
- 1 tsp cayenne pepper
- 1 tbsp canola oil
- 1 tbsp butter
- ½ tsp of lime zest

Steps to Cook

1. Melt the butter and combine it with the canola oil.
2. Whisk in the liquid and add chili, chili flakes, onion powder, garlic powder, cayenne pepper, and lime zest. Beat well.
3. Then sprinkle the lamb chops with the prepared oily marinade.
4. Leave the meat for at least 5 minutes in the fridge.
5. Preheat the air fryer to 400°F.
6. Place the marinated lamb chops in the air fryer and cook for 5 minutes.
7. After this, open the air fryer and turn the lamb chops on another side.
8. Cook the lamb chops for 5 more minutes.

Nutritional Information:

- Calories: 227
- Carbohydrates: 1g
- Fat: 11.6g
- Protein: 28.1g

Lamb Meatballs

Servings: 7

Preparation time: 10 min

Cook time: 14 minutes

Ingredients

- 1 clove garlic
- 1 tbsp butter
- 1 white onion
- ¼ tbsp of turmeric
- 1/3 tsp of cayenne pepper
- 1 tsp ground coriander
- ¼ tsp of bay leaf
- 1 tsp salt
- 1 lb. ground lamb
- 1 egg
- 1 tsp ground black pepper

Steps to Cook

1. Peel the garlic clove and mince it. Combine the minced garlic with the ground lamb. Next, Sprinkle the meat mixture with the turmeric, cayenne pepper, ground coriander, bay leaf, salt, and ground black pepper. Beat the egg into the meat for strength. Then grate the onion and add it in the lamb as well.
2. Mix to make the dough smooth.
3. Next, preheat the air fryer to 400°F.
4. Put the butter in the basket tray of the air fryer and melt. Then make the meatballs from the lamb mixture and place in the basket pan of the air fryer.
5. Cook the dish for 14 minutes.
6. Stir the meatballs twice during cooking

Nutritional Information:

- Calories: 134
- Carbohydrates: 1.8g
- Fat: 6.2g
- Protein: 16.9g

Greek Lamb Kleftiko

Servings: 6

Preparation time: 25 min

Cook time: 30 minutes

Ingredients

- 2 oz garlic clove, peeled
- 1 tbsp dried oregano
- ½ lemon
- ¼ tbsp of ground cinnamon
- 3 tbsp of frozen butter
- 18 oz. leg of lamb
- 1 cup heavy cream
- 1 tsp bay leaves
- 1 tsp dried mint
- 1 tbsp canola oil

Steps to Cook

1. Crush the garlic cloves and combine them with the dried oregano and ground cinnamon. Mix them. Then chop the lemon. Sprinkle the leg of lamb with the crushed garlic mixture Then rub with the chopped lemon. Combine the heavy cream, bay leaf, and dried mint. Beat the mixture well.
2. After this, add the canola oil and beat one more time. Then pour the cream mixture over the leg of lamb and stir carefully. Let the leg of lamb marinated for 10 minutes.
3. Preheat the air fryer to 380°F. Chop the butter and sprinkle on the marinated lamb. Next, place the leg of lamb in the basket tray of the air fryer and sprinkle with the remaining cream mixture.
4. Next, sprinkle the meat with the minced butter.
5. Cook the meat for 30 minutes. When the time is up, remove the meat from the air fryer and sprinkle gently with the remaining cream mixture

Nutritional Information:

- Calories: 318
- Carbohydrates: 4.9g
- Fat: 21.9g
- Protein: 25.1g

Swedish Meatballs

Servings: 6

Preparation time: 15 min

Cook time: 11 minutes

Ingredients

- 1 tbsp of almond flour
- 1 lb. ground beef
- 1 tsp parsley
- 1 tsp dried dill
- ½ tsp of nutmeg
- 1 oz. onion, minced
- 1 tsp garlic powder
- 1 tsp salt
- ½ cup of heavy cream
- ¼ cup of chicken broth
- 1 tsp mustard
- 1 tsp black pepper
- 1 tbsp butter

Steps to Cook

1. Put the ground beef and almond flour in the bowl.
2. Next, put the dried dill, dried parsley, ground nutmeg, garlic powder, minced onion, salt, ground black pepper, and mustard.
3. Mix to get the meat of quiet strength. After this, make the meatballs from the beef forcemeat.
4. Preheat the air fryer to 380°F.
5. Put the veal meatballs in the basket tray of the air fryer. Add the butter and cook the dish for 5 minutes. After this, turn the meatballs on another side. Sprinkle meatballs with heavy cream and chicken broth. Cook the meatballs for 6 more minutes. When the meatballs are cooked - serve immediately with the creamy sauce.

Nutritional Information:

- Calories: 227
- Carbohydrates: 2.7g
- Fat: 12.9g
- Protein: 24.6g

Shredded Beef With Herbs

Servings: 6

Preparation time: 15 min

Cook time: 23 minutes

Ingredients

- 1 tsp thyme
- 1 tsp ground black pepper
- 1 tsp salt
- 1 tsp dried dill
- 1 tsp of mustard
- 4 cups of chicken broth
- 2 lbs beef steak
- 1 garlic clove, peeled
- 3 tbsp of butter
- 1 bay leaf

Steps to Cook

1. Preheat the air fryer to 360°F. Combine thyme, ground black pepper, salt, dried dill, and mustard in the small mixing bowl. Sprinkle the steak with the spice mixture from both sides.
2. Massage the steak with the help of your fingertip to make the meat soak in the spices.
3. Next, pour the chicken broth into the air fryer. Add the prepared fillet of beef and bay leaf—Cook the steak for 20 minutes.
4. When the time is up - strain the chicken broth and discard the steak from the air fryer.
5. Shred the meat with the help of 2 forks and put it back in the basket tray of the air fryer. Add the butter and cook the meat for 2 minutes at 365°F.
6. Mix the grated meat carefully.

Nutritional Information:

- Calories: 265
- Carbohydrates: 1.2g
- Fat: 14g
- Protein: 32.4g

Roasted Beef Tongue

Servings: 6

Preparation time: 20 min

Cook time: 10 minutes

Ingredients

- 1 lb beef tongue
- 1 tsp salt
- 1 tsp ground black pepper
- 1 tsp of paprika
- 1 tbsp butter
- 4 cups of water

Steps to Cook

1. Preheat the air fryer to 365°F.
2. Place the veal tongue on the air fryer basket tray and add water.
3. Sprinkle the mixture with the salt, ground black pepper, and paprika.
4. Cook the beef tongue for 15 minutes.
5. After this, strain the water from the beef tongue.
6. Cut the beef tongue into strips.
7. Next, place the butter in the air fryer basket pan and add the beef strips.
8. Cook the beef tongue strips for 5 minutes at 360 degrees Fahrenheit.

Nutritional Information:

- Calories: 234
- Carbohydrates: 0.4g
- Fat: 18.8g
- Protein: 14.7g

Bacon With Cabbage

Servings: 4

Preparation time: 10 min

Cook time: 15 minutes

Ingredients

- 4 oz. bacon, chopped
- 10 oz. white cabbage, shredded
- ¼ of a white onion, cut into cubes
- ½ tsp of salt
- 1 tsp of paprika
- 1 tsp of butter
- ½ tsp of ground black pepper

Steps to Cook

3. Preheat the air fryer to 360^0F.
4. Place the chopped bacon on the air fryer basket tray. Sprinkle with salt and paprika-
5. Add the butter and cook the bacon for 8 minutes.
6. After this, add the shredded cabbage, diced onion, butter, and ground black pepper.
7. Stir the mixture carefully and cook for 7 more minutes.
8. When the time is up, and the cabbage is tender, remove and serve.

Nutritional Information:

- Calories: 184
- Carbohydrates: 5.6g
- Fat: 13g
- Protein: 11.6g

Bacon Wrapped Asparagus

Servings: 6

Preparation time: 15 min

Cook time: 10 minutes

Ingredients

- 7 oz bacon sliced
- 14 oz asparagus
- 1 tsp salt
- 1 tsp ground black pepper
- 1 tbsp of sesame oil
- 1 tsp of paprika

Steps to Cook

1. Wrap the asparagus in the sliced bacon.
2. Preheat the air fryer to 380°F.
3. Put the wrapped asparagus in the air fryer and sprinkle the vegetables with the salt, ground black pepper, paprika, and sesame oil.
4. Cook the asparagus for 5 minutes.
5. After this, turn the asparagus to the other side and cook for 5 more minutes.
6. Then transfer the cooked dish onto serving plates.
7. Serve the garnish only hot
8.

Nutritional Information:

- Calories: 214
- Carbohydrates: 3.5g
- Fat: 16.2g
- Protein: 13.8g

Corned Meat

Servings: 8

Preparation time: 10 min

Cook time: 7 minutes

Ingredients

- 1 onion
- 1 tsp black pepper
- ¼ tsp cayenne pepper
- 1 cup of water
- 1 lb beef
- 1 tsp of butter
- ½ tsp of ground paprika

Steps to Cook

1. Peel the onion and cut it finely.
2. Sprinkle the onion with black pepper, cayenne pepper, and ground paprika.
3. Then add water and mix the onion carefully.
4. Preheat the air fryer to 400°F and put the tray with the sliced onion in the air fryer basket.
5. Cook the onion for 4 minutes.
6. After this, remove the pan from the air fryer and add the minced garlic.
7. Mix the onion and meat mixture carefully and return it to the air fryer.
8. Cook the beef mixture for 7 minutes at the same temperature.
9. After this, mix the meat mixture carefully with the help of the fork and cook the ground meat mixture for 8 minutes plus point
10. Then remove the cooked meat from the air fryer and mix gently with the help of the fork. Accompany it with white rice.

Nutritional Information:

- Calories: 310
- Carbohydrates: 4.2g
- Fat: 10.8g
- Protein: 46.4g

Chapter 3

Poultry Recipes

Ground Chicken Casserole

Servings: 6

Preparation time: 15 min

Cook time: 18 minutes

Ingredients

- 9 oz of ground chicken
- 5 oz bacon, sliced
- ½ onion
- 1 tsp salt
- ½ tsp of black pepper
- 1 tsp of paprika
- 1 tsp of turmeric
- 6 oz cheddar cheese
- 1 egg
- ½ cup of cream
- 1 tbsp of almond flour
- 1 tbsp butter

Steps to Cook

1. Take the tray out of the air fryer basket and spread with the butter. Put the ground chicken in the large bowl and add salt and ground black pepper.
2. Add the paprika and turmeric and stir the mixture well with the help of the spoon.
3. After this, grated cheddar cheese.
4. Beat the egg into the ground chicken mixture until smooth. Then mix the cream and the almond flour.
5. Peel the onion and dice it.
6. Place the ground chicken on the bottom of the air fryer pan. Sprinkle the ground chicken with the diced onion and cream mixture.
7. Then make the layer from the grated cheese and sliced bacon.
8. Preheat the air fryer to 380°F.
9. Cook for 18 minutes. When the casserole is cooked - let it cool briefly.

Nutritional Information

- Calories: 396
- Carbohydrates: 3.8g
- Fat: 28.6g
- Protein: 30.4g

Chicken Hash

Servings: 4

Preparation time: 10 min

Cook time: 14 minutes

Ingredients

- 6 oz. cauliflower
- 7 oz chicken fillet
- 1 carrot
- 1 potatoe
- 1 tbsp cream
- 3 tbsp of butter
- 1 tsp ground black pepper
- ½ onion
- 1 green pepper
- 1 tbsp of water

Steps to Cook

1. Chop the cauliflower roughly and put it in the blender. Mix carefully until you get the cauliflower rice. Chop the chicken fillet into small pieces.
2. Sprinkle the chicken fillet with the ground black pepper and stir.
3. Preheat the air fryer to 380^0F.
4. Put the prepared chicken in the basket tray of the air fryer, add water and cream and cook for 6 minutes. Reduce the heat of the air fryer to 360^0F.
5. Cut the onion, carrot, potato, and the green pepper. Next, add the cauliflower rice, diced onion, the carrot, potato, and chopped green bell pepper. Add the butter and mix the mixture.
6. Cook the dish for 8 other minutes.

Nutritional Information:

- Calories: 261
- Carbohydrates: 7.1g
- Fat: 16.8g
- Protein: 21g

Fried Chicken Strips

Servings: 4

Preparation time: 10 min

Cook time: 12 minutes

Ingredients

- 1 tsp of paprika
- ½ tsp of ground black pepper
- 1 tbsp butter
- ½ tsp of salt
- 1 lb chicken fillet
- 1 tbsp cream

Steps to Cook

1. Cut the chicken fillet into strips.
2. Sprinkle the chicken strips with the ground black pepper and salt.
3. Next, preheat the air fryer to 365°F.
4. Put the butter on the tray of the air fryer basket and add the chicken strips.
5. Cook the chicken strips for 6 minutes.
6. Then turn the chicken strips to the other side and cook for 5 more minutes.
7. After this, sprinkle the chicken strips with the cream and let it rest for 1 minute.

Nutritional Information:

- Calories: 245
- Carbohydrates: 0.6g
- Fat: 11.5g
- Protein: 33g

Chicken Wrapped In Pandan Leaves

Servings: 4

Preparation time: 20 min

Cook time: 10 minutes

Ingredients

- 15 oz chicken
- 1 pandan leaf
- ½ onion cut into cubes
- 1 tsp minced garlic
- 1 tsp chili flakes
- 1 tsp of Stevia
- 1 tsp black pepper
- 1 tsp turmeric
- 1 tbsp butter
- ¼ cup of coconut milk
- 1 tbsp chives

Steps to Cook

1. Cut the chicken into 4 large cubes. Put the chicken cubes in the large bowl. Sprinkle the chicken with the minced garlic, minced onion, chili flakes, Stevia, ground black pepper, chives, and turmeric.
2. Mix the meat with the help of your hands. Then cut the pandan sheet into 4 parts. Wrap the chicken cubes in pandan foil. Pour the coconut milk into the bowl with the wrapped chicken and leave it for 10 minutes.
3. Preheat the air fryer to 380°F. Put the pandan chicken in the fryer basket and cook the dish for 10 minutes. When chicken is done - transfer to serving plates and chill for at least 2 to 3 minutes.

Nutritional Information:

- Calories: 250
- Carbohydrates: 3.1g
- Fat: 12.6g
- Protein: 29.9g

Bacon Wrapped Cream Cheese Chicken

Servings: 4

Preparation time: 20 minutes

Cook time: 10 minutes

Ingredients

- 1 lb chicken breast, skinless, boneless
- 4 oz bacon, sliced
- 1 tsp of paprika
- ¼ cup of almond milk
- 1 tsp salt
- ½ tsp of ground black pepper
- 1 tsp turmeric
- 1 tsp fresh lemon juice
- 2 butter spoons
- 1 tsp canola oil

Steps to Cook

4. Lightly beat the chicken breast. Then rub the chicken breast with the paprika, salt, ground black pepper, and turmeric. Sprinkle the chicken breast with fresh lemon juice. Put the butter in the center of the chicken breast and roll-up.
5. Wrap the chicken roll in the sliced bacon and sprinkle the bacon chicken with the almond milk and canola oil.
6. Preheat the air fryer to 380°F.
7. Put the bacon chicken in the basket of the air fryer and cook for 8 minutes. Turn the chicken breast to the other side and cook it for 8 more minutes.
8. Don't worry if the bacon will be too crispy - it gives it the juicy texture of the chicken breast.

Nutritional Information:

- Calories: 383
- Carbohydrates: 2.2g
- Fat: 25.4g
- Protein: 35.1g

Cheesy Chicken Drumsticks

Servings: 4

Preparation time: 18 minutes

Cook time: 13 minutes

Ingredients

- 1 lb chicken drumstick
- 6 oz cheese left, sliced
- 1 tsp of dried rosemary
- 1 tsp dried oregano
- ½ tsp of salt
- ½ tsp of chili flakes

Steps to Cook

1. Sprinkle the chicken drumsticks with the dried rosemary, dried oregano, salt, and chili flakes.
2. Gently massage the chicken drumsticks and marinate for 5 minutes.
3. Preheat the air fryer to 370°F.
4. Place the marinated chicken drumsticks on the fryer pan and cook for 10 minutes.
5. Turn the chicken drumsticks on another side and cover with the layer of the sliced cheese.
6. Cook the chicken for 3 more minutes at the same temperature.
7. Next, transfer the chicken drumsticks to the large serving plate.

Nutritional Information:

- Calories: 226
- Carbohydrates: 1g
- Fat: 9.8g
- Protein: 16.4g

Roasted Garlic Chicken

Servings: 4

Preparation time: 20 minutes

Cook time: 16 minutes

Ingredients

- 3 oz fresh coriander root
- 1 tsp of olive oil
- 3 tbsp minced garlic
- ¼ tsp of a lemon, sliced
- ½ tsp of salt
- 1 tsp black pepper
- ½ tsp of chili flakes
- 1 tbsp dried parsley
- 1 lb chicken

Steps to Cook

1. Peel the fresh coriander and grate it. Next, combine the olive oil with the minced garlic, salt, ground black pepper, chili flakes, and dried parsley.
2. Coat the mixture and sprinkle the chicken stockings.
3. After this, add the sliced lemon and the grated coriander root.
4. Mix the chicken stockings carefully and let them marinate for 10 minutes in the fridge.
5. Meanwhile, preheat the air fryer to 365°F.
6. Place the chicken stockings in the basket tray of the air fryer. Add all the remaining liquid from the chicken stockings and cook the meat for 15 minutes.
7. When the time is up, gently turn the chicken to another side and cook for 1 more minute.

Nutritional Information:

- Calories: 187
- Carbohydrates: 3.6g
- Fat: 11.4g
- Protein: 20g

Crispy Fried Chicken Skin

Servings: 6

Preparation time: 10 minutes

Cook time: 6 minutes

Ingredients

- 1 lb chicken skin
- 1 tsp dried dill
- ½ tsp of ground black pepper
- ½ tsp of chili flakes
- ½ tsp of salt
- 1 tsp of butter

Steps to Cook

1. Cut the chicken skin roughly and sprinkle with the dried dill, ground black pepper, chili flakes, and salt.
2. Mix in the chicken skin. Melt the butter and add it to the chicken skin mixture. Mix the chicken skin with the help of the spoon.
3. Next, preheat the air fryer to 360°F.
4. Put the prepared chicken skin in the basket of the air fryer. Cook the chicken skin for 3 minutes on each side, cook the chicken skin more if you want the crispy effect

Nutritional Information:

- Calories: 350
- Carbohydrates: 0.2g
- Fat: 31.4g
- Protein: 15.5g

Air Fryer Crispy Curry Chicken

Servings: 4

Preparation time: 10 minutes

Cook time: 15 minutes

Ingredients

- 1 tsp of olive oil
- 1 lb chicken thighs, skinless, boneless
- 1 onion
- 2 tsp minced garlic
- 1 tbsp of apple cider vinegar
- 1 tbsp lemongrass
- ½ cup of coconut milk
- ½ cup of chicken broth
- 2 tbsp curry paste

Steps to Cook

1. Peel the onion and dice it. Next, Combine the chicken and chopped onion in the basket tray of the air fryer.
2. Preheat the air fryer to 365°F.
3. Put the chicken mixture in the deep fryer and cook for 5 minutes. After this, add the minced garlic, apple cider vinegar, lemongrass, coconut milk, chicken broth, and curry paste.
4. Mix the mixture with the help of the wooden spatula—Cook the chicken curry for 10 more minutes at the same temperature.
5. When the time is up, and the chicken curry is cooked, remove it from the fryer and stir once more.

Nutritional Information:

- Calories: 275
- Carbohydrates: 7.2g
- Fat: 15.7g
- Protein: 25.6g

Chicken Meatball Casserole

Servings: 7

Preparation time: 15 minutes

Cook time: 21 minutes

Ingredients

- 1 eggplant
- 10 oz ground chicken
- 8 oz ground beef
- 1 tsp minced garlic
- 1 tsp white pepper
- 1 tomato
- 1 egg
- 1 tbsp of coconut flour
- 8 oz parmesan, grated
- 2 butter spoons
- 1/3 cup of cream

Steps to Cook

1. Combine ground chicken and ground beef in a large bowl. Add the minced garlic and ground white pepper. Then beat the egg in the bowl with the ground beef mixture and stir carefully until the batter is homogeneous. Then add the coconut flour and mix.
2. Make the little ground beef meatballs.
3. Preheat the air fryer to 360°F. Then sprinkle the fryer basket pan with the butter and pour in the cream. Peel the eggplant and chop it.
4. Put the meatballs on the cream and sprinkle them with the chopped eggplant. Then cut the tomato and place it on the eggplant. Make the layer of the grated cheese over the sliced tomato. After this, put the casserole in the fryer and cook it for 21 minutes. When the time is up - let it cool down.

Nutritional Information:

- Calories: 314
- Carbohydrates: 7.5g
- Fat: 16.8g
- Protein: 33.9g

Chicken Goulash

Servings: 6

Preparation time: 10 minutes

Cook time: 17 minutes

Ingredients

- 1 white onion
- 2 green bell peppers, chopped
- 1 tsp of olive oil
- 14 oz ground chicken
- 2 tomatoes
- ½ cup of chicken broth
- 2 garlic cloves, sliced
- 1 tsp salt
- 1 tsp black pepper
- 1 tsp of mustard

Steps to Cook

1. Peel the onion and chop it more or less. Next, spray the basket pan of the air fryer with the olive oil inside—Preheat the air fryer to 365°F.
2. Place the diced onion in the basket tray of the air fryer. Add the chopped green bell pepper and cook the vegetables for 5 minutes. Then add the ground chicken. Chop the tomatoes into the small cubes and add them to the air fryer mix as well.
3. Cook the mixture for 6 more minutes. After this, add the chicken broth, sliced garlic cloves, salt, ground black pepper, and mustard. Mix the mixture carefully to obtain a homogeneous texture.
4. Cook the goulash for 6 more minutes.
5. When done, cut the cooked dish into the bowls.

Nutritional Information:

- Calories: 275
- Carbohydrates: 7.2g
- Fat: 15.7g
- Protein: 25.6g

Turkey Meatloaf

Servings: 12

Preparation time: 15 minutes

Cook time: 25 minutes

Ingredients

- 3 tbsp of butter
- 10 oz ground turkey
- 7 oz of ground chicken
- 1 tsp dried dill
- ½ tsp of coriander
- 2 tbsp of almond flour
- 1 tbsp minced garlic
- 3 oz. of fresh spinach
- 1 tsp salt
- 1 egg
- ½ tbsp of paprika
- 1 tsp of sesame oil

Steps to Cook

1. Put the ground turkey and ground chicken in the large bowl. Sprinkle ground poultry mixture with dried dill, ground coriander, almond flour, minced garlic, salt, and paprika. Then grind the fresh spinach and add it to the ground poultry mixture.
2. After this, beat the egg into the meat mixture and mix until the mixture is smooth. Spray the air fryer basket pan with the olive oil.
3. Preheat the air fryer to 350°F. Gently roll the ground beef mixture to make the layer flat. Then place the butter in the center of the meat layer. Next, make the meatloaf shape from the ground beef mixture. Use your fingertips for this step. Place the prepared meatloaf on the tray of the air fryer basket.
4. Cook the dish for 25 minutes.
5. When the meatloaf is cooked - let it cool well.
6. Next, remove the meatloaf from the air fryer basket tray and cut it into portions.

Nutritional Information:

- Calories: 142
- Carbohydrates: 1.7g
- Fat: 9.8g
- Protein: 13g

Turkey Meatballs

Servings: 9

Preparation time: 15 minutes

Cook time: 11 minutes

Ingredients

- 1 lb ground turkey
- 1 tsp chili flakes
- ¼ cup of chicken broth
- 2 tbsp dried dill
- 1 egg
- 1 tsp salt
- 1 tsp of paprika
- 1 tsp of coconut flour
- 2 tbsp heavy cream
- 1 tsp canola oil

Steps to Cook

1. Beat the egg in the bowl and beat with the help of the fork. Add ground turkey and chili flakes.
2. Sprinkle the mixture with the dried dill, salt, paprika, coconut flour, and mix. Make the meatballs from the ground turkey mixture.
3. Preheat the air fryer to 360°F.
4. Spray the air fryer basket pan with the canola oil.
5. Then put the meatballs there—Cook the meatballs for 6 minutes - for 3 minutes on each side.
6. After this, sprinkle the meatballs with the heavy cream. Cook the meatballs for 5 more minutes.
7. When the turkey meatballs are cooked, let them cool for 2 to 3 minutes.

Nutritional Information:

- Calories: 124
- Carbohydrates: 1.2g
- Fat: 7.9g
- Protein: 14.8g

Roasted Chicken Poppers

Servings: 9

Preparation time: 15 minutes

Cook time: 11 minutes

Ingredients

- ½ cup of coconut flour
- 1 tsp chili flakes
- 1 tsp ground black pepper
- 1 tsp garlic powder
- 11 oz chicken breast, boneless and skinless
- 1 tbsp canola oil

Steps to Cook

1. Cut the chicken breast into medium cubes and put them in the large bowl. Sprinkle the chicken cubes with the chili flakes, ground black pepper, garlic powder, and stir well with the palms of your hands. After this, sprinkle the chicken cubes with the almond flour.
2. Shake the bowl in the chicken cubes gently to coat the meat—Preheat the air fryer to 365°F. Sprinkle the air fryer basket pan with the canola oil. Then use the chicken cubes there—Cook the chicken poppers for 10 minutes. Turn the chicken poppers to another side after 5 minutes of cooking. Let the cooked chicken poppers cool gently and serve!

Nutritional Information:

- Calories: 124
- Carbohydrates: 1.2g
- Fat: 7.9g
- Protein: 14.8g

Roasted Whole Chicken With Herbs

Servings: 9

Preparation time: 15 minutes

Cook time: 75 minutes

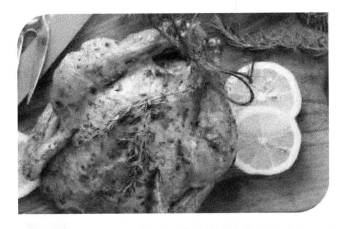

Ingredients

- A whole chicken, 6 lbs.
- Herbs for seasoning (basil, bay, cayenne, cumin, curry powder, dry mustard powder, oregano, rosemary, sage, and thyme.)
- 1 tsp kosher salt
- 1 tsp black pepper
- 1 tsp paprika
- 1 tbsp minced garlic
- 3 tbsp of butter
- 1 tsp canola oil
- ¼ cup of water
- ½ white onion

Steps to Cook

1. Rub the entire chicken with the kosher salt and ground black pepper and all the herbs inside and out. Then sprinkle with the ground paprika and minced garlic.
2. Peel the onion and dice it. Place the chopped onion inside the entire chicken. Then add the butter.
3. Rub the chicken with the canola oil outside.
4. Preheat the air fryer to 360°F and pour water into the air fryer basket.
5. Then place the rack and put all the chicken there.
6. Cook the chicken for 75 minutes.
7. When the chicken is cooked - it will have a little crispy skin.
8. Cut the cooked dish into portions.

Nutritional Information:

- Calories: 464
- Carbohydrates: 0.9g
- Fat: 20.1g
- Protein: 65.8g

Stuffed Turkey Rolls

Servings: 4

Preparation time: 10 minutes

Cook time: 12 minutes

Ingredients

- 1 lb. turkey fillet
- 2 tbsp garlic clove, sliced
- 1 tsp apple cider vinegar
- ½ white onion
- ½ tsp of salt
- 1 tsp of paprika
- 1 tsp dried dill
- 1 tsp chives
- 4 tsp of butter

Steps to Cook

1. Cut the turkey fillet into 4 parts. Next, beat each turkey fillet gently. Sprinkle the turkey fillets with the apple cider vinegar, salt, paprika and dried dill.
2. Chop the onion and combine it with the sliced garlic clove. Add the chives and butter. Mix the mixture until it is homogeneous. Next, place the scrambled garlic mixture in the center of each turkey fillet.
3. Roll up the steaks and secure the rolls tightly with the toothpicks.
4. Preheat the air fryer to 360°F. Place the turkey rolls on the air fryer basket tray and cook the dish for 12 minutes. Turn the rolls on another side once per cook.

Nutritional Information:

- Calories: 155
- Carbohydrates: 4.5g
- Fat: 20.1g
- Protein: 24.2g

Breast Chicken Stew

Servings: 6

Preparation time: 15 minutes

Cook time: 12 minutes

Ingredients

- 8 oz chicken breast
- 1 white onion
- ½ cup of spinach
- 2 cups of chicken broth
- 5 oz. white cabbage
- 6 oz. cauliflower
- 1/3 cup of heavy cream
- 1 tsp salt
- 1 green pepper
- 1 tsp of paprika
- 1 tsp cayenne pepper
- 1 tsp of butter
- 1 tsp ground coriander

Steps to Cook

1. Cut the chicken breast into large cubes. Sprinkle the chicken cubes with the salt, paprika, cayenne pepper, and ground coriander.
2. Preheat the air fryer to 365^0F.
3. Put the butter in the basket tray of the air fryer and melt. Then add the chicken cubes and cook for 4 minutes. Meanwhile, chop the spinach and chop the onion. Then shred the cabbage and cut the cauliflower into small florets.
4. Then chop the green pepper. When the time is up, add all the prepared ingredients to the air fryer basket tray. Pour in heavy cream and chicken broth.
5. Set the fryer to 360^0F and cook the stew for 8 more minutes. Stir gently with the help of the spatula.

Nutritional Information:

- Calories: 102
- Carbohydrates: 6.4g
- Fat: 4.5g
- Protein: 9.8g

Ground Chicken Pizza

Servings: 6

Preparation time: 15 minutes

Cook time: 12 minutes

Ingredients

- 10 oz ground chicken
- 1 tsp minced garlic
- 1 tsp of almond flour
- ½ tsp of salt
- 1 tsp black pepper
- 1 large egg
- 6 oz cheddar cheese, grated
- ½ tsp of dried dill

Steps to Cook

1. Put the ground chicken in the bowl. Sprinkle with minced garlic, almond flour, salt, ground black pepper, and dried dill. Then break the egg into the ground chicken mixture and mix it in with the help of the spoon when you get the smooth and homogeneous texture of the ground chicken.
2. Preheat the air fryer to 380°F.
3. Cover the pizza pan of the air fryer with the parchment. Next, place the ground chicken mixture on the pizza pan of the air fryer and make the shape of the pizza crust—Cook the chicken pizza crust for 8 minutes. Next, remove the chicken pizza and sprinkle with the grated cheese generously—Cook for 4 other minutes at 365°F.

Nutritional Information:

- Calories: 244
- Carbohydrates: 1.9g
- Fat: 16.1g
- Protein: 22.9g

Chicken And Eggplant Cheesy Lasagna

Servings: 8

Preparation time: 21 minutes

Cook time: 17 minutes

Ingredients

- 6 oz cheddar cheese, grated
- 7 oz Parmesan cheese, grated
- 2 eggplant
- 1 lb. ground chicken
- 1 tsp of paprika
- 1 tsp salt
- ½ tsp of cayenne pepper
- ½ cup of heavy cream
- 2 tsp butter
- 1 onion cut into cubes

Steps to Cook

1. Spread the butter on the tray of the air fryer basket. Then peel the eggplant and cut them. Separate the sliced eggplant into 3 parts.
2. Combine ground chicken with paprika, salt, cayenne pepper, and diced onion. Mix the mixture.
3. Separate the ground chicken mixture into 2 parts.
4. Make the layer of the first part of the sliced eggplant on the tray of the air fryer basket. Next, layer the ground chicken mixture.
5. Sprinkle the layer of ground chicken with half of the grated cheddar cheese. Then top the cheese with the second part of the sliced eggplant. The next step is to layer the ground chicken and all the shredded cheddar cheese. Cover the cheese layer with the last piece of the sliced eggplant. Then, sprinkle with grated Parmesan cheese. Pour in the heavy cream and add the butter.
6. Preheat the air fryer to 365°F. Cook the lasagna for 17 minutes.

Nutritional Information:

- Calories: 348
- Carbohydrates: 10.9g
- Fat: 20.6g
- Protein: 31.4g

Sweet Sour Chicken Breas

Servings: 4

Preparation time: 20 minutes

Cook time: 12 minutes

Ingredients

- 1 lb. chicken breast, boneless, skinless
- 3 tbsp Stevia extract
- 1 tsp white pepper
- ½ tsp of paprika
- 1 tsp cayenne pepper
- 1 tsp lemongrass
- 1 tsp lemon zest
- 1 tbsp of apple cider vinegar
- 1 tbsp butter

Steps to Cook

4. Sprinkle the chicken breast with the apple cider vinegar. After this, rub the chicken breast with the ground white pepper, paprika, cayenne pepper, lemongrass, and lemon zest.
5. Leave the chicken breast for 5 minutes to marinate.
6. After this, rub the chicken breast with the Stevia extract and leave it for 5 more minutes.
7. Preheat air fryers to 380°F.
8. Rub the prepared chicken breast with the butter and place it on the tray of the air fryer basket.
9. Cook the chicken breast for 12 minutes.
10. Turn the chicken breast to another side after 6 minutes of cooking.

Nutritional Information:

- Calories: 160
- Carbohydrates: 1g
- Fat: 5.9g
- Protein: 24.2g

Duck Legs With Lemon

Servings: 6

Preparation time: 25 minutes

Cook time: 25 minutes

Ingredients

- 1 lemon
- 2 lb. duck legs
- 1 tsp ground coriander
- 1 tsp ground nutmeg
- 1 tsp kosher salt
- ½ tsp of dried rosemary
- 1 tbsp of olive oil
- 1 tsp of Stevia extract
- ¼ tsp of sage

Steps to Cook

1. Squeeze the lemon juice and grate the zest. Combine lemon juice and lemon zest in a large bowl.
2. Add the ground coriander, ground nutmeg, kosher salt, dried rosemary, and sage. Sprinkle the liquid with the olive oil and the Stevia extract.
3. Beat carefully and put the duck feet there.
4. Stir the duck legs and leave for 15 minutes to marinate.
5. Meanwhile, preheat the air fryer to 380°F.
6. Put the marinated duck legs in the deep fryer and cook for 25 minutes. Turn the duck feet to another side after 15 minutes of cooking.

Nutritional Information:

- Calories: 296
- Carbohydrates: 1.6g
- Fat: 11.5g
- Protein: 44.2g

Chicken Kebab

Servings: 5

Preparation time: 15 minutes

Cook time: 10 minutes

Ingredients

- 14 oz. chicken fillet
- ½ cup of heavy cream
- 1 tsp kosher salt
- ½ tsp of ground black pepper
- 1 tsp turmeric
- 1 tsp curry powder
- 1 tsp of olive oil

Steps to Cook

1. Combine the heavy cream with the kosher salt, ground black pepper, turmeric, and curry powder.
2. Beat the mixture well.
3. Add the oil and praise it again.
4. Cut the chicken fillet into pieces.
5. Add the chicken pieces to the prepared heavy cream mixture and stir carefully.
6. Preheat the air fryer to 360°F.
7. Put the chicken kebab on the fryer shelf and cook for 10 minutes.

Nutritional Information:

- Calories: 204
- Carbohydrates: 1g
- Fat: 11.4g
- Protein: 23.3g

Chapter 4

Seafood Recipes

Salmon Pie With Egg

Servings: 8

Preparation time: 20 minutes

Cook time: 30 minutes

Ingredients

- ½ cup of cream
- 1 ½ cups of almond flour
- ½ tsp of baking soda
- 1 tbsp of apple cider vinegar
- 1 onion cut into cubes
- 1 lb salmon
- 1 tbsp chives
- 1 tsp dried oregano
- 1 tsp dried dill
- 1 tsp of butter
- 1 egg
- 1 tsp dried parsley
- 1 tbsp ground paprika

Steps to Cook

1. Beat the egg in the bowl and beat it.
2. Then add the cream and keep beating for 2 more minutes.
3. After this, add baking soda and apple cider vinegar.
4. Add the almond flour and knead the dough smooth and not sticky.
5. Then cut the salmon into small pieces.
6. Sprinkle the chopped salmon with the diced onion, chives, dried oregano, dried dill, dried parsley, and ground paprika. Mix well.
7. Next, cut the dough into 2 parts.
8. Cover the pan of the air fryer basket with the parchment.
9. Put the first part of the dough on the tray of the air fryer basket. And make the crust out of it with your fingertips.
10. Then add the salmon filling.

11. Roll the second part of the dough with the help of the rolling pin and cover the salmon filling.
12. Set the edges of the cake.
13. Preheat the air fryer to 360°F.
14. Place the air fryer basket tray in the fryer and cook the cake for 15 minutes.
15. After that, reduce the power to 355°F and cook the cake for 15 more minutes.

Nutritional Information:

- Calories: 134
- Carbohydrates: 3.3g
- Fat: 8.1g
- Protein: 13.2g

Salmon Casserole

Servings: 8

Preparation time: 20 min

Cook time: 12 minutes

Ingredients

- 7 oz cheddar cheese, grated
- ½ cup of cream
- 1 lb. salmon fillet
- 1 tbsp dried dill
- 1 tsp dried parsley
- 1 tsp salt
- 1 tsp ground coriander
- ½ tsp of black pepper
- 2 green bell peppers, chopped
- 1 onion cut into cubes
- 7 oz bok choy, chopped
- 1 tbsp canola oil

Steps to Cook

1. Sprinkle the salmon fillet with the dried dill, dried parsley, ground coriander, and ground black pepper.
2. Gently massage the salmon fillet and leave it for 5 minutes to let the fish roll the spices.
3. Meanwhile, sprinkle the pan of the air fryer with the canola oil inside. After this, cut the salmon fillet into cubes. Separate the salmon cubes into two parts.
4. Next, place the first part of the salmon cubes on the saucepan tray. Sprinkle the fish with the chopped bok choy, diced onion, and chopped green bell pepper. After this, place the second part of the salmon cubes on the vegetables. Then sprinkle the casserole with the grated cheese and heavy cream.
5. Preheat the air fryer to 380°F.
6. Cook the salmon casserole for 12 minutes.

Nutritional Information:

- Calories: 216
- Carbohydrates: 4.3g
- Fat: 14.4g
- Protein: 18.2g

Eggplant And Mushrooms Salad

Servings: 6

Preparation time: 20 min

Cook time: 23 minutes

Ingredients

- 1 cup of water
- 1 eggplant
- 6 oz white mushrooms
- 1 clove garlic, sliced
- 2 tbsp apple cider vinegar
- 1 tbsp of olive oil
- 1 tsp canola oil
- ½ tbsp flax seeds
- 1 tsp black pepper
- 1 tsp salt

Steps to Cook

1. Peel the eggplant and cut it into medium cubes.
2. Then sprinkle the eggplant cubes with the half teaspoon of salt.
3. Gently stir the eggplant cubes and leave for 5 minutes.
4. Meanwhile, cut the white mushrooms.
5. Preheat the air fryer to 400°F.
6. Pour water into the basket tray of the air fryer.
7. Add the chopped mushrooms, half a teaspoon of salt, and cook for 8 minutes.
8. Next, strain the water from the mushrooms and cool them.
9. Next, place the eggplant cubes in the air fryer and sprinkle with the canola oil.
10. Cook the eggplants for 15 minutes at 400°F.
11. Stir the eggplants after 7 minutes of cooking.
12. When the aubergines are cooked, let them cool slightly.
13. Combine the aubergines with the chopped mushrooms in the salad bowl.
14. Sprinkle the plate with the flax seeds, olive oil, sliced garlic clove, and ground black pepper.
15. After this, add the apple cider vinegar and stir the salad carefully.
16. Let the salad rest for 5 minutes.

Nutritional Information:

- Calories: 62
- Carbohydrates: 6.9g
- Fat: 3.5g
- Protein: 2g

Tuna In White Wine

Servings: 4

Preparation time: 5 minutes

Cook time: 40 minutes

Ingredients

- 1 lb. tuna in tacos
- 1 leek
- 1 green bell pepper
- 1 clove garlic
- 1 lb. chopped natural tomato
- 2 tbsp of olive oil
- ½ cup of white wine
- 3 bay leaves
- 1 tsp of sugar
- Salt

Steps to Cook

1. Open the jar of chopped natural tomato and drain the liquid.
2. Finely chop the garlic and chop the leek and bell pepper.
3. In a large skillet or casserole, fry the garlic and the leek for 5 minutes and then add the chopped green pepper—salt and cook over low heat for 10 minutes.
4. Then add the bay leaves and the chopped tomato, add the teaspoon of sugar and a little more salt, remove all the sauce, and continue cooking slowly for 15 more minutes. Stir occasionally to prevent sticking.
5. Add the white wine and the previously salted tuna tacos. Cover and leave 10 minutes until the tuna turns white, but without letting it dry.

Nutritional Information:

- Calories: 160
- Carbohydrates: 14.3g
- Fat: 7.6g
- Protein: 9.2g

Crab With White Mushrooms

Servings: 5

Preparation time: 15 minutes

Cook time: 5 minutes

Ingredients

- 7 oz. crab meat
- 10 oz. white mushrooms
- ½ tsp of salt
- ¼ cup of fish broth
- 1 tsp of butter
- ¼ tsp of ground coriander
- 1 tsp dried coriander
- 1 tsp of butter

Steps to Cook

1. Chop the crab meat and sprinkle with the salt and dried coriander. Mix the crab meat carefully.
2. Preheat the air fryer to 400°F.
3. Chop the white mushrooms and combine them with the crab meat.
4. After this, add the fish stock, ground coriander, and butter.
5. Transfer the garnish mixture into the air fryer basket pan.
6. Stir gently with the help of the plastic spatula.
7. Cook the garnish for 5 minutes.

Nutritional Information:

- Calories: 56
- Carbohydrates: 2.6g
- Fat: 1.7g
- Protein: 7g

Mayonnaise Baked Hake

Servings: 3

Preparation time: 10 min

Cook time: 20 minutes

Ingredients

- 1 lb. skinless hake fillets (frozen)
- ½ lb. light mayonnaise
- ½ lb. light cream
- 1 tbsp of olive oil
- Pepper to taste
- Salt to taste

Steps to Cook

1. Let the hake fillets thaw at room temperature.
2. Gently clean and pat dry each fillet with a kitchen paper napkin.
3. Add salt and pepper to each fillet on both sides and place them on a baking tray, brush with the tablespoon of olive oil so that the fillets do not stick when cooking.
4. In a bowl, mix the mayonnaise with the liquid cream and a little salt and pepper very well.
5. Next, place the mayonnaise and cream mixture on top of the hake fillets and cook in the oven, previously preheated to 400°F, for 20 minutes.
6. Serve hot accompanied by salad, tomato slices, steamed potatoes, or any other light garnish.

Nutritional Information:

- Calories: 97.7
- Carbohydrates: 2.4g
- Fat: 5.9g
- Protein: 17.4g

Chapter 5

Vegetable Recipes

Roasted Spiced Asparagus

Servings: 6

Preparation time: 9 minutes

Cook time: 6 minutes

Ingredients

- 1 lb. asparagus
- 1 tsp salt
- 1 tsp chili flakes
- ½ tsp of ground white pepper
- 1 tbsp of sesame oil
- 1 tbsp of flax seeds

Steps to Cook

1. Combine the sesame oil with the salt, chili flakes, and ground white pepper.
2. Coat the mixture.
3. Preheat the air fryer to 400°F.
4. Place the asparagus on the air fryer basket tray and sprinkle with the sesame oil and spice mixture.
5. Cook the asparagus for 6 minutes.
6. When the dish is cooked - let it cool for a few minutes.
7. Serve it

Nutritional Information:

- Calories: 42
- Carbohydrates: 3.4g
- Fat: 2.7g
- Protein: 1.9g

Shirataki Noodles

Servings: 4

Preparation time: 5 minutes

Cook time: 3 minutes

Ingredients

- 2 cups of water
- 1 tsp salt
- 1 tsp Italian seasoning
- 8 oz. shirataki noodles

Steps to Cook

1. Preheat the air fryer to 365°F.
2. Pour the water into the air fryer basket pan and preheat for 3 minutes. Then add the shirataki noodles, salt, and Italian seasoning.
3. Cook the shirataki noodles for 1 minute at the same temperature. Next, strain the noodles and cook for 2 more minutes at 360°F.
4. When the shirataki noodles are cooked, let them cool for 1 to 2 minutes. Gently stir the noodles.

Nutritional Information:

- Calories: 16
- Carbohydrates: 1.4g
- Fat: 1g
- Protein: 0g

Roasted Cauliflower Rice

Servings: 6

Preparation time: 8 minutes

Cook time: 10 minutes

Ingredients

- 1 white onion cut into cubes
- 3 tbsp of butter
- 1 tsp salt
- 1 lb. cauliflower
- 1 tsp minced garlic
- 1 tsp ground ginger
- 1 cup of chicken broth

Steps to Cook

1. Wash the cauliflower and chop it roughly.
2. Next, put the chopped cauliflower in the blender and blend until you get the rice texture of cauliflower. Transfer the cauliflower rice to the mixing bowl. Add the diced onion.
3. After this, sprinkle the vegetable mixture with the salt, turmeric, minced garlic, and ground ginger.
4. Mix.
5. Preheat the air fryer to 370°F. Put the cauliflower rice mixture there. Next, add the butter and chicken broth—Cook the cauliflower rice for 10 minutes.
6. When the time is up - remove the cauliflower rice from the air fryer and strain the excess liquid.
7. Stir gently.

Nutritional Information:

- Calories: 82
- Carbohydrates: 6.5g
- Fat: 6g
- Protein: 2g

Zucchini Gratin

Servings: 6

Preparation time: 15 minutes

Cook time: 13 minutes

Ingredients

- 2 zucchini
- 1 tbsp dried parsley
- 1 tbsp of coconut flour
- 5 oz. parmesan cheese, grated
- 1 tsp of butter
- 1 tsp ground black pepper

Steps to Cook

1. Combine the dried parsley, coconut flour, ground black pepper, and grated cheese in the large bowl.
2. Shake gently to make the dough homogeneous.
3. Then wash the zucchini and slice them.
4. Then cut the zucchini to make squares.
5. Spread the air fryer basket pan with the butter and place the zucchini squares there.
6. Preheat the air fryer to 400°F.
7. Sprinkle the zucchini squares with the dried parsley mixture—Cook the zucchini gratin for 13 minutes.
8. When cooked, the zucchini gratin will have a light brown surface color.

Nutritional Information:

- Calories: 98
- Carbohydrates: 4.2g
- Fat: 6g
- Protein: 8.6g

Winter Squash Spaghetti

Servings: 8

Preparation time: 10 minutes

Cook time: 10 minutes

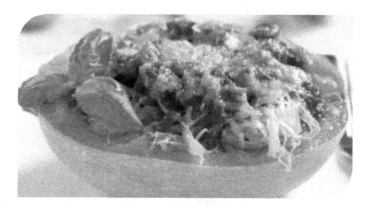

Ingredients

- 4 tbsp heavy cream
- 1 cup of chicken broth
- 1 lb. winter squash
- 1 tsp salt
- 1 tsp ground black pepper
- 1 tsp of butter

Steps to Cook

1. Peel the winter squash and grate to get the spaghetti.
2. Preheat the air fryer to 400°F.
3. Put the winter squash spaghetti in the basket tray of the air fryer. Sprinkle in the chicken broth and salt.
4. Add the ground black pepper and cook the dish for 10 minutes. When the time is up - strain the excess liquid from the winter squash spaghetti.
5. Then add the butter and heavy cream and stir.
6. Serve the garnish immediately.
7. Enjoy!

Nutritional Information:

- Calories: 55
- Carbohydrates: 6.4g
- Fat: 3.4g
- Protein: 0.7g

Kale Puree

Servings: 7

Preparation time: 10 minutes

Cook time: 12 minutes

Ingredients

- 1 lb. Italian dark leafy kale
- 7 oz. grated Parmesan
- 1 tsp salt
- 1 cup heavy cream
- 1 tsp of butter
- 1 tsp ground black pepper
- 1 white onion cut into cubes

Steps to Cook

1. Cut the kale carefully and place it on the air fryer basket tray.
2. Sprinkle the chopped kale with the salt, butter, ground black pepper, diced onion, and heavy cream.
3. Preheat the air fryer to 250°F.
4. Cook the kale for 12 minutes.
5. When the time is up - mix the kale puree carefully to make it homogeneous.
6. Serve the kale puree and enjoy it!

Nutritional Information:

- Calories: 180
- Carbohydrates: 6.8g
- Fat: 13.2g
- Protein: 10.9g

Roasted Celery Stalk

Servings: 6

Preparation time: 10 minutes

Cook time: 8 minutes

Ingredients

- 1 lb. celery size
- 1 tbsp butter
- 1 white onion, sliced
- 1 cup of chicken broth
- 2 tbsp heavy cream
- 1 tsp salt
- 1 tbsp of paprika

Steps to Cook

1. Cut the celery stalk roughly. Pour the chicken broth into the air fryer basket pan and add the sliced onion.
2. Preheat the air fryer to 400°F. Cook the onion for 4 minutes. After this, reduce the heat to 365°F.
3. Add the chopped celery stalk, butter, salt, paprika, and heavy cream. Mix the vegetable mixture.
4. Cook the celery for 8 more minutes.
5. When the time is up - the celery stalk should be very soft.
6. Cool the garnish to room temperature.
7. Serve it and enjoy it!

Nutritional Information:

- Calories: 59
- Carbohydrates: 4.9g
- Fat: 4.2g
- Protein: 1.1g

Eggplant Stew

Servings: 7

Preparation time: 10 minutes

Cook time: 13 minutes

Ingredients

- 1 eggplant
- 1 zucchini
- 1 onion
- 1 green pepper
- 2 garlic cloves, peeled
- 1 tsp turmeric
- 1 tsp of paprika
- 1 tsp dried dill
- 1 tsp dried parsley
- 1 cup of vegetable broth
- ½ cup of heavy cream
- 1 tsp kosher salt

Steps to Cook

1. Cut the zucchini and aubergine into cubes.
2. Then sprinkle the vegetables with the dried parsley, dried dill, paprika, and turmeric. Chop the garlic cloves.
3. Then chop the onion and green pepper.
4. Preheat the air fryer to 390^0F.
5. Pour the chicken broth into the air fryer and add the eggplants.
6. Cook the eggplants for 2 minutes.
7. After this, add the chopped onion and green pepper.
8. Next, add the minced garlic cloves and heavy cream.
9. Cook the stew for an additional 11 minutes at the same temperature.

Nutritional Information:

- Calories: 65
- Carbohydrates: 8.1g
- Fat: 3.6g
- Protein: 1.7g

Creamy White Mushrooms

Servings: 4

Preparation time: 10 minutes

Cook time: 12 minutes

Ingredients

- 9 oz. white mushrooms
- 1 tsp garlic sliced
- 1 onion, sliced
- 1 cup of cream
- 1 tsp of butter
- 1 tsp of olive oil
- 1 tsp ground red pepper
- 1 tsp chili flakes

Steps to Cook

1. Cut the white mushrooms. Sprinkle the white mushrooms with the chili flakes and ground red pepper.
2. Mix the mixture.
3. After this, preheat the air fryer to 400°F.
4. Pour the olive oil into the basket tray of the air fryer.
5. Then add the sliced mushrooms and cook the vegetables for 5 minutes. After this, add the sliced onion, cream, butter, sliced garlic, and mix the mushroom gently with the help of the spatula.
6. Cook the dish for 7 minutes at 365°F.
7. When the time is up, remember the garnish carefully

Nutritional Information:

- Calories: 84
- Carbohydrates: 7g
- Fat: 2.9g
- Protein: 2.9g

Green Bean Puree

Servings: 8

Preparation time: 10 minutes

Cook time: 12 minutes

Ingredients

- 1 cup green beans
- 6 oz. cheddar cheese, grated
- 7 oz. Parmesan cheese, grated
- ¼ cup of heavy cream
- 1 zucchini
- 1 tsp salt
- 1 tsp of paprika
- ½ tsp of cayenne pepper
- 1 tbsp dried parsley
- 1 tbsp butter

Steps to Cook

1. Cut the zucchini into cubes and sprinkle with the paprika and salt. Next, place the butter in the basket tray of the air fryer. Add the zucchini cubes in the butter.
2. Preheat the air fryers to 400°F and cook the zucchini for 6 minutes. Next, add the green beans, grated cheddar cheese, and cayenne pepper.
3. After this, sprinkle the casserole with the grated Parmesan cheese. Pour in the heavy cream.
4. Cook the casserole for 6 more minutes at 400 degrees Fahrenheit. When is cooked - let it cool well

Nutritional Information:

- Calories: 201
- Carbohydrates: 3.3g
- Fat: 15.3g
- Protein: 21.4g

Roasted Cabbage

Servings: 4

Preparation time: 10 minutes

Cook time: 5 minutes

Ingredients

- 9 oz. white cabbage, sliced
- 1 tsp salt
- 1 tsp of butter
- 1 tsp of olive oil
- 1 tsp of paprika
- ½ tsp of ground black pepper

Steps to Cook

1. Combine the olive oil and the paprika. Melt the butter and add it to the olive oil mixture. After this, add the ground black pepper and fasten it.
2. Rub the sliced white cabbage well with the spice mixture.
3. Then sprinkle the white cabbage slices with the salt.
4. Preheat the air fryer to 400°F.
5. Place the cabbage slices on the fryer rack and cook the dish for 3 minutes.
6. After this, turn the cabbage slices to the other side and cook for 2 more minutes.
7. When the cabbage slices are cooked, they will have a light brown surface.

Nutritional Information:

- Calories: 37
- Carbohydrates: 4.2g
- Fat: 2.3g
- Protein: 0.9g

Creamy Spinach

Servings: 6

Preparation time: 10 minutes

Cook time: 11 minutes

Ingredients

- 2 cups of spinach
- 1 cup of cream
- 2 butter spoons
- ¼ cup of coconut milk
- 1 oz. walnuts, crushed
- 5 oz. cheddar cheese shredded
- 1 tsp salt

Steps to Cook

1. Wash the spinach and slice it. Sprinkle the spinach with the salt and mix it to let the spinach give the juice.
2. Next, preheat the air fryer to 380°F.
3. Place the spinach in the basket tray of the air fryer.
4. Add the coconut milk, crushed walnuts, butter, and cream.
5. Cook the spinach for 8 minutes.
6. After this, stir the spinach with the wooden spatula.
7. Add the grated cheese and cook for 3 more minutes.
8. When the time is up, carefully mix the melted cheese and spinach.

Nutritional Information:

- Calories: 209
- Carbohydrates: 2.9g
- Fat: 19.1g
- Protein: 7.9g

Roasted Broccoli With Sriracha

Servings: 5

Preparation time: 10 minutes

Cook time: 6 minutes

Ingredients

- 1 tsp sriracha
- 1 tbsp canola oil
- 1 tsp flax seeds
- 1 tsp ground white pepper
- 1 tsp kosher salt
- 1 lb. broccoli
- 4 tbsp vegetable broth

Steps to Cook

1. Wash the broccoli and separate it into the florets.
2. Next, combine the chicken broth, ground white pepper, flax seeds, and sriracha.
3. Add the canola oil and beat the mixture.
4. Preheat the air fryer to 400°F.
5. Put the broccoli florets on the fryer basket rack and sprinkle the vegetables with the sriracha mixture.
6. Cook the broccoli for 6 minutes.
7. When the time is up, shake the broccoli gently and transfer it to the serving plates.

Nutritional Information:

- Calories: 61
- Carbohydrates: 6.7g
- Fat: 3.3g
- Protein: 2.7g

Cheesy Cauliflower

Servings: 7

Preparation time: 15 minutes

Cook time: 11 minutes

Ingredients

- 14 oz. cauliflower
- 6 oz. cheddar cheese, sliced
- 1 tsp salt
- 1 tsp ground black pepper
- 1 tsp of frozen butter
- 1 tsp dried dill
- 1 tbsp of olive oil

Steps to Cook

1. Wash the head of cauliflower carefully and cut it into portions. Sprinkle the sliced cauliflower with the salt, ground black pepper, and dried dill.
2. Grate the frozen butter. Next, sprinkle the cauliflower with the olive oil on both sides.
3. Preheat the air fryer to 400°F.
4. Place the cauliflower in the air fryer and cook for 7 minutes. After this, turn the cauliflower on another side and sprinkle with the grated frozen butter. Cook the cauliflower for 3 more minutes.
5. Next, place the cheese on the cauliflower and cook it for another minute.

Nutritional Information:

- Calories: 135
- Carbohydrates: 3.6g
- Fat: 10.7g
- Protein: 7.2g

Roasted Cauliflower

Servings: 6

Preparation time: 10 minutes

Cook time: 15 minutes

Ingredients

- 1 oz. cauliflower head
- 1 tsp onion powder
- ½ cup of heavy cream
- 5 oz. parmesan, grated
- 1 tsp garlic powder
- 1 tsp salt

Steps to Cook

1. Combine heavy cream, onion powder, garlic powder, salt, and grated Parmesan cheese in a large bowl. Mix the mixture. Next, place the cauliflower head in the heavy cream mixture.
2. Cover the cauliflower with the heavy cream mixture with your hands.
3. Next, preheat the air fryer to 360°F.
4. Place the cauliflower head in the fryer basket and cook for 12 minutes.
5. After this, increase the temperature to 390°F and cook the cauliflower head for 3 minutes.

Nutritional Information:

- Calories: 132
- Carbohydrates: 5.8g
- Fat: 8.8g
- Protein: 9.4g

Cheesy Zucchini

Servings: 8

Preparation time: 10 minutes

Cook time: 12 minutes

Ingredients

- 3 zucchini
- 1 tbsp canola oil
- ½ tsp of chili powder
- 1 tsp garlic powder
- 6 oz. cheddar cheese shredded

Steps to Cook

1. Cut the zucchini into cubes.
2. Sprinkle the zucchini cubes with eth chili powder, garlic powder, and olive oil.
3. Next, preheat the air fryer to 400°F.
4. Place the zucchini cubes in the air fryer and cook the vegetables for 10 minutes.
5. Then sprinkle the zucchini with the grated cheese.
6. Cook the garnish for two more minutes.
7. When zucchini is cooked - transfer it to serving plates.

Nutritional Information:

- Calories: 115
- Carbohydrates: 3.1g
- Fat: 9g
- Protein: 6.3g

Artichoke Stuffed With Spinach

Servings: 5
Preparation time: 15 minutes
Cook time: 40 minutes

Ingredients

- 4 tbsp fresh chopped spinach
- ½ tbsp of heavy cream
- 1 tsp of butter
- 1 tsp salt
- 1 lb. artichoke
- 1 tsp of olive oil
- ½ lemon
- 1 tsp ground black pepper

Steps to Cook

1. Prepare the artichokes and remove the core from them. Next, combine the chopped spinach with the heavy cream and butter. Mix the mixture.
2. After this, rub the artichokes with the salt, olive oil, ground black pepper, and half of the lemon.
3. Fill the artichokes with the cream of spinach mixture.
4. Then wrap the artichokes in the foil.
5. Preheat the air fryer to 350°F.
6. Put the wrapped artichokes in the basket of the air fryer and cook for 40 minutes.
7. When the time is up, and the artichokes are cooked, discard them from the fryer.
8. Remove foil and serve garnish immediately

Nutritional Information:

- Calories: 66
- Carbohydrates: 10.4g
- Fat: 2.4g
- Protein: 3.2g

Roasted Shredded Brussels Sprouts

Servings: 6

Preparation time: 10 minutes

Cook time: 15 minutes

Ingredients

- 17 oz. brussels sprouts
- 1 oz of butter
- 1 tbsp of olive oil
- 1 tsp ground white pepper
- 1 tsp salt
- 1 tbsp of apple cider vinegar

Steps to Cook

1. Place the brussels sprouts in the blender and crumbled.
   Next, preheat the air fryer to 380°F.
2. Place the grated brussels sprouts on the tray of the air fryer basket. Add the butter, olive oil, ground white pepper, salt, and apple cider vinegar.
3. Mix the grated Brussels sprouts carefully with the help of the spoon.
4. Cook the dish in the preheated air fryer for 15 minutes. When the time is up, remove the plate from the fryer and stir. Serve it immediately.

Nutritional Information:

- Calories: 90
- Carbohydrates: 7.6g
- Fat: 6.4g
- Protein: 2.8g

Cauliflower Rice With Parmesan And Pesto

Servings: 7

Preparation time: 10 minutes

Cook time: 13 minutes

Ingredients

- 1 lb. cauliflower head
- 2 tbsp pesto sauce
- 6 oz. grated Parmesan
- 1 tsp salt
- 1 tsp of olive oil
- ½ cup of heavy cream
- 1 tbsp butter
- 1 tbsp dried dill
- 1 tsp dried parsley
- 1 tsp chili flakes

Steps to Cook

1. Wash the cauliflower head carefully and chop it up more or less. Put the chopped cauliflower in the blender and mix well until you get the texture of cauliflower rice.
2. Then place the cauliflower rice in the air fryer and sprinkle with the salt, olive oil, butter, dried dill, dried parsley, and chili flakes. Carefully mix the cauliflower rice with the help of the wooden spatula.
3. After this, add the heavy cream and cook the dish 370°F for 10 minutes.
4. After this, add the grated Parmesan and the pesto sauce. Mix the cauliflower rice carefully and cook it for 3 more minutes at the same temperature.
5. Serve the garnish immediately.

Nutritional Information:

- Calories: 165
- Carbohydrates: 5.1g
- Fat: 12.6g
- Protein: 9.8g

Roasted Bok Choy

Servings: 6

Preparation time: 10 minutes

Cook time: 10 minutes

Ingredients

- 1 white onion, sliced
- 1 lb. bok choy
- 1 tsp minced garlic
- 1 tbsp mustard
- 1 tsp ground ginger
- 2 tbsp apple cider vinegar
- 2 tsp of olive oil
- 1 tbsp butter

Steps to Cook

1. Wash the bok choy cut it. Next, place the chopped bok choy in the basket tray of the air fryer.
2. Sprinkle the minced bok choy with the minced garlic, sliced onion, mustard, ground ginger, apple cider vinegar, olive oil, and butter.
3. Preheat the air fryer to 360°F.
4. Cook the bok choy for 10 minutes.
5. When the dish is cooked - stir carefully.
6. Then let the cooked dish cool slightly.

Nutritional Information:

- Calories: 59
- Carbohydrates: 4.4g
- Fat: 4.2g
- Protein: 1.9g

Roasted Green Peppers

Servings: 4

Preparation time: 10 minutes

Cook time: 15 minutes

Ingredients

- 1 tsp minced garlic
- 1 lb. green pepper
- 1 tsp salt
- 1 tbsp of olive oil

Steps to Cook

1. Wash the green peppers carefully and remove the seeds from them. After this, cut the green peppers into the medium squares (or the form you want them).
2. Preheat the air fryer to 320°F.
3. Next, place the green pepper squares in the large bowl. Sprinkle the green peppers with olive oil, salt, and minced garlic. Mix.
4. Place the prepared green bell peppers on the air fryer basket tray.
5. Cook the dish for 15 minutes.
6. Stir the green peppers after 8 minutes of cooking.

Nutritional Information:

- Calories: 54
- Carbohydrates: 5.5g
- Fat: 0.6g
- Protein: 1g

Zucchini Boats With Cheese

Servings: 2

Preparation time: 5 minutes

Cook time: 15 minutes

Ingredients

- 1 medium zucchini
- 3 oz bok choy
- 1 clove garlic, sliced
- 6 oz. cheddar cheese
- 4 tbsp heavy cream
- 1 tbsp of coconut flour
- ¼ of salt
- ½ tsp of ground black pepper
- 1 tsp of paprika
- 1 tsp of olive oil

Steps to Cook

1. Cut the zucchini into 2 pieces crosswise. Next, remove the meat from the zucchini halves.
2. Mix the zucchini meat and combine it with the sliced garlic clove. After this, sprinkle the zucchini meat with the salt, ground black pepper, and paprika. Mix. Combine heavy cream and coconut flour and whisk in liquid. Fill the zucchini halves with the zucchini meat mixture. Grind into bok choy and sprinkle with the heavy cream mixture—grated cheddar cheese. Add the bok choy mixture to the zucchini halves. Next, sprinkle the zucchini with the olive oil—Preheat the air fryer to 400°F.
3. Put the zucchini halves in the deep fryer and cook for 10 minutes. Then sprinkle the zucchini boards with the grated cheese and cook for 2 minutes.

Nutritional Information:

- Calories: 255
- Carbohydrates: 5g
- Fat: 21.2g
- Protein: 12.2g

Parsley Butter Mushrooms

Servings: 5

Preparation time: 10 minutes

Cook time: 7 minutes

Ingredients

- 10 oz. white mushrooms
- 1 white onion, sliced
- 1 tsp of olive oil
- 1/3 of garlic powder
- 3 tbsp of butter
- ½ cup of heavy cream
- 2 tbsp dried parsley
- ½ tsp of salt

Steps to Cook

1. Cut the white mushrooms and sprinkle them with the garlic powder and salt.
2. Preheat the air fryer to 400°F.
3. Place the sliced mushrooms on the air fryer basket tray. Next, sprinkle the mushrooms with the olive oil. Add sliced white onion.
4. Cook the mushrooms for 2 minutes. Then stir the sliced mushrooms carefully. Add the butter and heavy cream. Sprinkle the mushrooms with the dried parsley.
5. Stir the mushrooms carefully and cook for 5 more minutes.

Nutritional Information:

- Calories: 133
- Carbohydrates: 4.5g
- Fat: 12.5g
- Protein: 2.4g

Zucchini Noodles

Servings: 4

Preparation time: 15 minutes

Cook time: 5 minutes

Ingredients

- 1 green zucchini
- 1 cup of chicken broth
- 1 tsp of butter
- ½ tsp of salt
- ½ tsp of ground white pepper

Steps to Cook

1. Preheat the air fryer to $400°F$.
2. Make the zucchini noodles using the spiralizer.
3. Pour the chicken broth into the air fryer basket tray.
4. Add the chicken broth, salt, and ground white pepper.
5. Cook the zucchini broth for 2 minutes.
6. After this, add the zucchini noodles and cook for 3 minutes.
7. Then strain the chicken broth and add the butter.
8. Mix in the soft zucchini noodles so as not to damage them.

Nutritional Information:

- Calories: 19
- Carbohydrates: 2g
- Fat: 1.2g
- Protein: 0.8g

Cauliflower Puree

Servings: 5

Preparation time: 10 minutes

Cook time: 13 minutes

Ingredients

- 2 butter spoons
- 4 tbsp heavy cream
- 1 lb. cauliflower
- 1 tsp garlic powder
- ½ tsp of salt
- 1 tsp chili pepper
- 1 tsp of olive oil

Steps to Cook

1. Preheat the air fryer to 360°F.
2. Chop the cauliflower roughly and place in the basket tray of the air fryer.
3. Sprinkle the vegetables with the garlic powder, salt, chili powder, and olive oil.
4. Cook the cauliflower for 10 minutes.
5. After this, stir the cauliflower gently, add the heavy cream, and cook for 3 more minutes at 390°F.
6. Then transfer the cooked soft cauliflower into the blender.
7. Mix well until you get a smooth and smooth texture.
8. Add the butter and stir carefully.

Nutritional Information:

- Calories: 115
- Carbohydrates: 5.6g
- Fat: 10.1g
- Protein: 2.2g

Zucchini Pâté Bites

Servings: 4

Preparation time: 15 minutes

Cook time: 12 minutes

Ingredients

- 2 garlic cloves, minced
- 1 tbsp butter
- 1 tsp salt
- ½ tsp of ground black pepper
- 2 zucchini
- ½ tbsp of olive oil

Steps to Cook

1. Peel the zucchini and grate it.
2. Next, combine the grated zucchini with the salt and ground black pepper.
3. Stir in the zucchini.
4. Preheat the air fryer to $390°F$.
5. Place the grated zucchini in the air fryer basket tray, add the olive oil and minced garlic clove and cook for 8 minutes.
6. Then stir the zucchini carefully and add the butter.
7. Cook the zucchini pate for 4 more minutes at $400°F$.
8. When the time is up, and the zucchini pâté is smooth and smooth, remove it from the air fryer and cool to room temperature.

Nutritional Information:

- Calories: 59
- Carbohydrates: 4g
- Fat: 4.8g
- Protein: 1.4g

Sweet Sour Chinese Greens

Servings: 5

Preparation time: 10 minutes

Cook time: 10 minutes

Ingredients

- 1 tbsp chives
- 1 tsp sesame seeds
- 1 tbsp of apple cider vinegar
- 2 butter spoons
- 1 tbsp canola oil
- ½ tsp of salt
- 8 oz bok choy
- 1 tbsp garlic, sliced
- ½ tsp of Stevia extract

Steps to Cook

1. Preheat the air fryer to 360°F.
2. Slice the bok choy and place it on the tray of the air fryer basket. Then sprinkle the sliced bok choy with the salt and butter.
3. Cook the bok choy for 10 minutes.
4. When the bok choy is done - let cool gently and transfer to the serving bowl.
5. Combine the chives, sesame seeds, apple cider vinegar, canola oil, and Stevia extract in the shallow bowl.
6. Add the sliced garlic and mix.
7. Then sprinkle the cooked bok choy with the prepared garlic mixture

Nutritional Information:

- Calories: 78
- Carbohydrates: 1.8g
- Fat: 7.8g
- Protein: 1g

Turnip Puree

Servings: 6

Preparation time: 10 minutes

Cook time: 14 minutes

Ingredients

- 5 turnips
- 3 oz. of butter
- ½ grated white onion
- 1 tsp salt
- 1 cup heavy cream

Steps to Cook

1. Preheat the air fryer to 400°F.
2. Peel the turnips and chop them.
3. Place the chopped turnips in the basket tray of the air fryer.
4. Add the butter, grated onion, salt, and heavy cream.
5. Cook the dish for 14 minutes.
6. When time is up, and turnip is cooked - let cool for 5 minutes.
7. After this, mix the turnip mixture into the puree. Use the hand blender for this step.
8. Serve the cooked turnip puree hot. Add more salt if desired.

Nutritional Information:

- Calories: 203
- Carbohydrates: 8g
- Fat: 19g
- Protein: 1.6g

Roasted Daikon

Servings: 8

Preparation time: 20 minutes

Cook time: 20 minutes

Ingredients

- 1 lb. daikon
- ½ tsp of sage
- 1 tsp salt
- 1 tbsp of olive oil
- 1 tsp dried oregano

Steps to Cook

1. Peel the daikon and cut it into cubes.
2. Sprinkle the daikon cubes with the sage, salt, and dried oregano.
3. Mix.
4. Preheat the air fryer to 360°F.
5. Place the daikon cubes on the fryer rack and sprinkle the vegetables with the olive oil.
6. Cook the daikon for 6 minutes.
7. After this, turn the daikon cubes to the other side and cook the dish for 4 more minutes.
8. When the time is up - the daikon cubes should be soft and a little golden.
9. Serve immediately.

Nutritional Information:

- Calories: 43
- Carbohydrates: 3.9g
- Fat: 2.8g
- Protein: 1.9g

Eggplant With Cheese

Servings: 7

Preparation time: 15 min

Cook time: 11 minutes

Ingredients

- 2 eggplant
- 1 tsp minced garlic
- 1 tsp of olive oil
- 5 oz cheddar cheese shredded
- ½ tsp of ground black pepper

Steps to Cook

1. Wash the eggplants carefully and slice them.
2. Rub the sliced aubergine with the minced garlic, salt, and ground black pepper.
3. Leave the eggplant slices for 5 minutes to marinate.
4. After this, preheat an air fryer to 400°F.
5. Place the eggplant circles in the air fryer and cook for 6 minutes.
6. Then turn the eggplant circles to the other side and cook for 5 more minutes,
7. Sprinkle the eggplant with the grated cheese and cook for another 30 seconds.

Nutritional Information:

- Calories: 127
- Carbohydrates: 9.7g
- Fat: 7.7g
- Protein: 6.6g

Sesame Okra With Egg

Servings: 4

Preparation time: 8 min

Cook time: 4 minutes

Ingredients

- 1 tbsp of sesame oil
- 1 tsp sesame seeds
- 11 oz. okra
- ½ tsp of salt
- 1 egg

Steps to Cook

1. Wash the okra and chop it more or less.
2. Break the egg into the bowl and beat it.
3. Add the beaten egg into the chopped okra.
4. Sprinkle with the sesame seeds and salt.
5. Preheat the air fryer to 400^0F.
6. Mix the okra mixture carefully.
7. Place the okra mixture in the basket of the air fryer.
8. Sprinkle with the olive oil.
9. Cook the okra for 4 minutes.
10. When the time is up, stir the cooked dish.
11. Transfer to serving plates

Nutritional Information:

- Calories: 81
- Carbohydrates: 6.1g
- Fat: 5g
- Protein: 3g

Roasted Garlic Heads

Servings: 8

Preparation time: 7 minutes

Cook time: 10 minutes

Ingredients

- 1 lb. garlic heads
- 2 tbsp olive oil
- 1 tsp dried oregano
- 1 tsp dried basil
- 1 tsp ground coriander
- ¼ tsp of ground ginger

Steps to Cook

1. Cut off the ends of the garlic heads.
2. Place each head of garlic on the foil.
3. Then sprinkle the garlic heads with the olive oil, dried oregano, dried basil, ground coriander, and ground ginger.
4. Preheat the air fryer to 400°F.
5. Wrap the garlic heads in the foil and place it in the air fryer.
6. Cook the garlic heads for 10 minutes.
7. When the time is up, the garlic heads should be soft.
8. Let them cool for at least 10 minutes

Nutritional Information:

- Calories: 115
- Carbohydrates: 17.9g
- Fat: 3.8g
- Protein: 3.6g

Parmesan Cheese Sticks

Servings: 3

Preparation time: 10 min

Cook time: 8 minutes

Ingredients

- 8 oz. parmesan
- 1 egg
- ½ cup of heavy cream
- 4 tablespoons of almond flour
- ¼ tsp of ground black pepper

Steps to Cook

1. Beat the egg in the bowl and beat it.
2. Add the heavy cream and the almond flour.
3. Next, sprinkle the mixture with the ground black pepper.
4. Mix gently or use the hand mixer.
5. After this, cut the cheese into the short thick sticks.
6. Dip the cheese sticks in the heavy cream mixture.
7. Next, place the cheese sticks in the plastic bags and freeze them.
8. Preheat the air fryer to 400°F.
9. Place the cheese sticks on the fryer shelf.
10. Cook the cheese sticks for 8 minutes.

Nutritional Information:

- Calories: 389
- Carbohydrates: 5.5g
- Fat: 29.5g
- Protein: 28.6g

Snow Peas Puree

Servings: 4

Preparation time: 7 minutes

Cook time: 5 minutes

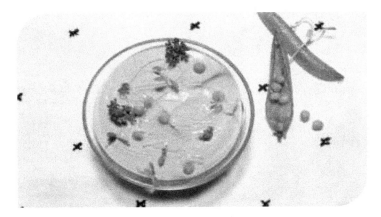

Ingredients

- ½ a cup of heavy cream
- 1 tsp of butter
- 1 tsp salt
- 1 tsp of paprika
- 1 lb. snow peas
- ¼ tsp of nutmeg

Steps to Cook

1. Preheat the air fryer to 400°F.
2. Wash the snow peas carefully and place them in the air fryer basket tray.
3. Then sprinkle the snow peas with the butter, salt, paprika, nutmeg, and heavy cream.
4. Cook the snow peas for 5 minutes.
5. When the time is up, gently shake the snow peas and transfer to serving plates.

Nutritional Information:

- Calories: 110
- Carbohydrates: 8.8g
- Fat: 6.9g
- Protein: 4.1g

Fennel Wedges

Servings: 5

Preparation time: 15 minutes

Cook time: 6 minutes

Ingredients

- 1 tsp of Stevia extract
- ½ tsp of fresh thyme
- ½ tsp of salt
- 1 tsp canola oil
- 14 oz. fennel
- 1 tsp of butter
- 1 tsp dried oregano
- ½ tsp of chili flakes

Steps to Cook

1. Cut the fennel into wedges.
2. Melt the butter.
3. Combine the butter, canola oil, dried oregano, and chili flakes in the bowl.
4. Coat the mixture.
5. Add salt, fresh thyme, and Stevia extract.
6. Whisk gently.
7. Next, brush the fennel wedges with the rotated mixture.
8. Preheat the air fryer to 370°F.
9. Place the fennel wedges on the fryer rack.
10. Cook the fennel wedges for 3 minutes on each side.

Nutritional Information:

- Calories: 41
- Carbohydrates: 6.1g
- Fat: 1.9g
- Protein: 1g

Kohlrabi Fritters

Servings: 5

Preparation time: 10 min

Cook time: 7 minutes

Ingredients

- 8 oz kohlrabi
- 1 egg
- 1 tbsp of almond flour
- ½ tsp of salt
- 1 tsp of olive oil
- 1 tsp ground black pepper
- 1 tbsp dried parsley
- ¼ tsp of chili.

Steps to Cook

1. Peel the kohlrabi and grate it.
2. Combine the grated kohlrabi with the salt, ground black pepper, dried parsley, and chili.
3. Beat the egg into the mixture and beat it.
4. After this, make the medium fritters from the mixture.
5. Preheat the air fryer to 380^0F.
6. Spray the basket tray of the air fryer with the olive oil inside and place the fritters there.
7. Cook the fritters for 4 minutes.
8. After this, turn the fritters to the other side and cook for 3 more minutes.

Nutritional Information:

- Calories: 66
- Carbohydrates: 4.4g
- Fat: 4.7g
- Protein: 3.2g

Delicious Bamboo Shoots

Servings: 2

Preparation time: 8 min

Cook time: 4 minutes

Ingredients

- 8 oz. bamboo shoots
- 2 garlic cloves, sliced
- 1 tbsp of olive oil
- ½ tsp of chili flakes
- 2 tbsp chives
- ½ tsp of salt
- 3 tbsp of fish broth

Steps to Cook

1. Preheat the air fryer to 400°F.
2. Cut the bamboo shoots into strips.
3. Combine the sliced garlic cloves, olive oil, chili flakes, salt, and fish broth in the air fryer basket tray.
4. Cook for 1 minute.
5. After this, gently stir the mixture.
6. Add the strips of bamboo shoots and chives.
7. Stir the dish carefully and cook for 3 more minutes.
8. Next, stir the cooked garnish carefully.
9. Transfer it to the service plates.

Nutritional Information:

- Calories: 100
- Carbohydrates: 7g
- Fat: 7.4g
- Protein: 3.7g

Summer Vegetables

Servings: 4

Preparation time: 15 minutes

Cook time: 15 minutes

Ingredients

- 1 eggplant
- 1 tomato
- 1 zucchini
- 1 white onion
- 2 green peppers
- 1 tsp of paprika
- 1 tbsp canola oil
- ½ tsp of ground nutmeg
- ½ tsp of ground thyme
- 1 tsp salt

Steps to Cook

1. Preheat the air fryer to 390°F.
2. Carefully wash the eggplant, tomato, and zucchini.
3. Peel the onion. Chop up all the prepared vegetables more or less. Next, place the chopped vegetables in the basket tray of the air fryer.
4. Sprinkle the vegetables with the paprika, canola oil, ground nutmeg, ground thyme, and salt.
5. Stir the vegetables carefully with the help of two spatulas.
6. Cut the green peppers into squares. Next, add the pepper squares to the vegetable mixture. Stir gently.
7. Cook the dish for 15 minutes. Stir the vegetables after 10 minutes carefully

Nutritional Information:

- Calories: 96
- Carbohydrates: 14.8g
- Fat: 4.1g
- Protein: 2.4g

Chapter 6

Dinner Recipes

Zucchini Chips

Servings: 5

Preparation time: 8 min

Cook time: 13 minutes

Ingredients

- 2 zucchini
- 1 tsp of olive oil
- ½ tsp of salt
- 1 tsp of paprika

Steps to Cook

1. Wash the zucchini carefully and cut it into chips.
2. Preheat the air fryer to 370°F.
3. Sprinkle the zucchini slices with the salt and paprika. After this, place the zucchini slices in the air fryer. Gently spread the zucchini slices with the olive oil— Cook the zucchini strips for 13 minutes.
4. Turn the zucchini strips to another side during cooking if desired. When the zucchini fries are cooked, let them cool well.

Nutritional Information:

- Calories: 22
- Carbohydrates: 2.9g
- Fat: 1.1g
- Protein: 1g

Radish Chips

Servings: 12

Preparation time: 8 minutes

Cook time: 15 minutes

Ingredients

- 1 lb. radish
- 2 tbsp olive oil
- 1 tsp salt

Steps to Cook

1. Wash the radish carefully and cut it to the size of the chips.
2. After this, sprinkle the radish shavings with the salt.
3. Drizzle the radish shavings with the olive oil.
4. Preheat the air fryer to 375^0F.
5. Place the radish slices in the air fryer and cook the chips for 15 minutes.
6. When the radish shavings get the desired texture, they are cooked.
7. Chill the chips and serve.

Nutritional Information:

- Calories: 26
- Carbohydrates: 1.3g
- Fat: 2.4g
- Protein: 0.3g

Squid Rings

Servings: 4

Preparation time: 12 min

Cook time: 8 minutes

Ingredients

- 1 cup of almond flour
- 9 oz. squid
- 1 egg
- ½ tsp of lemon zest
- 1 tsp fresh lemon juice
- ½ tsp of turmeric
- ¼ tsp of salt
- ¼ tsp of ground black pepper

Steps to Cook

1. Wash and peel the squid. Then cut the squid into thick rings. Beat the egg in the bowl and beat it.
2. Sprinkle the beaten egg with the lemon zest, turmeric, salt, and ground black pepper.
3. Sprinkle the squid rings with the fresh lemon juice.
4. After this, put the squid rings in the beaten egg and stir carefully.
5. Leave the squid rings in the egg mixture for 4 minutes. Next, coat the squid rings well in the almond flour mixture.
6. Preheat the air fryer to 360°F.
7. Transfer the calamari rings to the fryer rack.
8. Cook the squid rings for 8 minutes.

Nutritional Information:

- Calories: 190
- Carbohydrates: 7g
- Fat: 15.7g
- Protein: 8.7g

Roasted Almond

Servings: 4

Preparation time: 12 min

Cook time: 8 minutes

Ingredients

- ¼ cup of hazelnuts
- ¼ cup of walnuts
- ½ a cup of walnuts
- ½ a cup of macadamia nuts
- 1 tbsp of olive oil
- 1 tsp salt

Steps to Cook

1. Preheat the air fryer to 320 degrees Fahrenheit.
2. Place the hazelnuts, walnuts, walnuts, and macadamia nuts in the air fryer.
3. Cook the walnuts for 8 minutes.
4. Stir the walnuts after 4 minutes of cooking.
5. At the end of cooking, sprinkle the nuts with the olive oil and salt and shake well.
6. Cook the walnuts for 1 more minute.
7. Then transfer the cooked walnuts into the serving ramekins.

Nutritional Information:

- Calories: 230
- Carbohydrates: 3.9g
- Fat: 23.9g
- Protein: 3.9g

Almond Butter Bread

Servings: 22

Preparation time: 30 min

Cook time: 30 minutes

Ingredients

- 6 eggs
- 5 oz. almond flour
- 4 tbsp butter, melted
- 3 tsp baking powder
- 1 lemon wedge
- 1 tsp salt
- 6 drops liquid stevia

Steps to Cook

1. Preheat the air fryer to 375°F.
2. Separate the yolks from the whites. Beat the egg whites to the point of snow. When they start to rise, add 3 drops of lemon. Keep beating until "peaks" and is like a meringue.
3. In a separate bowl, add the yolks, melted butter, almond flour, baking powder, and salt. Mix everything well; a compact mass will remain.
4. To this mixture, add 1/3 of the egg whites and mix with enveloping movements. Keep adding the whites little by little, always wrapping them.
5. You will get a fluffy dough. Grease the mold with a little butter and pour the batter.
6. Bake 30 minutes at 375°F.
7. After 30 minutes, insert a needle or knife into the bread: if it comes out clean, that's it. If not, leave it in the oven for a few more minutes.
8. Let cool 30 minutes before unmolding. Unmold the bread and leave to cool on a rack for another 30 minutes. Cut it into slices and enjoy!

Nutritional Information:

- Calories: 184.2
- Carbohydrates: 4.6g
- Fat: 15.8g
- Protein: 8.9g

Lemon Coconut Pudding

Servings: 5

Preparation time: 8 minutes

Cook time: 25 minutes

Ingredients

- 3 ½ oz. grated coconut
- ½ cup of sugar
- ½ lb. self-rising flour
- 1 lemon (juice and zest)
- 2 tbsp cornstarch
- 1 egg
- 1 tsp vanilla essence
- ¼ cup sunflower oil

Steps to Cook

1. Preheat the air fryer to 360°F.
2. Beat the egg with the sugar, then add the lemon juice and oil.
3. Add the lemon zest and vanilla essence.
4. Mix the dry ingredients and add them to the preparation.
5. Place the mixture in a buttered and floured pan.
6. Bake in the preheated air fryer for 25 minutes or until a toothpick sticks in it comes out dry.

Nutritional Information:

- Calories: 167.2
- Carbohydrates: 16.3g
- Fat: 13.8g
- Protein: 3.2g

Roasted Avocados With Mozzarella

Servings: 2

Preparation time: 5 minutes

Cook time: 15 minutes

Ingredients

- 1 avocado
- Lemon juice
- ½ tomato
- 1 oz. Mozzarella cheese
- ½ tsp Salt flakes pinch
- 2 tsp Extra virgin olive oil
- 8 Fresh oregano (leaves)

Steps to Cook

1. Cut the avocado in half lengthwise, carefully remove the seed, and brush each half with lemon juice. Cut the meat of the avocado halves making a rhomboid pattern and deep cuts that come to the base.
2. Drain the mozzarella and cut two pieces the same size as the cavities of the avocados. Fill them with the cheese.
3. Put them in the preheated air fryer to 360°F with heat up and down, for 15 minutes or until the mozzarella has melted well.
4. Meanwhile, wash the tomato and cut one of its halves into small dice. When the avocado is ready, remove it from the oven and place the tomato cubes on the surface. Sprinkle salt flakes, fresh oregano leaves, and drizzle with extra virgin olive oil before serving.

Nutritional Information:

- Calories: 220
- Carbohydrates: 9g
- Fat: 18g
- Protein: 7g

Mini Muffins With Blueberries

Servings: 8

Preparation time: 10 minutes

Cook time: 12 minutes

Ingredients

- 2 Eggs
- 60 ml Milk or vegetable alternative
- ½ lb. ground almonds
- 1 tsp Vanilla essence
- 1 tsp yeast
- A pinch of Salt
- Sweetener suitable for liquid cooking, equivalent to about 2 oz. g of sugar (optional)
- Fresh blueberries
- Chia seeds (optional)

Steps to Cook

1. Preheat the air fryer to 360°F and prepare a tray with suitable molds.
2. In a bowl, beat the eggs, milk, and vanilla essence with a whisk. Reserve.
3. Mix the almond flour with the yeast and salt, and form a hole. Pour in the liquid dough, add the sweetener if using and combine gently.
4. When the dough is homogeneous, distribute it into the molds without filling them to the top. Introduce 3-4 fresh blueberries previously washed and dried, pressing gently, and add some chia seeds on top, if desired.
5. Bake for about 10-12 minutes or until they have risen and are firm to the touch, slightly golden. Wait for a little out of the air fryer before unmolding.

Nutritional Information:

- Calories: 218
- Carbohydrates: 6.1g
- Fat: 19.3g
- Protein: 6.9g

Eggplant Chips

Servings: 2

Preparation time: 5 minutes

Cook time: 15 minutes

Ingredients

- ½ eggplant
- ½ cup almond flour
- ¼ tsp. Cayenne pepper
- salt and pepper
- ½ egg
- ½ tbsp. coconut oil in spray form

Steps to Cook

1. Preheat the air fryer to 400°F.
2. Peel the eggplant and cut into the shape of French fries. Sprinkle a little salt on all sides. Reserve.
3. In a shallow bowl, mix the ground almonds, cayenne pepper, salt, and black pepper. Break the eggs into another bowl and beat until foamy.
4. Dip the pieces of eggplants in the ground almond mixture, then in the beaten eggs, and then again in the almond mixture.
5. After bathing, place the eggplant "potatoes" on a greased baking sheet and drizzle melted coconut oil on top.
6. Bake for 15 minutes or until crisp and golden.

Nutritional Information:

- Calories: 257
- Carbohydrates: 5g
- Fat: 21g
- Protein: 8g

Chocolate Muffins

Servings: 6
Preparation time: 10 minutes
Cook time: 15 minutes

Ingredients

- 1 ½ oz. granulated sugar
- ½ cup coconut milk or soy milk
- 1/3 cup coconut oil, liquid
- 1 tsp of vanilla extract
- 4 oz. all-purpose flour
- 3 tsp cocoa powder
- 1 tsp baking powder
- ½ tsp of baking soda
- a pinch of salt
- 3 oz. of chocolate chips
- 1 oz. pistachios, cracked (optional)
- Non-stick spray oil

Steps to Cook

1. Put the sugar, coconut milk, coconut oil, and vanilla extract in a small bowl. Set aside.
2. Mix the flour, cocoa powder, baking powder, baking soda, and salt in a separate bowl and set aside.
3. Mix the dry ingredients with the wet ingredients gradually, until smooth. Then mix with the chocolate and pistachio.
4. Select Preheat, in the air fryer, adjust the temperature to 300°F.
5. Grease the muffin tins with cooking spray and pour the mixture until they are full to ¾.
6. Carefully place the muffin tins in the preheated air fryer. Select Desserts set the time to 15 minutes.
7. Remove the muffins when the cooking is done and let them cool for 10 minutes before serving.

Nutritional Information:

- Calories: 690
- Carbohydrates: 79.2g
- Fat: 38g
- Protein: 9.9g

Sweet Sponge Cake

Servings: 10

Preparation time: 10 min

Cook time: 50 min

Ingredients

- ½ lb. flour for
- yeast pastry
- ½ lb. of sugar
- 3 medium eggs
- 3 tbsp olive oil
- Orange zest
- ¾ lb. chopped pistachio
- 1 envelope of yeast

Steps to Cook

1. Separate the yolks from the eggs. Mount the egg whites until stiff with the mixer and gradually incorporate the sugar.
2. Mix until you get a thick white cream.
3. Separately, beat the yolks with the oil and the orange zest. Incorporate this mixture with the whites, mix in an enveloping way, and finally incorporate the flour and yeast with a sieve. When everything is well mixed, add the pistachios. You can use a circular mold greased with oil and flour or kitchen paper that is more comfortable. Add the cake batter to the pan.
4. Preheat the air fryer for a few minutes at 320°F. Put the mold in the basket of the Air fryer and program the timer for about 30 minutes at 320°F temperature.
5. While it is cooking, prepare the lemon cream.
6. To do this, gradually mix the white with the sugar, add the lemon juice and add the sour cream and mix until obtaining a thick cream and ready.

Nutritional Information:

- Calories: 110
- Carbohydrates: 23g
- Fat: 1g
- Protein: 2.1g

Egg Custard

Servings: 4

Preparation time: 10 min

Cook time: 60 minutes

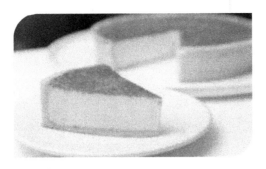

Ingredients

- 1 ¼ cup milk
- 3 eggs
- 3 oz. of sugar

Steps to Cook

1. Put the sugar in a saucepan, reserving two tablespoons for later. Add a little water. With very low heat, melt the sugar until it is all liquid and caramelized.
2. Immediately pour into the pudding molds. It is essential to do it right away because the caramel solidifies very quickly on cooling.
3. In a separate bowl, beat the eggs with the help of some rods. When they start frothing, add the milk and mix everything very well.
4. Once the mixture is homogeneous, pour into the molds you will have previously put the caramel.
5. Then preheat the Air fryer for a few minutes to 360°F.
6. Then cook the custards in a bain-marie in the Air fryer. To do this, arrange the custards inside the basket of the Air fryer in a container with water ensuring that the water reaches half of the containers but ensuring that no water enters them.
7. Put the container with the flan and the medium water bathing them in the air fryer and cook everything at medium temperature 320°F for about 1 hour.
8. To check if the flans are cooked, shake gently, and if they have the consistent appearance of the flans when they are moved, they are ready. Otherwise, if they look very liquid, bake them in a bain-marie a little more.

Nutritional Information:

- Calories: 146.6
- Carbohydrates: 15.5g
- Fat: 6.5g
- Protein: 7.1g

Cheddar Cheese Bites

Servings: 8
Preparation time: 1 min
Cook time: 20 minutes

Ingredients

- 1 8 squares of cheddar cheese
- Mashed potatoes
- Flour
- Egg and breadcrumbs
- Extra virgin olive oil

Steps to Cook

1. Make the mashed potatoes as you like.
2. Cut the cheddar cheese into small squares.
3. Take a piece of cheese and wrap it with a thin layer of mashed potatoes.
4. When you have the 8 pieces wrapped in the mashed potatoes, take it to the freezer for about 30 minutes.
5. Go through the flour and shake.
6. Go through the beaten egg, breadcrumbs, again through the beaten egg and through the breadcrumbs.
7. Take to the refrigerator at least 30 minutes.
8. Place in the basket of the Air fryer and paint well with extra virgin olive oil.
9. Select 20 minutes at 360°F.

Nutritional Information:

- Calories: 130
- Carbohydrates: 20g
- Fat: 3.5g
- Protein: 3g

Mini Potato And Egg Pizza

Servings: 6-8
Preparation time: 10 min
Cook time: 35 minutes

Ingredients

- ½ lb. of wheat flour
- ¼ lb. of water
- 5 tsp of extra virgin olive oil
- 2 tsp of salt
- 2 tsp of yeast
- 8 eggs
- 2 potatoes
- extra virgin olive oil
- Salt
- Ketchup
- Oregano
- Bacon
- Grated cheese

Steps to Cook

1. Peel the potatoes and cut them into a long, thick stick. Put salt, a little oil, and mix.
2. Put them in the pan of the Air fryer and select 30 minutes. Reserve.
3. Continue with the pizza dough. For this, put in the food processor with a kneading hook, the flour, water, oil, salt, and yeast. Knead at low speed for at least 5 minutes. Make a ball and let it rest for 30 minutes. Divide the dumpling into 8 equal parts.
4. Spread the masses. Put a small layer of tomato sauce and sprinkle with oregano. Place the potatoes on the edge of the pizza dough. Press a little so that they are well fixed in the dough. Take to the preheated air fryer, 360^0F, 15 minutes.
5. Remove the mini pizza slices and add a layer of chopped bacon and on the bacon, crack an egg in each mini pizza. Cover with grated cheese on the part of the white, leaving the yolk in sight. Return to the air fryer, 360^0F, another 10 to 20 minutes.

Nutritional Information:

- Calories: 179.7
- Carbohydrates: 34.2g
- Fat: 3.3g
- Protein: 5.2g
- Sugar: 0.6g
- Cholesterol: 0mg

Chocolate And Walnut Cake

Servings: 2-4

Preparation time: 5 minutes

Cook time: 20 minutes

Ingredients

- 2 ¼ oz dark chocolate
- 2 butter spoons
- 1 egg
- 3 tbsp of sugar
- 2 oz. flour
- 1 envelope Royal yeast
- Chopped walnuts

Steps to Cook

1. Melt the dark chocolate with the butter over low heat. Once melted, put in a bowl.
2. Incorporate the egg, sugar, flour, yeast, and finally, the chopped nuts.
3. Beat well by hand until a uniform dough is obtained.
4. Put the dough in a silicone mold or oven suitable for incorporation in the basket of the Air fryer.
5. Preheat the air fryer for a few minutes at 1800C.
6. Set the timer for 20 minutes at 1800C and when it has cooled, remove from the mold.

Nutritional Information:

- Calories: 310
- Carbohydrates: 44g
- Fat: 14g
- Protein: 5g

Light Cheese Cake

Servings: 8
Preparation time: 5 minutes
Cook time: 55 minutes

Ingredients

- 1 lb. of cottage cheese
- 3 whole eggs
- 2 tbsp of sweetener powder
- 2 tbsp of oat bran
- ½ tbsp of baking yeast
- 2 tbsp of cinnamon
- 2 tbsp vanilla flavoring
- 1 lemon (the skin)

Steps to Cook

1. Mix the cottage cheese, the sweetener, the cinnamon, the vanilla flavor, and the lemon zest in a bowl. Mix very well until you get a homogeneous cream.
2. Incorporate the eggs one by one.
3. Finally, add the oats and yeast, mixing well.
4. Put all the mixture in a container so that it fits in the Air fryer.
5. Preheat the air fryer for a few minutes at 360°F.
6. Put the mold in the basket of the Air fryer and adjust the timer for about 20 minutes at 360°F.

Nutritional Information:

- Calories: 222
- Carbohydrates: 9g
- Fat: 14g
- Protein: 18g

Blackberry Pie With Cheese

Servings: 4
Preparation time: 5 min
Cook time: 20-30 min

Ingredients

- 2 cups blackberry
- 1 cup of sugar
- 1 tbsp of lemon juice
- enough flour to spread
- ½ lb. of puff pastry
- ½ cups cream cheese, diced
- enough egg, to varnish
- enough of icing sugar to decorate

Steps to Cook

1. Preheat the air fryer to 400°F.
2. In a saucepan, cook the blackberries with the sugar for about 30 minutes over low heat or until it has a thick consistency, add the lemon juice and mix well. Let cool and reserve.
3. On a floured surface, spread the puff pastry approximately 3 mm thick and with the help of a 10 cm diameter round cutter, cut discs.
4. Fill the puff pastry discs with the blackberry jam and cream cheese, close and with your hands, make a fold, place on a tray, and garnish with egg.
5. Put in the air fryer for 20 minutes or until golden, let cool and decorate with icing sugar.

Nutritional Information:

- Calories: 470
- Carbohydrates: 57 g
- Fat: 27g
- Protein: 6g

Apple Pie And Sweet Milk

Servings: 6-8
Preparation time: 5 minutes
Cook time: 20 minutes

Ingredients

- 3 apples
- 1/3 cups cranberry
- ½ cups of walnut
- ½ cups of rum
- enough flour to spread
- ½ lb. of puff pastry
- ¾ cups of sweet milk
- 1 egg, to varnish
- enough walnut, finely chopped, to decorate

Steps to Cook

1. Preheat the air fryer to 400°F.
2. For the filling, peel and cut the apples into very thin sheets, place in a bowl and mix with the walnuts, blueberries, and rum. Macerate for 30 minutes, drain very well, and reserve.
3. Spread the puff pastry on a floured surface 3 mm thick, with a 10 cm diameter cutter that cuts discs.
4. Fill the puff pastry discs with the apples and a little sweet milk, with your hands, make folds to close the empanadas. Place on a tray, garnish with egg, and sprinkle with walnuts.
5. Put in the air fryer for 20 minutes or until golden. Serve with milk or coffee.

Nutritional Information:

- Calories: 750
- Carbohydrates: 82g
- Fat: 37g
- Protein: 15g

Lemon Cake

Servings: 6
Preparation time: 5 minutes
Cook time: 30 minutes

Ingredients

- ¼ lb. all-purpose flour
- 1 tsp baking powder
- a pinch of salt
- 3 oz. unsalted butter, softened
- ¼ lb. granulated sugar
- 1 large egg
- ½ oz. of fresh lemon juice
- 1 lemon, lemon zest
- 2 oz. of whey

Steps to Cook

1. Mix the flour, baking powder, and salt in a bowl. Set aside. Add the softened butter to an electric mixer and beat until smooth and fluffy—a—approximately 3 minutes. Beat the sugar in the butter for 1 minute.
2. Whisk the flour mixture in the butter until entirely united, for about 1 minute. Add the egg, lemon juice, and lemon zest. Mix until everything is completely united. Slowly pour in the buttermilk while mixing on medium speed.
3. Add the mixture to a greased mini-loaf pan on top.
4. Select Preheat; in the air fryer. Adjust the temperature to 320^0F. Place the cake in the preheated air fryer. Select Pan set the time to 30 minutes.

Nutritional Information:

- Calories: 326
- Carbohydrates: 12.1g
- Fat: 25.2g
- Protein: 13.4g

Healthy Carrot Chips

Servings: 3
Preparation time: 5 minutes
Cook time: 20-25 minutes

Ingredients

- carrots to taste
- 2 tablespoons extra virgin olive oil
- salt to taste

Steps to Cook

1. Wash the carrots very well and remove the ends.
2. Cut the carrots into very thin slices, either using a mandolin or with a food processor.
3. Add the oil and, with clean hands, spread it over all the carrots. Put the carrot slices in the basket of your air fryer and program it at 330°F for 20-25 minutes, depending on the number of carrots you make.
4. Every 5-7 minutes, open the basket and shake it vigorously so that they are removed, and put the basket back inside to continue to be made. Watch from the 15th minute that they do not burn, since it depends on the amount you do can be done before. Take out the carrots, put some salt on them, and ready.

Nutritional Information:

- Calories: 35
- Carbohydrates: 8g
- Fat: 2g
- Protein: 1g

Focaccia

Servings: 4
Preparation time: 45 min
Cook time: 20 minutes

Ingredients

- ½ oz. dry yeast
- ½ cup of warm water
- 1 cup baker's flour

Mass:
- ½ oz. dry yeast
- ½ pound baker's flour
- Warm water

Steps to Cook

1. Assemble the sponge for 40 minutes. Assemble the dough, unite with the sponge for 45 minutes, knead degassing until the dough joins, and becomes smooth.
2. Assemble the pastries, they can roll 1 ½ tbsp loaves, or in a source place the extended dough, let it take half an hour. In the extended dough, drip olive oil, rosemary, tomatoes, onion into slices, and bake at 360°F 10 minutes approximately both bread and focaccia.

Nutritional Information:

- Calories: 387.9
- Carbohydrates: 64.4g
- Fat: 9.9g
- Protein: 9g

Chocolate Cake

Servings: 2
Preparation time: 5 min
Cook time: 40 minutes

Ingredients

- 2 eggs
- 1 homemade chocolate soy yogurt
- 1 container of yogurt sugar
- 2 containers of sponge cake flour
- ½ container of oil
- ½ sachet baking powder
- Orange zest

Steps to Cook

1. Preheat deep fryer to 250°F for 5 minutes.
2. In a bowl, put the eggs, the yogurt, and sugar, beat and then add the flour, the yeast, the oil, and the orange zest.
3. Mix all.
4. In the bucket of the fryer, mold on purpose for the fryer but also a mold that burns inside. Put the oven paper down the mold and add the dough.
5. Put in a fryer Cupcakes program 15 minutes at 300°F. Then make some crosscuts on the cake and put another 15 minutes with the same temperature. If it is not cooked inside, add about 5 minutes more at 280°F.

Nutritional Information:

- Calories: 424
- Carbohydrates: 58g
- Fat: 22g
- Protein: 3.8g

Roasted Pears

Servings: 4
Preparation time: 10 min
Cook time: 20 minutes

Ingredients

- 4 pears in shell, well washed
- ¼ cup of raisins
- 2 tbsp sugar-free jam, the one you like the most
- 1 tsp honey
- 1 pinch cinnamon powder

Steps to Cook

1. Wash the pears, hollowed out by removing the core.
2. Separate the pulp.
3. Mix the chosen jam with the pulp of the pears, honey, and raisins, and cinnamon.
4. Fill the pears with that mixture.
5. Place the pears in the fryer.
6. In the container, place a glass of water.
7. Cook for 20 minutes at 360^0F.
8. Serve them alone or accompanied with a scoop of vanilla ice cream.

Nutritional Information:

- Calories: 84
- Carbohydrates: 22g
- Fat: 1g
- Protein: 1g

Tatin Mini Cake

Servings: 6
Preparation time: 10 min
Cook time: 30 minutes

Ingredients

- 3 ½ oz. flour
- 1 ½ oz. cold butter
- 5 tsp water
- 1 pinch of salt
- 1 apple
- Lemon juice
- 1 oz. Sugar
- ½ oz. butter

Steps to Cook

1. Put the salt in the flour and the cold butter. Mix everything until it is like sand. Add the 5 tsp of water and mix it until obtaining a homogeneous mass. Wrap it in transparent paper and reserve. In a clay pot, put the sugar and butter and let it melt and toast. Peel the apple, use the lemon juice to spread it. When your sugar and butter are already browned, put the apples on top, and place them tightly, cover the entire surface very well. Leave the apples caramelizing for 15 to 20 minutes; control them.
2. While stretch the dough. You can do it as you find it more manageable. Once the apples are caramelized, top with the short-crust pastry. Cut what is left and adjust to the contour.
3. Preheat the fryer to 220^0F, and put the cake for about 15 minutes.

Nutritional Information:

- Calories: 355.7
- Carbohydrates: 62.9g
- Fat: 12.3g
- Protein: 2.1g

Gluten-Free Yogurt Cupcake

Servings: 3
Preparation time: 3 min
Cook time: 40 minutes

Ingredients

- 1 Greek yogurt
- 3 eggs
- 4 ½ oz. sugar
- 3 oz. cream
- 1 ½ oz. sunflower oil
- 1 ½ oz. butter
- 6 oz. gluten-free flour
- Salt
- 1 sachet yeast

Steps to Cook

1. Put the eggs, yogurt, and sugar in the air fryer. Mix well. Add the rest of the ingredients and mix.
2. Put the dough in the cake container, previously brushed with oil. Preheat the fryer and put the mold with the dough for 40 minutes at 240⁰F.
3. When it cools, we unmold and decorate to taste.

Nutritional Information:

- Calories: 131
- Carbohydrates: 16g
- Fat: 6.3g
- Protein: 2.4g

Rabas

Servings: 2
Preparation time: 5 min
Cook time: 10 minutes

Ingredients

- 16 rabas
- 1 egg
- Bread crumbs
- Condiments: salt, pepper, sweet paprika

Steps to Cook

1. If they are frozen put them in hot water and they boil for 2 minutes.
2. Remove and dry well.
3. Beat the egg and season to taste, salt, pepper and sweet paprika. Place in the egg.
4. Bread with breadcrumbs. Place on sticks.
5. Place in the fryer for 5 minutes at 320^0F. Remove
6. Sprinkle with fritolin and place 5 more minutes at 400^0F.

Nutritional Information:

- Calories: 200
- Carbohydrates: 1g
- Fat: 1g
- Protein: 1g

Conclusion

In this eBook, we have seen a lot about an air fryer. As we have seen in chapter 1; the concept of air fryer; which is simply a revolutionary kitchen appliance for cooking food through the circulation of superheated air. They're also significant advantages using this appliance. For this reason, we gave you some tips so that you can take advantage of using it.

Oil-free fryers are all the rage in the kitchen. It is a simple but innovative cooking method. You can cook any type of food that would otherwise get soaked in deep fat.

So, you have just seen in the preceding chapters, a great variety of recipes that you can take advantage of with your air fryer. Don't let time kill you by working on cooking traditionally. Take advantage of your time, health, and, above all, the flavor cooking with an air fryer.

PART- II

The Complete Air Fryer Cookbook

Foolproof, Quick & Easy Air Fryer Recipes for Beginners and Advanced Users

Jennifer Newman

Introduction

Generally, frying food involves dipping it in a bowl of boiling oil. The food becomes crispy on the outside, and it usually tastes delicious, but it's also full of oil, and that much oil isn't healthy for the human body.

With air fryers, a pulsating hot air cooking system is used, which is similar to the operation of a convection oven. This leads to results where the food is crispy on the outside and tender on the inside, without the need for oil (or perhaps just one spoonful).

It almost seems too good to be true! For those who love French fries, it is a much less oily alternative that allows you to eat more often without the adverse health effects.

Again, good news! Most models allow not only frying but also cooking, baking, and roasting food. Therefore, you can use your fryer to prepare vegetables, meats, fish, and even a whole chicken, as well as cookies or cakes. In short, an air fryer can do what a conventional oven does, but only by using little to no oil.

The Pros and Cons of the Air Fryer

Pros

There are many good things about using an air fryer. Here are some of the advantages:

- Low oil use, which makes our favorite fried foods healthier
- The air fryer doesn't smell like oil, keeping the overwhelming odor out of the house when it's used
- The ability to cook an unlimited amount of food

Cons

Among the disadvantages, the cooking time of food is generally much longer with this type of fryer than in the oven or with a conventional fryer. In addition, space is more limited, which means you must cook less food at a time.

But is it really an essential accessory?

Unless you fry a lot at home, an oven also cooks most foods, not to mention potato chips are also very good. And, above all, if we limit our consumption of fries to a few occasions, we can afford to eat those cooked in a fryer!

Tips for Using Your Air Fryer

1-Attach the Control Panel

For safety reasons, if the control panel of your semi-professional fryer is not properly connected to the appliance (on both sides), your fryer will not turn on. It is important always to press the control panel down until you hear a click. In other fryers, always check that all accessories are well fixed or recessed.

2-Adding Oil

Pour oil or grease into the fryer before turning it on. Warning: without oil, the resistance may burn and damage the device.

Pour enough oil into the fryer before turning it on. The oil level must at least reach the minimum level without exceeding the maximum level. If it exceeds the prescribed amount, the oil may spill out of the fryer as soon as you dip the basket in, which could result in burns.

3-Oil Level

Take the opportunity to renew the oil. If you prefer to wait, be sure to add the same type of oil or grease. We do not recommend mixing different oils, as they can react with each other when they heat up. Each oil has its own cooking temperature and shelf life.

Important: when you add oil or grease, it is not extending the shelf life of what is already in the fryer.

If you use solid grease, melt it according to the instructions in your user manual. Keep in mind: not all fryers are suitable for using solid fats. Opt-in this case, preferably for a model equipped with a special indicator that controls the oil melting.

4-Kinds of Oil

Oil quality is an essential element. There are two types of frying oils:

Vegetable oils such as peanut oil is very suitable for frying. In addition, they are better for health because they are less abundant in bad cholesterol.

You can also prepare your fries with lard (beef fat or pork) that gives potatoes a distinctive flavor. But as shown above, not all fryers can be used with solid fat.

5-When to Change the Oil

The oil should never be dirty. Renew the oil approximately every ten uses, or sooner if it starts to get dark, smelly, or smoky. Remember that if you also use your fryer to fry sandwiches, croquettes, or donuts, you should renew the fat more often.

In the case of cold zone fryers, you will find that the oil gets dirty less quickly and can keep longer. How does a cold zone work? Under the resistance, there is an area that does not heat directly, where the temperature remains lower. Waste and crumbs are deposited at the bottom of the fryer and do not burn. Your oil stays clean for longer, and it is better for your health! Does your fryer have no cold zone? Don't panic! Filter your oil with a special paper filter, and that's it!

6-How to Make Perfect French Fries

If you put too many fries in the fryer at the same time, the oil temperature may drop too quickly, which would not guarantee optimal results. Always read the instructions on your device carefully before using it, and do not exceed the recommended amount of potato slices.

Do you want to make crispy fries on the outside and soft on the inside? Choose floury potatoes like Bintje. Later, rinse your fries thoroughly in cold water to remove as much starch as possible, then dry them at once with a clean, dry towel. Preferably cook twice. Start by previously cooking your fresh fries for 4 to 8 minutes at 150°C, and then let them cool for half an hour. Then cook them a second time at 180-190°C.

Do you use frozen fries? The first cooking is not necessary because they are already precooked. Nor is it necessary for fries to be cooked beforehand because they are very thin.

Good to know: cooking time varies depending on the type of potato used.

7-Do you use an oil-free fryer?

In principle, you should not preheat your fryer without oil, but it will take a while for the appliance to reach the desired temperature. How do you know if the fryer is ready? An indicator light comes on, or a signal is activated which indicates that the temperature has been reached and you can now adjust the preparation time.

It is not necessary to add oil. You will only need to add a tablespoon of oil if you are preparing fresh dishes such as chicken without marinade or fresh French fries. All pre-cooked foods, such as frozen fries, croquettes, and snacks, can be cooked without oil. Use peanut oil, sunflower oil, or olive oil, but never taste bad nut oil.

On some models, you should never pour the oil directly into the bowl or basket. Pour the oil over the ingredients after placing them in the pan. For models with a basket, mix the fries and oil in advance in a bowl. For best operation, do not overload the appliance and do not forget that the capacity decreases when cooking frozen food.

Cleaning

To keep the device efficient, it requires minimum maintenance. Reading the instructions is also essential, even if not all of them offer the same quality of information, advice, and warnings.

1-Anti-Odor/Anti-Grease Filters

The covers are equipped with a filter that retains steam and grease. It is metallic and permanent (fixed or removable depending on the case) and should be changed regularly: grease activated carbon anti-odor. Some fryers have a combined filter (grease and activated carbon) and another metal and permanent. The effectiveness of the filters varies depending on the device. If you retain odors during cooking, you cannot prevent them from escaping when you soak the basket in oil and when you take it out. Ideally, use the fryer in a well-ventilated room, or make sure it is equipped with an efficient hood. Logically, oil-free devices emit less odors, and hot pulsed air is recovered in the cooking chamber. Then, the odors are trapped there.

Oil must be filtered with each use to extract the crumbs that accelerate its degradation and carry risks of inflammation. In some devices, the systems facilitate the operation (filter or box). It is recommended to keep the filtered oil cold (for example, in a bottle, in the refrigerator) and change it after eight to ten uses, or as soon as it shows certain signs. If it turns brown, become viscous, smokes during heating, if foam appears, etc..

What do you do with the used oil? Do not dispose of it in the sewer or the toilet, as it contaminates while it can be recycled (biofuels). You can deposit it in a recycling center or your trash cans (in a closed bottle).

How to Make Good French Fries

When making French fries in the air fryer, golden and crispy at will, you must choose the right materials. Several varieties of potatoes are suitable: bintje, Caesar, manon or victoria. For frozen French fries, not all of them are in the same boat.

For the oil, "special frying" should be chosen. It can be sunflower, rapeseed, or olive oil for best results.

The ideal conditions for frying range is between 160 and 190°C. Under that, it is necessary to cook the fries for an extended, which makes them absorb more oil. If you cook it at higher temps,, the oil tends to decompose and release toxic compounds, such as acrylamide, in starchy foods. To prevent fries from being too greasy and limit damage, it is better to cook small amounts and cut relatively large fries (the surface area/volume ratio counts). Remove them quickly after cooking, shake the basket, and then drain on absorbent paper. At this point, they will be crispier. Baking small amounts at a time offers a second advantage in terms of color. French fries need space, since squeezing them in the basket does not suit them.

Security Questions

The precautionary statements are not useless; about fifty accidents occur every year (oil splashes, spills, fryers fire, contact burns, etc.). Do not use the device without supervision, ensure its stability, and that the cable does not drag. Use a grounded electrical outlet. Be careful when dipping frozen potato chips in oil, as water droplets can cause splashing. Gradually introduce them and remove the basket if the bath boils too much. Keep children away, and don't forget to turn your air fryer off after use. If the oil ignites, never use water! Unplug the appliance and close the lid.

Enjoy!

Chapter 1

Breakfast Recipes

Fried Zucchini

Preparation time: 15 minutes;

Cooking time: 15 minutes; Serve: 2

Ingredients:

- 2 zucchinis cut into French fries
- ½ cup flour
- 2 beaten eggs
- 1 cup (250 ml) breadcrumbs
- ½ cup grated Parmesan cheese
- ¾ tsp salt, garlic, pepper to taste

Direction:

1. Preheat the air fryer to 390°F (200°C).
2. Put the flour, eggs and breadcrumbs in three different bowls.
3. Dip the fries in the flour, then the eggs and finally in the breadcrumbs. Work with about 10 French fries at a time and fry for 5 to 7 minutes or until crispy. Serve with a Caesar dressing.

Nutrition Value (Amount per serving):

- Calories 296
- Fat 15g
- Carbohydrates 31g
- Sugars 7g
- Protein 9.2g
- Cholesterol 134mg

Fried Pickles

Preparation time: 20 minutes;

Cooking time: 15 minutes; Serve: 8

Ingredients:

- 32 dill pickles
- 3 large beaten eggs
- 2 tbsp dill pickle juice
- ½ cup all-purpose flour
- ½ tsp salt
- ½ tsp cayenne pepper
- ½ tsp garlic powder
- 2 cups Panko breadcrumbs
- 2 tbsp fresh dill
- Oil sprayer (optional)
- Ranch dressing

Direction:

1. Preheat the hot air fryer to 425°F (220°C).
2. Let the pickles rest on paper towels until the liquid has been absorbed (about 15 minutes).
3. In a bowl, combine the flour and salt.
4. In another bowl, whisk the eggs, pickle juice, cayenne pepper and garlic powder.
5. Combine breadcrumbs and dill in another bowl.
6. Dip each pickle in the flour on both sides and shake the excess well.
7. Dip in egg mixture, then in breadcrumbs.
8. Transfer to your fryer basket and spray with oil.
9. Fry for 7-10 minutes.
10. Serve with ranch dressing if desired.

Nutrition Value (Amount per Serving):

- Calories 32
- Fat 1.2g
- Carbohydrates 4.4g
- Sugars 0.1g
- Protein 0.8g
- Cholesterol 2.5m

Onion Rings

Preparation time: 5 minutes;

Cooking time: 16 minutes;

Serve: 1

Ingredients:

- 1 large white onion
- 1 cup and ¼ flour
- 1 tsp of baking powder
- 1 beaten egg
- 1 cup milk
- ¾ cup breadcrumbs
- Seasoned salt or a mixture of paprika, salt, pepper
- 1 tbsp olive oil

Direction:

1. Spray some oil in the bottom of your fryer. If you have a temperature setting, set it to 370°F (190°C).
2. Cut the onion into rings. In a bowl, combine the flour, baking powder and add the seasoning salt (to taste).
3. Add the milk and mix well. Place the breadcrumbs on a plate.
4. Dip each slice in the dough, then in breadcrumbs and place them in the basket.
5. Add the tablespoon of oil. Cook for 8 minutes on one side, turn, and bake for another 8 minutes or until crispy.

Nutrition Value (Amount per Serving):

- Calories 580
- Fat 29g
- Carbohydrates 74g
- Sugars 19g
- Protein 8g
- Cholesterol 0mg

Potatoes + Smoked Diots Sausages

Preparation time: 10 minutes;

Cooking time: 40 minutes; Serve: 2

Ingredients:

- 800 g of potatoes
- 4 Savoy smoked diots sausages
- 2 chopped onions (or 2 shallots) +10 cherry tomatoes
- 1 sprig of thyme and rosemary+1 tbsp of parsley/chopped garlic
- 3 tbsp olive oil
- 5 ml of water + white wine
- 1 tbsp of Provencal herbs + salt 5 berries
- 4 tbsp mustard tomato

Direction:

1. Peel the potatoes and cut them into cubes.
2. In the bowl of the air fryer pour the olive oil and put the onions, with the potatoes, parsley, the herbs of Provence and the salt of 5 berries. Program the fryer manually 180°C to 15 minutes.
3. When the onions and potatoes start to brown, add the sausages, cherry tomatoes, thyme, rosemary, and white wine + water. Stir with a wooden spoon.
4. Close and continue cooking. Set to 180°C - 30 minutes.
5. With a knife, check the cooking of the potatoes; otherwise, increase the cooking time by a few more minutes.
6. Remove the dish from the fryer with the tongs.
7. Enjoy this dish with mustard tomato

Nutrition Value (Amount per Serving):

- Calories 482
- Fat 37g
- Carbohydrates 24g
- Sugars 1g
- Protein 25g
- Cholesterol 57mg

Poached Egg

Preparation time: 10-20 minutes;

Cooking time: 45-60 minutes; Serve: 6

Ingredients:

- 500g Eggplant
- 200g of celery
- ½ onion
- 90g olives
- 15g capers
- 40g pine nuts
- 300g ripe tomatoes
- 30g sugar
- 250g broth
- 60g vinegar
- 2 tsp olive oil
- Leave at discretion

Direction:

1. Cut the eggplant, celery and chop the onions.
2. Attach the mixing paddle to the tank.
3. Pour the oil and onion into the basket. Set the air fryer to 150°C and brown the onion for 4 minutes.
4. Add celery, eggplant, broth and cook for another 25 minutes.
5. Season with salt and pepper. Add the pine nuts, tomato pieces, capers and olives and cook for another 15 minutes.
6. Add the sugar and vinegar at the end and cook for another 15 minutes.

Nutrition Value (Amount per Serving):

- Calories 73
- Fat 4.95g
- Carbohydrates 0.38g
- Sugars 0.38g
- Protein 6.26g
- Cholesterol 210mg

Cheeseburger

Preparation time: 0-10 minutes;

Cooking time: 15-30 minutes;

Serve: 4

Ingredients:

- 4 chopped steak
- 4 hamburger buns
- Salad to taste
- 1 large tomato
- Mayonnaise, ketchup, or mustard to taste
- 4 slices of cheese
- Taste oil
- Salt to taste
- Pepper to taste

Direction:

1. Season the fillets and place them in the basket. Set the air fryer 180°C.
2. Cook the chopped steaks for 20 min. depending on their size turning 1-2 times during cooking.
3. Add a slice of cheese to each chopped steak and simmer for 1 minute.
4. Remove the chopped fillets from the air fryer wipe any liquid left in the basket with a cloth and heat the hamburger bread in the middle for about 1 minute.
5. Start composing the cheeseburger; spread the mayonnaise, ketchup or mustard on the bread, a salad leaf, the chopped steak with the cheese and finally the tomato slices; cover with the other slice of bread and serve.

Nutrition Value (Amount per Serving):

- Calories 343
- Fat 16.4g
- Carbohydrates 32g
- Sugars 6.7g
- Protein 17g
- Cholesterol 50mg

Strasbourg Sausage Croissants

Preparation time: 0-10 minutes,

Cooking time: 15-30 minutes;

Serve: 4

Ingredients:

- 1 round puff pastry roll
- 4 small sausages from Strasbourg
- Mustard to taste
- Poppy seeds to taste

Direction:

1. Unroll the puff pastry and define 16 triangles. Spread the mustard over the dough, place a small piece of Strasbourg sausage at the base of each triangle and roll until it reaches the tip. Press well to adhere.
2. Place the mini croissants in the pan, previously covered with parchment paper, well separated with the tip down; otherwise they may open during cooking.
3. Brush the mini croissants with water and sprinkle with poppy seeds.
4. Set the air fryer to 150°C. Simmer for 13 minutes and then turn the mini croissants half a turn.
5. Simmer for another 7 min.

Nutrition Value (Amount per Serving):

- Calories 570
- Fat 40g
- Carbohydrates 32g
- Sugar 3g
- Protein 20g
- Cholesterol 275mg

Sausage Fondues

Preparation time: 10 – 20 minutes;

Cooking time: 15 – 30 minutes;

Serve: 4

Ingredients:

- 3 large sausages from Strasbourg
- 200g of bread dough
- Mustard (optional) to taste

Direction:

1. To prepare the poached Strasbourg sausages, start by dividing the dough into 3 equal parts (or even 6 if you want to cut the Strasbourg sausages in half).
2. Spread the dough with a rolling pin so you can completely roll up the Strasbourg sausage. Spread the mustard and place the Strasbourg sausage in the center of the rectangle, rolled up completely.
3. Moisten the bread dough to make it easier to close. Remove the excess on the sides and with a small sharp knife form transverse lines on the surface of the dough.
4. Place the Strasbourg sausages in the basket covered with parchment paper.
5. Set the temperature to 180°C and simmer for 30 minutes.

Nutrition Value (Amount per serving):

- Calories 20
- Fat 0g
- Carbohydrates 4g
- Sugars 3g
- Protein 0.3g
- Cholesterol 0mg

Patty Mozzarella

Preparation time: 10 – 20 minutes;

Cooking time: 0 – 15 minutes;

Serve: 4

Ingredients:

- 12 slices of sandwich bread
- 3 eggs
- Flour to taste
- Breadcrumbs
- Leave to taste
- 12 anchovies (optional)
- 12 slices of mozzarella
- 6 slices of cooked ham

Direction:

1. Take the slices of bread and remove the crust. Cut 2 rectangles on each slice. Fill each rectangle with a slice of mozzarella, ½ slice of ham and 1 anchovy.
2. Then close everything with a slice of bread.
3. Put the eggs in a bowl, in another the flour and in a third the breadcrumbs.
4. Take the sandwiches and pass them on both sides first in the flour, then in the egg and finally in the breadcrumbs, welding well to prevent the mozzarella from coming out during cooking.
5. If you prefer, you can iron the sandwiches in the egg and in the breadcrumbs.
6. Grease the basket and preheat it for 1 minute at 150°C.
7. Add mozzarella and continue cooking for 8 minutes, turning halfway through cooking.

Nutrition Value (Amount per Serving):

- Calories 290
- Fat 15 g
- Carbohydrates 24 g
- Sugars 2g
- Protein 11 g
- Cholesterol 35 mg

Strasbourg Potatoes and Sausages with Curry

Preparation time: 10-20 minutes;

Cooking time: 15-30 minutes;

Serve: 6

Ingredients:

- 750 g of fresh potatoes
- 3 Strasbourg sausages
- 2 small spoons of curry
- Salt to taste

Direction:

1. Peel the potatoes and cut them into cubes of approximately 1 cm per side. Put the Perl apples to soak in water, drain them and dry them well with a paper towel.
2. After spraying the air fryer with cooking spray, pour potatoes, salt.
3. Set the temperature to 150°C and simmer the potatoes for 20 minutes.
4. Add the Strasbourg sausages cut into small pieces, curry, and cook for another 10 minutes.

Nutrition Value (Amount per Serving):

- Calories 418.5
- Fat 17.6 g
- Carbohydrate 42.1 g
- Sugars 2.1 g
- Protein 18.0 g
- Cholesterol 44.5 mg

Treviso Chicory Sauce

Preparation time: 10-20 minutes,

Cooking time: 15-30 minutes;

Serve: 6

Ingredients:

- 400g of Treviso chicory
- 1 leek
- ½ red wine
- Salt to taste

Direction:

1. Chop the leek and place it in the basket previously greased.
2. Cook for 3 minutes at 160°C.
3. Add the previously cleaned chicory cut into large pieces, pour the red wine and salt. Cook for an added 12 minutes. Ideal for filling pancakes, lasagna, savory cakes, etc.

Nutrition Value (Amount per Serving):

- Calories 20
- Fat 0g
- Carbohydrates 4g
- Protein 1g

Sausages and Peppers

Preparation time: 0-10 minutes,

Cooking time: 15-30 minutes;

Serve: 4

Ingredients:

- 4 sausages
- 2 peppers

Direction:

1. Pour the sausages and peppers cut into pieces in the basket.
2. Cook for 20 minutes at 150°C.

Nutrition Value (Amount per Serving):

- Calories 339
- Fat 27g
- Carbohydrates 5.8g
- Sugars 3g
- Protein 17g
- Cholesterol 84mg

Brioche Sausage

Preparation time: 0 – 10 minutes

Cooking time: 0 – 15 minutes; Serve: 4

Ingredients:

- 2 sausages
- 2 bread sticks

Direction:

1. Remove the crumb from the bread to obtain a hollow cylinder (make pieces of about 10 cm, otherwise it will be difficult to work them).
2. Place the sausage in half the bread, then make slices about 2 cm thick.
3. Place the slices at the bottom of the basket (6 per batch).
4. Set the temperature to 160°C.
5. Cook for 10 minutes, turning the crispy rolls on themselves after 5/6 minutes.
6. Serve while it is still hot.

Nutrition Value (Amount per Serving):

- Calories 546
- Carbohydrates 37g
- Fat 35g
- Sugars 6g
- Protein 20g
- Cholesterol 0mg

Stuffed Potato Recipe

Preparation time: 20 minutes;

Cooking time: 14 minutes; Serve: 4

Ingredients:

- 150g Potatoes
- Ham
- Cheese
- Olive oil
- Salt
- Garlic powder

Direction:

1. Cut your potato into strips but don't get to the end.
2. Paint your potato with a little oil so it doesn't burn.
3. Add salt and pepper.
4. Put the potato 35 minutes at 180°C without preheating.
5. Fill each cut with ham and cheese to taste.
6. Put the potato back 10 minutes more at 180°C.

Nutrition Value (Amount per Serving):

- Calories 379.6
- Fat 17.6 g
- Carbohydrate 40.7 g
- Sugars 4.0 g
- Protein 14.0 g
- Cholesterol 25.4 mg

Chapter 2

Snacks and Appetizers

Corn with Bacon

Preparation time: 0-10;

Cooking time: 15-30; Serve: 4

Ingredients:

- 4 Precooked corn on the cob
- 8 Sliced Bacon

Direction:

1. Roll up the corn cobs with 2 slices of bacon each.
2. Place the corn cobs inside, close the lid.
3. Set the air fryer to 180°C and Cook the corn on the cob for 15 minutes.

Nutrition Value (Amount per Serving):

- Calories 90
- Fat 7g
- Carbohydrate 0g
- Sugars 0g
- Protein 5g
- Cholesterol 15mg

Brussels Sprouts With Bacon

Preparation time: 0-10 minutes;

Cooking time: 15-30 minutes; Serve: 6

Ingredients:

- 350g Brussels sprouts
- 100g of bacon
- 20g butter

Direction:

1. Clean the Brussels sprouts by removing the outer leaves and the base. Steam for about 20 min.
2. Place the bacon and butter in the bowl. Set the air fryer to 150°C and brown for 5 min.
3. Add the puff pastry, salt, and simmer for 10 min. additional, depending on the size of the cabbage.

Nutrition Value (Amount per Serving):

- Calories 287
- Fat 18g
- Carbohydrates 16g
- Sugars 3.8g
- Protein 18g
- Cholesterol 36m

Frozen Croissants

Cooking time: 30-45 minutes;

Serve: 4

Ingredients:

- 4 pieces of frozen croissants

Direction:

1. Preheat the air fryer at 150°C for 5 minutes.
2. Place the croissants in the basket.
3. Cook everything for 35 minutes. Turn it to 180°C (using parchment paper) after about 25 min.

Nutrition Value (Amount per Serving):

- Calories 201
- Carbohydrates 19g
- Fat 11g
- Sugars 2g
- Protein 4g
- Cholesterol 0mg

Frozen Potato Croquettes

Cooking time: 15-30 minutes;
Serve: 6

Ingredients:

- 750 g frozen potato croquette
- Fine salt to taste

Direction:

1. Preheat the air fryer at 180°C for 5 minutes.
2. Pour the potatoes in the basket. Cook everything for 24 minutes.
3. Salt and serve.

Nutrition Value (Amount per Serving):

- Calories 54
- Carbohydrates 6g
- Fat 2g
- Sugars 0g
- Protein 0.5g
- Cholesterol 0mg

Endives with Ham

Preparation time: 20-30 minutes;

Cooking time: 15-30 minutes; Serve: 6

Ingredients:

- 6 endives
- 500 ml of bechamel
- 6 slices of cooked ham
- 100g grated cheese

Direction:

1. Clean the Belgian chicory and steam for 15 min. Let them cool.
2. Separately, prepare ½ liter of bechamel and, as soon as it is ready, pour half the grated cheese and mix.
3. Pour the béchamel sauce in the bottom of the tank, roll each endive with a slice of ham, and place them too. Cover everything with the remaining bechamel and sprinkle with grated cheese.
4. Set the temperature to 150°C and cook for 15 minutes depending on the degree of gold desired.

Nutrition Value (Amount per Serving):

- Calories 106
- Fat 5.77 g
- Carbohydrates 5.69 g
- Sugars 2.67 g
- Proteins 6.2 g
- Cholesterol 0mg

4 Cheese Puffs

Preparation time: 10-20 minutes;

Cooking time: 15-30 minutes; Serve: 4

Ingredients:

- 1 rectangular puff pastry
- 250 g cheese mix
- Poppy seeds

Direction:

1. Unroll the puff pastry roll and cut it into 4 equal parts. Fill each rectangle with the cheeses cut into pieces and close the dough, welding the edges so that it does not open during cooking. This is the area of the puff pastry with water and sprinkle with poppy seeds.
2. Place 2 or 4 puff pastry (depending on its size) on the baking paper inside the basket.
3. Set the temperature to 150^0C.
4. Cook for 20 minutes or until desired browning is achieved.

Nutrition Value (Amount per Serving):

- Calories 140
- Fat 6g
- Carbohydrates 19g
- Sugars 1g
- Protein 2g
- Cholesterol 160mg

Treviso Chicory Puff Pastry

Preparation time: 0-10 minutes,

Cooking time: 15-30 minutes; Serve: 4

Ingredients:

- 1 stalk of Treviso chicory
- 1 roll of puff pastry
- Grated cheese to taste
- Salt to taste
- 1 tsp olive oil

Direction:

1. Cut the chicory of Treviso in 4 parts, wash carefully and dry.
2. Unwind the puff pastry on a work surface and cut it into small wide strips of approximately 1 cm. Roll the chicory in a spiral with the puff pastry, and more particularly outside, which would otherwise dry during cooking.
3. Cover the bottom of the basket with parchment paper. Place the chicory inside, sprinkle with grated cheese and salt.
4. Set the temperature to 180°C.
5. Simmer for 18 minutes; before serving, pour a drizzle of olive oil in each puff pastry.

Nutrition Value (Amount per Serving):

- Calories 170
- Carbohydrates 11g
- Fat 13g
- Sugars 0g
- Protein 2g
- Cholesterol 35 mg

Chocolate Muffins

Preparation time: 10-20 minutes;

Cooking time: 15-30 minutes; Serve: 10

Ingredients:

- 300g of flour 00:
- 300g of sugar
- 150g of butter
- 70g bitter cocoa powder
- 6g baking powder
- 180 ml of whole fresh milk
- 1g of salt
- Eggs
- 2g of baking soda
- 100g dark chocolate
- 1 vanilla pod

Direction:

1. In a food processor, beat the butter of the ointment with the sugar and then combine the seeds of a vanilla bean.
2. When the mixture is clear and foamy enough, add the eggs at room temperature, one at a time. Work all the ingredients for a few minutes and then add the flour, bitter cocoa, yeast, baking soda and salt (all sifted), alternating with milk at room temperature.
3. Finally, combine the dark chocolate chips
4. Fill the molds with the mixture and place them inside the air fryer (7 to 8 lots) previously preheated at 180°C.
5. Cook for about 25 minutes. In the end let cool. You can, at discretion, sprinkle with icing sugar.

Nutrition Value (Amount per Serving):

- Calories
- Fat 38g
- Carbohydrates 79.2g
- Sugars 47.9g
- Protein 9.9g
- Cholesterol 125mg

Pasticciata Pasta

Preparation time: 20 - 30 minutes,

Cooking time: 0 - 15 minutes; Serve: 6

Ingredients:

- 300g of macaroni
- 500 ml of bechamel
- 350 g minced meat
- 100 g cooked ham
- 30 g grated cheese

Direction:

1. Prepare the béchamel and cook the macaroni, making sure that they are firm when biting, once cooked, season them with separately cooked ground beef and ¾ of bechamel.
2. Pour the béchamel in the bowl, add half of the seasoned dough, cut the ham into small pieces, and pour the remaining dough. Sprinkle with grated cheese.
3. Set the air fryer to 150°C cook for about 10 min. or until the desired gold is obtained.

Nutrition Value (Amount per Serving):

- Calories 576
- Carbohydrates 58g
- Fat 25g
- Sugars 0g
- Protein 26g
- Cholesterol 0mg

Shepherd's Pie

Preparation time: 10-20 minutes;

Cooking time: more than 60 minutes; Serve: 8

Ingredients:

- 700 g of minced meat
- 350 g of tomato coulis
- 1 carrot
- 1 celery stalk
- 1 shallot
- Salt to taste
- Black pepper to taste
- 300 g of frozen peas

Ingredients for the cover:

- 1 kg of potatoes
- 200 g of milk
- 80 g butter
- 2 egg yolks
- Nutmeg to taste

Direction:

1. Divide the carrots, celery and chopped onions and then spray the basket. Brown for 5 minutes at 160°C.
2. Add the minced meat and cook for 5 minutes (during this time, using a wooden spoon, possibly separate the pieces of meat that can form). Add the tomato, salt and pepper coulis and cook for 45 minutes, mixing 3 to 4 times during cooking.
3. Finally, add the frozen peas and cook for another 10 to 15 minutes until the peas are tender.
4. Remove the blade (be careful that it is hot!) And spread the sauce with a tablespoon. Prepare the mash (according to the indicated doses) and then, using a bag of fluted puff pastry, make a lot of mash in the meat.
5. Brown everything for another 10 to 15 minutes. Let stand for 10 minutes before serving.

Nutrition Value (Amount per Serving):

- Calories 272
- Fat 8.21g
- Carbohydrate 34.46g
- Sugars 3.26g
- Protein 15.55g
- Cholesterol 34mg

Tomino With Speck

Preparation time: 0 – 10 minutes,

Cooking time: 0 – 15 minutes; Serve: 4

Ingredients:

- 4 tominos
- 8 speck slices

Direction:

1. Wrap the tominos with two slices of speck each, crossing them.
2. Cook the tominos for 5 minutes at 150°C.
3. Turn them on and cook for another 3 minutes.

Nutrition Value (Amount per Serving):

- Calories 361
- Carbohydrates 2g
- Fat 30g
- Sugars 0g
- Protein 20g
- Cholesterol 0mg

Chickpeas for Snack

Preparation time: 10 minutes;

Cooking time: 25 minutes; Serve: 6

Ingredients:

- 1 can (15 ounces) unsalted chickpeas, washed and drained
- Cooking spray oil
- ½ tsp garlic powder
- ½ tsp thyme powder
- ½ tsp coarsely ground black pepper
- 1/8 tsp red pepper or to taste

Direction:

1. Pour the chickpeas in a medium bowl. Dry them with a paper towel. Spray the chickpeas with the cooking spray oil for 2 seconds and stir to cover all the chickpeas. Pour them into the fryer basket.
2. In a small bowl, mix the garlic powder, the thyme powder, the pepper, and the red pepper; Set the bowl aside.
3. Adjust the temperature to 375°F and fry in air for 10 to 15 minutes or until the chickpeas are golden and crispy. Shake the fryer basket every 5 minutes. Halfway through the cooking time, sprinkle the chickpeas with cooking spray oil for 1 second.
4. Place the hot chickpeas in a bowl. Mix them with the seasoning immediately. Serve them warm or let the crispy chickpeas cool and dry completely, then store them in an airtight container at room temperature.

Nutrition Value (Amount per Serving):

- Calories 80
- Fat 1.5 g
- Carbohydrates 13 g
- Fiber 4g
- Sugar 2g
- Protein 4g

Crispy Cauliflower Snacks

Preparation time: 5 minutes;

Cooking time: 10 minutes; Serve: 4

Ingredients:

- 3 cups small cauliflower florets
- 1 tbsp olive oil
- ¼ tsp garlic powder
- 3 tbsp whole grain breadcrumbs
- 2 tbsp wing sauce

Direction:

1. In a medium bowl, mix the cauliflower florets with olive oil, garlic powder and breadcrumbs.
2. Place the cauliflower in the fryer basket. Set the temperature to 400°F and fry in air for 3 to 4 minutes. Shake the basket. Fry in air for 2 to 4 minutes or until the cauliflower is tender and the edges are crispy.
3. Transfer the cauliflower to a bowl and mix with the wing sauce. Serve warm.

Nutrition Value (Amount per Serving):

- Calories 70
- Fat 4g
- Carbohydrates 9g
- Fiber 2g
- Sugars 3g
- Protein 4g

Profiteroles

Preparation time: 25 minutes;

Cooking time 25 minutes; Serve: 10

Ingredients:

- 100 g flour
- 100 g of butter
- 200 g of water
- 200 g large eggs
- ¼ tsp of salt

Filling:

- 1 package vanilla pudding instant mix
- 240 ml milk
- 1 cup thick cream

Direction:

1. Mix the contents of the instant vanilla pudding mixture with 240 ml of cold milk in a bowl. Beat these ingredients with the double accessory to mix for 2 minutes. Cover and refrigerate to sit for at least 5 minutes.

2. Beat the thick cream with the whisk or the double mixing accessory. Add the whipped cream to the pudding mixture. Cover and refrigerate.

3. In a large pot, place water and butter until they boil. Over medium heat, stir so that it boils. Over medium heat, add flour and salt. Stir vigorously until the dough forms a ball in the center of the pan. Transfer the dough to a large mixing bowl and let stand for 5 minutes. With the double accessory to mix, beat the eggs one by one and mix well. Pour per tablespoon, 5 cm/2 apart, on an ungreased baking sheet.

4. Bake for 25 minutes at 218°C (425°F) until it reaches a golden-brown hue. The centers must be dry.

5. When the profiteroles are cold, you can split them and fill them with the pudding mix or use a pastry bag to introduce the pudding into the profiteroles.

Nutrition Value (Amount per Serving):

- Calories 170
- Fat 13g
- Carbohydrates 11g
- Fiber 0g
- Sugars 6g
- Protein 2g

Feta Cheese Triangles

Preparation time: 20 minutes;

Cooking time: 9 minutes; Serve: 3

Ingredients:

- 1 egg yolk
- 100 g feta cheese
- 2 tbsp chopped parsley
- 1 chive in thin rings
- Freshly ground black pepper
- 5 sheets of frozen phyllo dough

Direction:

1. Beat the egg yolk in a bowl and mix it with feta cheese, parsley, and chives; Season with pepper to taste.
2. Cut each sheet of phyllo dough into three strips.
3. Take a teaspoon full of the feta mixture and place it on the inside of a strip of pasta.
4. Fold the tip of the dough over the filling to form a triangle, and then fold the zigzag tip until the filling is wrapped in a dough triangle.
5. Fill the other strips of pasta with feta in the same way. Preheat the air fryer to 200°C. Spread the triangles with a little oil and place five of them in the basket. Insert the basket in the air fryer and set the timer to 3 minutes.
6. Bake the feta triangles until golden brown. Bake the rest of the triangles in the same way. Serve the triangles on a tray.

Nutrition Value (Amount per Serving):

- Calories 89
- Fat 3.6g
- Carbohydrates 11.7g
- Sugar 0.3g
- Protein 3g

Boudin meat

Preparation time: 10 minutes;

Cooking time: 25 minutes; Serve: 4

Ingredients:

- 400 g lean minced beef
- 1 lightly beaten egg
- 3 tbsp breadcrumbs
- 50 g of salami or chorizo well chopped
- 1 small onion, well chopped
- 1 tbsp fresh thyme
- Freshly ground pepper
- 2 mushrooms in thick slices
- 1 tbsp olive oil

Direction:

1. Preheat the air fryer to 200°C.
2. Mix the minced meat in a bowl with the egg, breadcrumbs, salami, onion, thyme, 1 teaspoon of salt and a generous amount of pepper. Knead it all right.
3. Pass the minced meat to the tray or platter and smooth the top. Place the mushrooms by pressing a little and cover the top with olive oil.
4. Place the tray or dish in the basket and insert it into the air fryer. Set the timer to 25 minutes and roast the meat pudding until it has a nice toasted color and is well done.
5. Let the pudding stand at least 10 minutes before serving. Then cut it into wedges. It is delicious with chips and salad.

Nutrition Value (Amount per Serving):

- Calories 200
- Carbohydrates 10g
- Fat 15g
- Sugars 0g
- Protein 5g
- Cholesterol 0mg

Chapter 3

Seafood and Fish recipes

Grilled Sardines

Preparation time: 5 minutes;

Cooking time: 21 minutes; Serve: 2

Ingredients:

- 5 sardines
- Herbs of Provence

Direction:

1. Preheat the air fryer to 160°C.
2. Spray the basket and place your sardines in the basket of your fryer.
3. Set the timer for 14 minutes. After 7 minutes, remember to turn the sardines so that they are roasted on both sides.

Nutrition Value (Amount per Serving):

- Calories 189g
- Fat 10g
- Carbohydrates 0g
- Sugars 0g
- Protein 22g
- Cholesterol 128mg

Spicy Squids Healthy

Preparation time: 10 minutes;

Cooking time: About fifteen minutes; Serve: 2

Ingredients:

- 300 g of squid slices, about 20
- ½ cup milk or vegetable drink (me, almond)
- 2 cloves garlic, pressed
- 2 pinches of salt
- Curry lining
- 4g breadcrumbs
- 4g cornmeal (semolina no. 400, texture close to polenta)
- 4 g freshly grated Parmesan cheese
- ¼ tsp Curry powder Madras
- ¼ tsp turmeric
- 1/8 tsp of garam masala
- Salt and pepper to taste
- 2 tbsp olive oil

Direction:

1. Rinse the squids in cold water, put them in a bowl and cover them with milk. Add salt and garlic and mix well. Cover the bowl and let it rest in the fridge for 1 hour, then let it cool 30 minutes before cooking.

2. Clean the squid with paper towels without insisting. In a bowl, combine the ingredients of the coating, except the oil. Roll the squid one by one in the dry pie to cover them well. Place them on a plate and lightly apply a little oil on each washer.

3. Heat the air fryer to 400°F. As soon as it is cooked, place the squid in the fryer basket. Cook for 5 minutes, remove the basket, and shake well. Repeat these operations two or three times more, always counting 5 minutes of cooking and stirring the basket. I left yesterday 15 minutes in total; the squid would have preferred 5 more.

4. Accompanied here of fried pak-choy, rice and a small sauce made with mayonnaise and yogurt.

Nutrition Value (Amount per Serving):

- Calories 264
- Carbohydrates 18g
- Fat 9g
- Protein 20g
- Sugars 11g
- Cholesterol 0mg

Frog Thighs

Preparation time: 15 minutes;

Cooking time: 20 minutes; Serve: 2

Ingredients:

- 1 454 g bag of frog legs, thawed and dried
- 3 tsp flour
- 1 beaten egg
- 1 tbsp of neutral oil, such as grape seed
- Clementine marinade
- The juice of 2 Clementine
- ½ orange zest
- 2 tbsp neutral oil
- 1 tsp rice vinegar
- 1 tsp tamari or soy sauce, reduced in salt
- 1 tsp fish sauce
- Crunchy coating
- ½ cup panko
- ½ orange zest
- 3 tsp Parmesan
- 2 tbsp unsweetened coconut flakes

Direction:

1. On a plate that can contain frog legs, prepare the marinade by combining all the ingredients. Using a fork for fondue, pierce the skin of the thighs in several places before macerating in the refrigerator, the dish covered with a plastic wrap, between 6 and 8 hours or overnight, and not just 2 hours.

2. 30 minutes before cooking, remove the thighs from the refrigerator. Prepare three deep plates, one with the flour, one second with the beaten egg, the last with the crunchy layer.

3. Start by flouring a thigh, soak it in the beaten egg and then roll it in the crunchy layer before placing it on a plate. Do the same with the other thighs. With a pastry brush, finish with a light layer of oil on each of its two sides.

4. Heat the air fryer to 400°F, place all thighs in the basket and cook for 5 minutes. Remove the basket, shake it, and replace it for another 3 minutes, remove it and shake it, then another 2 minutes.

5. Served here with grilled bok-choy mini petals and basmati rice.

Nutrition Value (Amount per Serving):

- Calories 75
- Carbohydrates 0g
- Fat 0.3g
- Protein 16.4g
- Sugars 0g
- Cholesterol 50mg

Exquisite Shrimp

Preparation time: 10 minutes;

Cooking time: 7 minutes; Serve: 2

Ingredients:

- 20 raw shrimp 31-40, thawed and well dried
- 3 tsp flour
- 1 egg
- 2 tbsp of neutral oil, grapeseed or other
- Crunchy coating
- 2/3 cup panko (uncooked Japanese breadcrumbs)
- 3 tsp freshly grated Parmesan cheese
- 2 tbsp unsweetened coconut flakes
- ½ tsp turmeric
- ½ tsp curry powder

Direction:

1. In a small bowl, put the flour. In another small bowl, beat the egg. In a third larger bowl, for example, a deep dish, combine the ingredients for the crispy coating and mix well.
2. Press a shrimp in the flour on both sides, soak it in the egg, then press it again on both sides, this time in the crunchy layer.
3. Place on a plate and do the same with all shrimp to cook.
4. With a brush, lightly brush all shrimp with oil, turn them over and brush the other side.
5. Place them one by one in the basket of the preheated air fryer at 180°C and replace them in the appliance. Wait 7 minutes, remove the basket, and place it on a heat resistant surface. Using a pair of silicone tweezers, remove the shrimp and serve.

Nutrition Value (Amount per Serving):

- Calories 6
- Fat 0.1g
- Carbohydrate 0.05g
- Protein 1.22g
- Sugars 0g
- Cholesterol 9mg

Shrimp Fritters

Preparation time: about 15 minutes;

Cooking time: 10 to 15 minutes; Serve: 4

Ingredients:

- 100g of flour
- 50g of cornstarch
- 50 ml of milk (to adapt to not have a paste too liquid)
- 1 sachet of baking powder
- 2 eggs
- 1 tbsp peanut or sunflower oil
- Salt and pepper
- Spices at your convenience
- 20 to 25 shrimp

Direction:

1. In a bowl, mix the flour, cornstarch, and baking powder.
2. Create a well in the middle and pour the eggs you have already beaten. Add salt, pepper, and spices if you choose to add them.
3. Mix everything while beating the dough so that it is very uniform and then let stand for 1:30.
4. Peel your shrimp while keeping your tail.
5. Once the dough is rested, dip each shrimp in it to cover it perfectly.
6. Cook:
7. Place the donuts in the fryer without oil for 10 to 15 minutes at 150^0C. Check the cooking and take them out as soon as the dough is golden brown.

Nutrition Value (Amount per Serving):

- Calories 137
- Carbohydrates 8g
- Fat 9g
- Protein 4g
- Sugars 1g
- Cholesterol 32mg

Cod Meatballs with Sauce

Preparation time: 10 – 20;

Cooking time: 15 – 30, 6 people.

Ingredients:

- 350g cod heart
- 50g breadcrumbs
- 1 bunch of parsley
- Thyme to taste
- 1 egg
- 1 clove garlic
- 40g grated cheese
- Salt, pepper, flour to taste
- Tartar sauce to taste

Direction:

1. To prepare the meatballs, start by mixing the breadcrumbs in a food processor. Then add the fish, thyme, chopped parsley, garlic, grated cheese, eggs and add (at discretion) salt and pepper.
2. Collect the preparation and form balls by hand. Flour each dough ball and roll them into a skewer (3 balls of dough per skewer).
3. Place the skewers in the basket of the air fryer. Close to cook at 180°C for 10 minutes by turning the skewers while cooking.
4. Cook for an additional 10 minutes.
5. Serve with tartar sauce.

Nutrition Value (Amount per Serving):

- Calories 40
- Fat 2.9 g
- Carbohydrates 0.9 g
- Sugars 0.5 g
- Protein 2.7 g
- Cholesterol 15 mg

Cod with Cherry Tomatoes and Green Olives

Preparation time: 10-20;

Cooking time: 30-45; Serve: 4

Ingredients:

- 400g cod
- 250 g cherry tomatoes
- 350 g of potatoes in pieces
- 100 g of green olives
- Salt to taste
- 1 clove garlic
- 1 tsp olive oil

Direction:

1. Put the cod in the center. Add small tomatoes, cut in half, olives, chopped potatoes, garlic clove, oil, and salt.
2. Set the air fryer to 150°C and Cook everything for 25 min. and then mix the vegetables with a wooden spoon to homogenize the cooking.
3. Cook for an additional 15 minutes; the cooking time varies according to the size at which you will cut the potatoes

Nutrition Value (Amount per Serving):

- Calories 226.0
- Fat 2.7 g
- Carbohydrate 6.9 g
- Sugars 2.4 g
- Protein 40.6 g
- Cholesterol 99.1 mg

Breaded Cod

Preparation time: 10-20;

Cooking time: 15-30; Serve: 4

Ingredient:

- 400g cod
- 2 eggs
- Flour at discretion
- Unlimited Breadcrumbs
- Parsley at discretion
- Chives at discretion
- Leave at discretion
- 1 tsp olive oil

Direction:

1. Clean the cod and cut it into pieces according to the desired size.
2. Beat the eggs on a first plate with a pinch of salt; in a second dish put the flour and in a third mix the breadcrumbs, parsley, and chives.
3. Pour the oil into the basket of the air fryer and distribute it throughout the surface.
4. Pass each slice of cod first in the flour, then in the beaten egg and finally in the breadcrumbs; arrange the slices in the tank.
5. Set the air fryer to 150^0C and cook for 10 minutes.
6. Turn the fish over and cook for another 6 minutes. Ideal accompanied by a sauce (yogurt, mayonnaise, etc.)

Nutrition Value (Amount per Serving):

- Calories 156
- Fat 2.3g
- Carbohydrates 16.4g
- Sugars 1.9g
- Protein 16.6g
- Cholesterol 0mg

Baked Scallops with Cheese

Preparation time: 10 – 20;

Cooking time: 15 – 30; Serve: 4

Ingredients:

- 4 scallops
- 40 g of breadcrumbs: 40 g
- 25 g grated cheese
- 1 tbsp parsley
- 1 tsp oil
- Salt to taste
- 1 clove of garlic (optional)

Direction:

1. Combine breadcrumbs, parsley, cheese, garlic, and salt in a bowl.
2. Place the scallops in the tank and cover them with the previously made filling, covered with a drizzle of olive oil.
3. Preheat the air fryer to 150°C for 5 minutes.
4. Cook for 17 min. or until the desired cooking is obtained; before serving, add a drizzle of olive oil.

Nutrition Value (Amount per Serving):

- Calories 218.2
- Fat 14.0 g
- Carbohydrate 12.5 g
- Sugars 1.3 g
- Protein 10.0 g
- Cholesterol 35.0 mg

Zucchini with Tuna

Preparation time: 10 – 20;

Cooking time: 15 – 30; Serve: 2

Ingredients:

- 4 medium zucchini
- 120g of tuna in oil (canned) drained
- 30g grated cheese
- 1 tsp pine nuts
- Salt, pepper to taste

Direction:

1. Cut the zucchini in half lengthwise and empty it with a small spoon (set aside the pulp that will be used for filling); place them in the basket.
2. In a food processor, put the zucchini pulp, drained tuna, pine nuts and grated cheese. Mix everything until you get a homogeneous and dense mixture.
3. Fill the zucchini. Set the air fryer to 180°C.
4. Simmer for 20 min. depending on the size of the zucchini. Let cool before serving

Nutrition Value (Amount per Serving):

- Calories 389
- Carbohydrates 10g
- Fat 29g
- Sugars 5g
- Protein 23g
- Cholesterol 40mg

Caramelized Salmon Fillet

Preparation time: 0-10;

Cooking time: 15-30; Serve: 4

Ingredients:

- 2 salmon fillets
- 60g cane sugar
- 4 tbsp soy sauce
- 50g sesame seeds
- Unlimited Ginger

Direction:

1. Preheat the air fryer at 180°C for 5 minutes.
2. Put the sugar and soy sauce in the basket.
3. Cook everything for 5 minutes.
4. In the meantime, wash the fish well, pass it through sesame to cover it completely and place it inside the tank and add the fresh ginger.
5. Cook for 12 minutes.
6. Turn the fish over and finish cooking for another 8 minutes.

Nutrition Value (Amount per Serving):

- Calories 569
- Fat 14.9 g
- Carbohydrates 40 g
- Sugars 27.6 g
- Protein 66.9 g
- Cholesterol 165.3 mg

Breaded Swordfish

Preparation time: 10-20;

Cooking time: 15-30; Serve:

Ingredients:

- 500g swordfish ranches:
- Breadcrumbs to taste
- 1 tsp peanut oil
- 1 tsp olive oil
- ½ lemon juice:
- Salt to taste
- Pepper to taste
- Parsley to taste

Direction:

1. Clean and rinse the fish; grease each slice and pass it in lightly salted breadcrumbs to cover it completely.
2. Preheat the air fryer at 160°C for 5 minutes.
3. Place the breaded fish in the basket. Cook the fish for 10 minutes.
4. Turn the fish over and cook for another 8 minutes.
5. Meanwhile, prepare the marinade with olive oil, lemon juice, salt, pepper and chopped parsley; Mix with a fork.
6. Once ready, place the fish slices on the plate and pour 1 to 2 tablespoons of marinade.

Nutrition Value (Amount per Serving):

- Calories 67
- Fat 3.79g
- Carbohydrates 2.23g
- Sugars 0.22g
- Protein 5.67g
- Cholesterol 16mg

Fish and French Fries

Preparation time: 10-20;

Cooking time: 30-45; Serve: 2

Ingredients:

- 400g cod fillets
- 2 eggs
- Breadcrumbs
- Leave to taste
- Flour to taste
- 1 tsp peanut oil
- 500g of frozen French fries

Direction:

1. Clean the fish and cut it into rectangles of about 8 to 10 cm by 4 cm. Pass each slice first in the flour, then in the egg (beaten with salt) and finally in the breadcrumbs; in the end, pass them again in the egg and in the breadcrumbs to obtain a double pie.
2. Grease the basket and preheat the air fryer at 160^0C for 5 minutes.
3. Cook the fish for 10 minutes.
4. Turn the fish over and cook for another 5 minutes.
5. At the end, clean the tank and insert the mixing paddle inside and then the potatoes.
6. Cook the French fries for 20 minutes or according to the desired degree of cooking.
7. At the end of cooking, remove the preparation paddle, place the previously cooked fish in the fries and reheat it for approximately 2 to 3 minutes.

Nutrition Value (Amount per Serving):

- Calories 79
- Fat 3g
- Carbohydrates 12.2g
- Sugars 0g
- Protein 0.8g
- Cholesterol 167mg

Deep Fried Prawns

Preparation time: 10 – 20;

Cooking time: 0 – 15; Serve: 6

Ingredients:

- 12 prawns
- 2 eggs
- Flour to taste
- Breadcrumbs
- 1 tsp oil

Direction:

1. Remove the head of the prawns and shell carefully.
2. Pass the prawns first in the flour, then in the beaten egg and then in the breadcrumbs.
3. Preheat the air fryer for 1 minute at 150°C.
4. Add the prawns and cook for 4 minutes. If the prawns are large, it will be necessary to cook 6 at a time.
5. Turn the prawns and cook for another 4 minutes.
6. They should be served with a yogurt or mayonnaise sauce.

Nutrition Value (Amount per Serving):

- Calories 2385.1
- Fat 23
- Carbohydrates 52.3g
- Sugar 0.1g
- Protein 21.4g

Mussels with Pepper

Preparation time: 10 - 20,

Cooking time: 0 - 15; Serve: 6

Ingredients:

- 700g mussels
- 1 clove garlic
- 1 tsp oil
- Pepper to taste
- Parsley Taste

Direction:

1. Clean and scrape the mold cover and remove the byssus (the "beard" that comes out of the mold).

2. Pour the oil, clean the mussels and the crushed garlic in the basket. Set the temperature to 200^0C and simmer for 12 minutes. Towards the end of cooking, add black pepper and chopped parsley.

3. Finally, distribute the mussel juice well at the bottom of the basket, stirring the basket.

Nutrition Value (Amount per Serving):

- Calories 150
- Carbohydrates 2g
- Fat 8g
- Sugars 0g
- Protein 15g
- Cholesterol 0mg

Scallops in Butter with Leaves

Preparation time: 10 - 20,

Cooking time: 15 - 30, 4 people, Calories: 127

Ingredients:

- 400g scallops
- 20g butter
- 1 clove garlic
- Leafs to taste
- Pepper to taste
- Parsley to taste
- ½ lemon juice

Direction:

1. Clean the scallops and dry them on a paper towel.
2. Place the butter and chopped garlic inside the basket. Set the temperature to 150°C.
3. Melt the butter for 2 to 3 minutes.
4. Add the scallops, salt, pepper and cook for 8 minutes.
5. Then add the lemon juice, parsley, and finish cooking for another 3 to 4 minutes.
6. Very good as an appetizer to serve inside the shells.

Nutrition Value (Amount per Serving):

- Calories 315.6
- Fat 13.8 g
- Carbohydrate 11.0 g
- Sugars 0.1 g
- Protein 38.7 g
- Cholesterol 114.8 mg

Scallops in Butter

Preparation time: 10 - 20,

Cooking time: 15 - 30, 4 people, Calories: 127

Ingredients:

- 400 g Scallops
- 20 g butter
- 1 clove garlic
- Salt to taste
- Pepper to taste
- Parsley to taste
- ½ lemon juice

Direction:

1. Remove the scallops by deciphering them, clean them and put them to dry on a paper towel.
2. Heat the air fryer at 150°C for 5 minutes.
3. Melt the butter for 2 to 3 minutes.
4. Add the scallops, salt, pepper and cook for 8 minutes.
5. Then add the lemon juice, parsley, and finish cooking for another 3 to 4 minutes.
6. Very good as an appetizer to serve inside the shells.

Nutrition Value (Amount per Serving):

- Calories 315.6
- Fat 13.8 g
- Carbohydrate 11.0 g
- Sugars 0.1 g
- Protein 38.7 g
- Cholesterol 114.8 mg

Monkfish with Olives and Capers

Preparation time: 10 – 20;

Cooking time: 30 – 45; Serve: 4

Ingredients:

- 1 monkfish
- 10 cherry tomatoes
- 50 g cailletier olives
- 5 capers

Direction:

1. Spread aluminum foil inside the basket and place the monkfish clean and skinless.
2. Add chopped tomatoes, olives, capers, oil, and salt.
3. Set the temperature to 160°C.
4. Cook the monkfish for about 40 minutes (depending on the size of the fish).

Nutrition Value (Amount per Serving):

- Calories 404
- Fat 29g
- Carbohydrates 36g
- Sugars 7g
- Protein 24g
- Cholesterol 36mg

Shrimp, Zucchini and Cherry Tomato Sauce

Preparation time: 0-10,

Cooking time: 15-30; Serve: 4

Ingredients:

- 2 zucchinis
- 300 shrimp
- 7 cherry tomatoes
- Pepper to taste
- Salt to taste
- 1 clove garlic

Direction:

1. Pour the oil, add the garlic clove and diced zucchini.
2. Cook for 15 minutes at 150°C.
3. Add the shrimp and the pieces of tomato, salt, and spices.
4. Cook for another 5 to 10 minutes or until the shrimp water evaporates.

Nutrition Value (Amount per Serving):

- Calories 214.3
- Fat 8.6g
- Carbohydrate 7.8g
- Sugars 4.8g
- Protein 27.0g
- Cholesterol 232.7mg

Spinach Crusted Salmon

Preparation time: 10-20,

Cooking time: 30-45; Serve; 6

Ingredients:

- 350 g salmon fillet
- 200 g bleached spinach
- 20g pine nuts
- 2 rolls of puff pastry
- 20 g butter
- 1 clove garlic
- Salt to taste
- Pepper to taste
- 1 egg

Direction:

1. Place the salmon, previously salted and spicy in the basket.
2. Cook for 15 minutes at 150°C. Once cooked, remove the salmon from the basket and let it cool. Put the butter, garlic clove, spinach (previously bleached), pine nuts, sole and pepper, and cook for 5 minutes.
3. Unwind the puff pastry on a work surface. Place the fillet in the center of the puff pastry (the skin will have been removed before the fillet has cooled) and cover with the earlier preparation.
4. Brush the 4 sides with the beaten egg and then cover with the other puff pastry. Pinch the sides to adhere the two pastes. Cut the excess puff pastry. Make a chimney on top of the puff pastry to facilitate the release of steam during cooking, then brush it with the egg.
5. Place the liner at the bottom of the basket on the baking paper (without the mixing).
6. Cook for 20/25 minutes depending on the degree of browning desired. Let cool before slicing.

Nutrition Value (Amount per Serving):

- Calories 186
- Fat 8.24g
- Carbohydrates 4.87g
- Sugars 3.22g
- Protein 23.67g
- Cholesterol 80mg

Salmon with Pistachio Bark

Preparation time: 10 - 20,

Cooking time: 15 - 30; Serve: 4

Ingredients:

- 600 g salmon fillet
- 50g pistachios
- Salt to taste

Direction:

1. Place the parchment paper on the bottom of the basket and place the salmon fillet in it (it can be cooked whole or already divided into four portions).

2. Cut the pistachios in thick pieces; grease the top of the fish, salt (little because the pistachios are already salted) and cover everything with the pistachios.

3. Set the air fryer to 180°C and simmer for 25 minutes.

Nutrition Value (Amount per Serving):

- Calories 371.7
- Fat 21.8 g
- Carbohydrate 9.4 g
- Sugars 2.2g
- Protein 34.7 g
- Cholesterol 80.5 mg

Salmon in Papillote With Orange

Preparation time: 10 – 20,

Cooking time: 15 – 30; Serve: 4

Ingredients:

- 600g salmon fillet
- 4 oranges
- Salt to taste
- 2 cloves of garlic
- Chives to taste
- 1 lemon

Direction:

1. Pour the freshly squeezed orange juice, the lemon juice, the zest of the two oranges into a bowl. Add two tablespoons of oil, salt, and garlic. Dip the previously washed salmon fillet and leave it in the marinade for one hour, preferably in the refrigerator

2. Place the steak and part of your marinade on a sheet of foil. Salt and sprinkle with chives and a few slices of orange.

3. Set to 160°C. Simmer for 30 minutes. Open the sheet, let it evaporate and serve with a nice garnish of fresh orange.

Nutrition Value (Amount per Serving):

- Calories 229
- Fat 11g
- Carbohydrates 5g
- Sugar 3g
- Protein 25g
- Cholesterol 62mg

Salted Marinated Salmon

Preparation time: 0-10,

Cooking time: 15-30; Serve: 2

Ingredients:

- 500g salmon fillet
- 1 kg coarse salt

Direction:

1. Place the baking paper on the basket and the salmon on top (skin side up) covered with coarse salt.
2. Set the air fryer to 150°C.
3. Cook everything for 25 to 30 minutes. At the end of cooking, remove the salt from the fish and serve with a drizzle of oil.

Nutrition Value (Amount per Serving):

- Calories 290
- Fiber 0g
- Fat 13g
- Protein 40g
- Carbohydrates 3g
- Cholesterol 196mg

Sautéed Trout with Almonds

Preparation time: more than 30,

Cooking time: 15 – 30; Serve:

Ingredients:

- 700 g salmon trout
- 15 black peppercorns
- Dill leaves to taste
- 30g almonds
- Salt to taste

Direction:

1. Cut the trout into cubes and marinate it for half an hour with the rest of the ingredients (except salt).
2. Cook for 17 minutes at 160°C. Pour a drizzle of oil and serve.

Nutrition Value (Amount per Serving):

- Calories 238.5
- Fat 20.1 g
- Carbohydrate 11.5 g
- Sugars 1.0 g
- Protein 4.0 g
- Cholesterol 45.9 mg

Stuffed Cuttlefish

Preparation time: 10 - 20,

Cooking time: 15 – 30; Serve: 4

Ingredients:

- 8 small cuttlefish
- 50 g of breadcrumbs
- Garlic to taste
- Parsley to taste
- 1 egg
- Salt to taste
- Pepper to taste

Direction:

1. Clean the cuttlefish, cut, and separate the tentacles. In a blender, pour the breadcrumbs, the parsley (without the branches), the egg, the salt, a drizzle of olive oil and the sepia tentacles.
2. Blend until you get a dense mixture. Fill the sepia with the mixture obtained.
3. Place the cuttlefish in the bowl.
4. Set the air fryer to 150°C and cook for 20 minutes. At the end of cooking, add a drizzle of olive oil and serve.

Nutrition Value (Amount per Serving):

- Calories 67.1
- Fat 0.6g
- Carbohydrates 0.7g
- Protein 13.8g
- Cholesterol 95.2mg

Sicilian Tuna Slices

Preparation time: 10 - 20,

Cooking time: 15 - 30; Serve: 4

Ingredients:

- 600 g of tuna slices
- 1 red onion stumbles
- 200 g chopped tomato
- 50 g boneless black olives
- 20 g desalted capers
- Salt to taste
- Pepper to taste
- Parsley to taste

Direction:

1. Pour sliced onion, tomato, olives, and capers in the basket.
2. Set the temperature to 150^0C and cook for 10 minutes.
3. Mix the sauce with a wooden spoon and add the slices of tuna, salt, and pepper.
4. Cook the fish for 10 minutes, turning it halfway through cooking.
5. Dress with chopped parsley.

Nutrition Value (Amount per Serving):

- Calories 233
- Carbohydrates 12g
- Fat 6g
- Sugars 0g
- Protein 29g
- Cholesterol 51 mg

Fish in Air Fryer

Preparation time: 5 minutes;

Cooking time: 10 minutes; Serve: 1

Ingredients:

- 1 lemon juice
- 3 fish fillets
- 1 tbsp full seasoning with achiote
- 1 tbsp ground garlic
- 1 tbsp ground onion
- Chickpea flour needed
- Water

Direction:

1. Rinse the fish. And cut them into pieces. Dry with paper towels. Spread with lemon and season.
2. In a bowl add the chickpea flour and little water to form a thick cream.
3. Batter the fish pieces. Spread the pan of the fryer with oil and place the fish. Cook for 10 minutes at 160°C.
4. Also, the cooking time will depend on the equipment you use.

Nutrition Value (Amount per Serving):

- Calories 280
- Fat 12.5g
- Carbohydrates 0g
- Fiber 0g
- Sugars 0g
- Protein 39.2g

Rabas

Preparation time: 5 minutes;

Cooking time: 12 minutes; Serve: 4

Ingredients:

- 16 rabas
- 1 egg
- Breadcrumbs
- Salt, pepper, sweet paprika

Direction:

1. Put the rabas boil for 2 minutes.
2. Remove and dry well.
3. Beat the egg and season to taste. You can put salt, pepper and sweet paprika. Place in the egg.
4. Bread with breadcrumbs. Place in sticks.
5. Place in the fryer 5 minutes at 160^0C. Remove
6. Spray with a cooking spray and place 5 more minutes at 200^0C.

Nutrition Value (Amount per Serving):

- Calories 200
- Fat 1g
- Carbohydrates 1g
- Sugars 0g
- Protein 1g
- Cholesterol 0mg

Prawns in Ham with Red Pepper Sauce

Preparation time: 15 minutes;

Cooking time: 13 minutes; Serve: 5

Ingredients:

- 1 red bell pepper cut in half
- 10 prawns (frozen), already thawed
- 5 slices of ham
- 1 tbsp olive oil
- 1 clove garlic, minced
- ½ tbsp paprika
- Freshly ground black pepper

Direction:

1. Preheat the air fryer to 200°C. Place the pepper in the basket and place it in the air fryer. Set the timer to 10 minutes. Roast the pepper until the skin is slightly burned. Place the pepper in a bowl and cover it with a lid or with transparent film. Let stand about 15 minutes.

2. Peel the prawns, make an incision in the back, and remove the black vein. Divide the slices of ham into two halves lengthwise and roll each shrimp into a slice of ham.

3. Apply a thin layer of olive oil to the packets and place them in the basket. Insert it into the air fryer and set the timer to 3 minutes. Fry the prawns until they are crispy and ready.

4. Meanwhile, peel the halves of peppers, remove the seeds, and chop them. Beat them in the blender together with the garlic, paprika and olive oil. Pour the sauce on a plate and season with salt and pepper to taste.

5. Serve the prawns with ham on skewers and add a small plate with the red pepper sauce.

Nutrition Value (Amount per Serving):

- Calories 187
- Fat 17g
- Carbohydrates 9g
- Fiber 2g
- Sugar 2g
- Protein 2g

Chapter 4

Poultry

Chopped Chicken Olive Tomato Sauce

Preparation time: 10 minutes;

Cooking time: 30 minutes; Serve: 4

Ingredients:

- 500 g chicken cutlet
- 2 minced shallots+1 degermed garlic clove
- 75 g of tomato sauce + 15 g of 30% liquid cream
- 1 bay leaf+salt+pepper+1 tsp Provence herbs
- 20 pitted green and black olives

Direction:

1. Cut the chicken cutlets into strips and put them in the fryer basket with the garlic and the shallots. Do not put oil. Salt/pepper.
2. Set the timer and the temperature to 10-12 minutes at 200°C
3. Add the tomato sauce, the cream, the olives, the bay leaf, and the Provence herbs. Salt if necessary. Mix with a wooden spoon.
4. Close the air fryer and program 20 minutes at 180°C.
5. Eat hot with rice or pasta.

Nutrition Value (Amount per Serving):

- Calories 220.2
- Fat 7.0 g
- Carbohydrate 8.5 g
- Sugars 4.5 g
- Protein 28.9 g
- Cholesterol 114.8 mg

Chicken Thighs in Coconut Sauce, Nuts

Preparation time: 10 minutes;

Cooking time: 30 minutes; Serve: 4

Ingredients:

- 8 skinless chicken thighs
- 2 chopped onions
- 25 ml of coconut cream + 100 ml of coconut milk
- 4 tbsp coconut powder + 1 handful of dried fruit mix+ 5 dried apricots, diced + a few cashew nuts and almonds
- Fine salt + pepper

Direction:

1. Put the onions, chopped with the chicken thighs, in the air fryer (without oil). Add salt and pepper. Program 10 minutes at 200°C.
2. Stir alone with a wooden spoon.
3. Add coconut cream and milk, coconut powder, dried fruits, and apricots. Get out if necessary. Continue cooking by programming 20 minutes at 200°C. You don't have anything to do; it cooks alone, without any problem.
4. With the tongs, remove the bowl and serve hot with rice, vegetables, Chinese noodles............... A delight. Perfect kitchen

Nutrition Value (Amount per Serving):

- Calories 320.4
- Fat 11.6 g
- Carbohydrate 9.0 g
- Sugars 2.1 g
- Protein 44.0 g
- Cholesterol 102.7 mg

Forest Guinea Hen

Preparation time: about 15 minutes;

Cooking time: 1 h 15 - 1 h 30; Serve: 4

Ingredients:

- A beautiful guinea fowl farm weighing 1 to 1.5 kilos
- 100g of dried or fresh porcini mushrooms according to the season
- 8 large potatoes Béa
- 1 plate
- 2 cloves of garlic
- 1 shallot
- Chopped parsley
- A pinch of butter
- Vegetable oil
- Salt and pepper

Direction:

1. Put the dried mushrooms in water to rehydrate them or simply clean them if they are fresh porcini mushrooms. Peel the potatoes and cut them finely. Chop the garlic and parsley and set aside.

2. Prepare the guinea fowl by cutting the neck and removing all the giblets inside. Garnish with stuffed dough, garlic cloves and parsley.

3. Place guinea fowls in the air fryer at 200°C without oil of sufficient capacity. Simply add the butter knob and a tablespoon of cooking oil. Allow approximately one hour of cooking per kilo, so you will have to check after a certain period.

4. When the guinea fowl is ready, prepare the porcini mushrooms in the oil-free fryer by adding the shallot. This preparation is very fast, and you should not forget salt and pepper.

5. When everything is ready, place each of the preparations in the air fryer, sprinkle with the cooking juices and cook for another 15 minutes.

6. Serve hot to enjoy all the flavors of the dish.

Nutrition Value (Amount per Serving):

- Calories 110
- Fat 2.5g
- Carbohydrate 0g
- Sugars 0g
- Protein 21g
- Cholesterol 63mg

Fried and Crispy Chicken

Preparation time: 15 minutes;

Cooking time: 35-40 minutes; Serve: 4

Ingredients:

- 4 chicken breasts
- 1 tbsp olive oil
- 1 tbsp breadcrumbs
- 1 tbsp of a spice mixture
- Salt
- 250g of potatoes per person

Direction:

1. Cut chicken breasts into 4 slices
2. Mix them with the other ingredients so that the chicken is perfectly covered with the preparation.
3. Peel and cut the potatoes in the same way as the fries, trying to make a regular cut to cook better.
4. Place the strips in the air fryer without oil and cook at 200^0C for 15 to 20 minutes to get a crispy chicken.
5. For French fries, wait 30 minutes to cook.

Nutrition Value (Amount per Serving):

- Calories 227
- Carbohydrates 23g
- Fat 18g
- Sugars 0g
- Protein 12g
- Cholesterol 63mg

Orange Turkey Bites

Preparation time: 10-20;

Cooking time: 15-30; Serve: 8

Ingredients:

- 750 g turkey
- 1 shallot
- 2 oranges
- Thyme to taste
- 1 tsp oil
- Salt and pepper to taste

Direction:

1. Cut the turkey into pieces and peel the oranges, cutting the skin into strips.
2. Put the chopped shallot, the orange peel, the thyme, and the oil in the basket of the preheated air fryer at 150 for 5 minutes. Brown all for 4 min.
3. Add ½ glass of water, lightly floured turkey, salt, and pepper; simmer for 6 more minutes.
4. Then add the orange juice and cook at 200°C for 15 minutes until a thick juice is obtained.
5. Serve garnished with some thyme leaves and slices of orange.

Nutrition Value (Amount per Serving):

- Calories 80
- Fat 5g
- Carbohydrates 1g
- Sugar 0g
- Protein 7g
- Cholesterol 25mg

Chicken Thighs with Potatoes

Preparation time: 0-10;

Cooking time: 45-60; Serve: 6

Ingredients:

- 1kg chicken thighs
- 800g of potatoes in pieces
- Salt to taste
- Pepper to taste
- Rosemary at ease
- 1 clove garlic

Direction:

1. Preheat the air fryer at 180°C for 15 minutes.
2. Place the chicken thighs in the basket and add the previously peeled and washed potatoes, add a clove of garlic, rosemary sprigs, salt, and pepper.
3. Set the temperature 200°C and cook everything for 50 min. Mix 3-4 times during cooking (when they are well browned on the surface) and chicken 1-2 times.

Nutrition Value (Amount per Serving):

- Calories 419.4
- Fat 9.5 g
- Carbohydrate 44.8 g
- Sugars 2.0 g
- Protein 39.1 g
- Cholesterol 115.8 mg

Chicken Blanquette With Soy

Preparation time: 10-20;

Cooking time: 15-30; Serve:

Ingredients:

- 600g Chicken breast
- 300g Potatoes
- 100g Bean sprouts
- 150g Broth
- 50g Onion
- 1tsp Olive oil
- 25g Soy sauce

Direction:

1. Cut the meat and potatoes into pieces.
2. Pour the sliced oil and onion into the bottom of the tank, close the lid.
3. Set the air fryer at 150°C to brown for 5 minutes.
4. Add the floured chicken, potatoes, broth, salt, and pepper and cook for another 13 minutes.
5. Then pour the sprouts and the soy sauce and cook for another 10 minutes.

Nutrition Value (Amount per Serving):

- Calories 250
- Carbohydrates 19g
- Fat 11g
- Sugars 7g
- Protein 16g
- Cholesterol 0mg

Fish Sticks

Cooking time: 15-30;

Serve: 6

Ingredients:

- 18 pieces Fish patties

Direction:

1. Remove the mixing paddle from the tank.
2. Heat the air fryer at 150°C for 5 minutes
3. Cook everything for 20 min.

Nutrition Value (Amount per Serving):

- Calories 281
- Total Fat 15 g
- Carbohydrates 23.9 g
- Sugars 2.8 g
- Protein 12.5 g
- Cholesterol 36 mg

Vegetarian Curry with Pumpkin and Chickpeas

Preparation time: 20-30;

Cooking time: 15-30; Serve: 6

Ingredients:

- 600g pumpkin, cleaned
- 300g chicken weights already cooked
- 1 tsp oil
- 1 tsp paprika
- 1 tsp curry
- ½ onion
- 1 clove garlic
- 1 tsp tomato puree
- 200 ml of broth
- 1 tsp turmeric
- 480g basmati rice

Direction:

1. Remove the skin of the pumpkin and the seeds inside. Cut it into small pieces, the same size as the chickpeas to have the same cooking time.
2. Pour the chopped onion and garlic, oil, and spices (paprika - curry - turmeric - saffron) in the basket.
3. Set the temperature to 150°C and brown all for 4 min.
4. Add the pumpkin and brown for 6 min. additional.
5. Then pour the chickpeas, tomato puree, broth and cook for 10 min. additional.
6. Meanwhile, boil basmati rice in saltwater, drain and serve with vegetarian curry.

Nutrition Value (Amount per Serving):

- Calories 249.6
- Fat 11.7 g
- Carbohydrate 27.8 g
- Sugars 9.6 g
- Protein 8.1 g
- Cholesterol 0.0 mg

Turkey Diced with Ginger, Apples and Vegetables

Preparation time: 10-20;

Cooking time: 30-45; Serve: 4

Ingredients:

- 600g turkey breast
- 150g carrots
- 100g of celery
- 50g onion
- 200g of potatoes
- Ginger to taste
- Flour at discretion
- 200ml broth
- 1 tsp olive oil
- Leave at discretion
- Black pepper to taste
- 1 apple

Direction:

1. Preheat the air fryer at 150°C for 5 minutes.
2. Cut the meat and vegetables into small pieces.
3. Pour the sliced oil and onion into the bottom of the basket and cook for 5 minutes.
4. Add carrots, celery, potatoes, and broth, then cook for another 15 minutes.
5. Add the floured turkey, salt, and pepper, then cook for another 15 minutes (if necessary, add some water).
6. Add the apple pieces and ginger at the end and continue cooking for another 5 minutes.

Nutrition Value (Amount per Serving):

- Fat 13.6g
- Carbohydrates 2.3g
- Sugars 0g
- Protein 42.4g
- Cholesterol 124.9mg Value (Amount per Serving):

Ligurian Rabbit

Preparation time: 10-20,

Cooking time: 45-60, 6 people, Calories: 440

Ingredients:

- 1 kg of rabbit pieces
- 150g green olives
- 2 tbsp pine nuts
- 100ml broth
- 1 shallot
- 1 clove garlic
- 1 rosemary branch
- 1 glass of red wine
- 1 tsp olive oil
- 2-3 bay leaves
- Salt to taste

Direction:

1. Put the chopped onion, oil, and garlic in the basket. Set the temperature to 200^0C and brown for 2 min.
2. Add meat, red wine and cook for another 8 min.
3. Finally add the green olives, pine nuts, broth, herbs, salt and pepper and simmer for another 50 min. (until the rabbit becomes tender, the meat should easily detach from the bone) turning 2-3 times (if the bottom is too dry, add the broth).

Nutrition Value (Amount per Serving):

- Calories 795
- Fat 8g
- Carbohydrates 0g
- Sugars 0g
- Protein 20.8g
- Cholesterol 82mg

Frozen Chicken Nuggets

Cooking time: 15-30;

Serve: 8

Ingredients:

- 750 g of frozen chicken nuggets
- Fine salt to taste

Direction:

1. Pour the chicken nuggets in the basket
2. Cook for 18 min at 200°C.
3. Salt and serve.

Nutrition Value (Amount per Serving):

- Calories 33
- Fat 1g
- Carbohydrates 2.8g
- Sugar 0g
- Protein 3.3g
- Cholesterol 9mg

Chicken with Cacciatore (Chicken Hunter)

Preparation time: 10-20,

Cooking time: 30-45; Serve: 6

Ingredients:

- 1 kg of chicken pieces
- 1 onion:
- 2 carrots
- 3 celery stalks
- 1 clove garlic
- 1 glass of red wine
- 400 g peeled tomatoes
- 50 g of olives
- Salt, pepper, parsley to taste

Direction:

1. Clean the chicken and place it inside the basket previously greased with the cooking spray.
2. Set the temperature to 180°C and cook the chicken pieces for 15 minutes.
3. Add the celery mince, carrots, onions, garlic, red wine, salt, pepper, and simmer for an additional 5 minutes.
4. Then pour the tomato and olives and finish simmering for additional 20 minutes stirring chicken and sauce.
5. Once cooked, add a handful of chopped parsley, and serve hot with mash or polenta.

Nutrition Value (Amount per Serving):

- Calories 233
- Fat 7g
- 10g carbohydrates
- Sugars 2.2g
- Protein 34.7g
- Cholesterol 98.5mg

Devil Chicken

Preparation time: 10-20,

Cooking time: 45-60; Serve: 4

Ingredients:

- 1 kg of whole chicken
- Salt to taste
- Black pepper to taste
- Chili pepper

Direction:

1. Thoroughly clean the chicken and cut it along the white. Flatten it well on the work surface and then massage with oil and spices.
2. Cook the chicken for 35 minutes at 200^0C.
3. Turn the chicken and cook another 25 minutes.

Nutrition Value (Amount per Serving):

- Calories 429.7
- Fat 17.3 g
- Carbohydrate 19.5 g
- Sugars 5.1 g
- Protein 51.1 g
- Cholesterol 155.0 mg

Chicken with Pineapple

Preparation time: 10 - 20,

Cooking time: 15 – 30; Serve: 6

Ingredients:

- 600g chicken breast
- 350 g canned pineapple
- 50 ml pineapple juice
- 1 tbsp of starch
- ½ tbsp ginger
- ½ tbsp curry
- 15 ml soy sauce
- Salt to taste
- Pepper to taste
- Flour (sufficient quantity)

Direction:

1. The floured chicken cut into small pieces, salt, and pepper in the basket previously greased.
2. Simmer for 8 minutes at 180°C (If, at the end of cooking, the chicken pieces stick together, separate them with a wooden spoon).
3. Add the pineapple into small pieces, ginger and curry and simmer for added 3 minutes.
4. Finally, add water, soy sauce and diluted starch to pineapple juice. Simmer for another 6 minutes until the sauce has thickened.
5. Ideal accompanied with basmati rice.

Nutrition Value (Amount per Serving):

- Calories 222
- Fat 7.1g
- Carbohydrates 11g
- Sugars 9.7g
- Protein 27g
- Cholesterol 85mg

Chicken Curry

Preparation time: 10-20,

Cooking time: 15-30; Serve: 6

Ingredients:

- 600g chicken breast
- 1 onion
- 2 carrots
- 150 ml
- 200 ml of fresh cream
- 100 ml of milk
- Salt to taste
- 2 spoons of curry
- Flour 00 (sufficient quantity)

Direction:

1. Chop the onion in a food processor and cut the carrots into cubes or slices.
2. Spray the basket and distribute the onion and carrots evenly in the basket.
3. Brown for 5 minutes at 150°C.
4. Add the floured chicken, cut into small pieces, the broth, salt, and simmer for another 5 min.
5. Finally pour the fresh cream, the milk and finish cooking for another 15 min. Ideal accompanied with basmati rice.

Nutrition Value (Amount per Serving):

- Calories 243
- Fat 11g
- Carbohydrates 7.5g
- Sugars 2g
- Protein 28g
- Cholesterol 74mg

Chicken with Yogurt and Mustard

Preparation time: 10 - 20,

Cooking time: 15 - 30; 6

Ingredients:

- 500 g chicken breast
- 100 g of white yogurt
- 40 g mustard
- 1 shallot
- Salt to taste
- Pepper to taste

Direction:

1. Place the chopped shallot inside the basket previously greased.
2. Brown for 3 minutes at 150°C
3. Add the chicken pieces, salt, pepper and cook for another 15 minutes at 180°C.
4. Then pour the mustard and yogurt and cook for another 5 minutes.

Nutrition Value (Amount per Serving):

- Calories 287.1
- Fat 8.9g
- Carbohydrate 4.3 g
- Sugars 1.7 g
- Protein 43.6 g
- Cholesterol 99.9 mg

Almond Chicken

Preparation time: 10 - 20,

Cooking time: 15 – 30; 6

Ingredients:

- 500 g chicken breast
- 130g crushed almonds
- ½ onion
- 1 tbsp grated fresh ginger
- 60 g of soy sauce
- Water (sufficient quantity)

Direction:

1. Pour the almonds into the basket.
2. Roast the almonds for 5 minutes at 150°C.
3. Remove the almonds and pour the chopped onion and ginger, the oil into the tank and brown for about 2 minutes.
4. Add lightly floured chicken, salt, pepper and cook for additional 13 minutes.
5. Pour the soy sauce, a ladle of hot water, the roasted almonds and simmer for additional 5 minutes.

Nutrition Value (Amount per Serving):

- Calories 458
- Fat 34g
- Carbohydrates 22g
- Sugars 7.3g
- Protein 20g
- Cholesterol 24mg

Mushroom Chicken

Preparation time: 10-20,

Cooking time: 15-30; Serve: 6

Ingredients:

- 500 g chicken breast
- Mushroom 300g
- 100 g of fresh cream
- 1 shallot

Direction:

1. Cut the chicken into pieces and sliced mushrooms. Spray the basket and chopped shallot into the basket. Set the temperature to 150^0C and lightly brown for 5 minutes.
2. Add the mushrooms and cook for additional 6 minutes.
3. Finally pour the chicken, salt, pepper, and simmer for another 10 minutes.
4. Then add the fresh cream and cook for 5 min. until the sauce has thickened.

Nutrition Value (Amount per Serving):

- Calories 220
- Fat 14g
- Carbohydrates 11g
- Sugar 4g
- Protein 12g
- Cholesterol 50mg

Pepper Chicken

Preparation time: 10-20;

Cooking time: 45-60; Serve: 6

Ingredients:

- 1 kg of chicken pieces
- 500 g of red and yellow peppers
- Salt to taste
- 50g onion

Direction:

1. Pour the chopped onion into the bowl with the chopped peppers and chicken. Add salt and pepper.
2. Set the temperature to $150°C$.
3. Cook everything for about 50 minutes, mixing 3 to 4 times during cooking, both meat and peppers.

Nutrition Value (Amount per Serving):

- Calories 281
- Fat 12g
- Carbohydrates 21g
- Sugars 3.4g
- Protein 23g
- Cholesterol 102mg

Stuffed Chicken and Baked Potatoes

Preparation time: 10-20,
Cooking time: 45-60; Serve: 4

Ingredients:

- 800 g boneless chicken
- 300 g minced meat
- 150 g sausage
- 80 g French toast
- 1 tbsp chopped parsley

Direction:

1. Bone the chicken (or bone directly by the butcher).

Prepare the filling:

2. Put in a food processor the meat, the sausage, the French toast bathed in milk to soften it, the parsley, the eggs, the grated cheese, the salt, the pepper and mix until obtaining a homogeneous and compact mixture.

3. Fill the boneless chicken and tie it well with a kitchen rope so that the filling does not come out.

4. Place the chicken inside the bowl, add the chopped potatoes, oil, salt, and pepper.

5. Set the air fryer to 160°C. Cook everything for 60 minutes over mix the potatoes 2-3 times to cook evenly and turn the chicken about once in the middle of cooking.

Nutrition Value (Amount per Serving):

- Calories 223.8
- Fat 6.5 g
- Carbohydrate 19.8 g
- Sugars 1.9 g
- Protein 21.2 g
- Cholesterol 48.8 mg

Tandoori Chicken

Preparation time: more than 30,

Cooking time: 15 – 30; Serve: 4

Ingredients:

- 600 g chicken pieces
- 125 g whole yogurt
- 1 tbsp curry
- 3 tsp of spices for roasted meats

Direction:

1. Place all ingredients in a bowl, flame well and let stand for 1 hour in the refrigerator.
2. Place the pieces of meat in the basket and set the temperature to 160^0C
3. Cook the meat for 30 minutes, turning it 1-2 times to brown the chicken on both sides.

Nutrition Value (Amount per Serving):

- Calories 263
- Fat 12g
- Carbohydrates 6.1g
- Sugars 3.7g
- Protein 31g
- Cholesterol 135mg

Crispy Chicken Fillets in Brine in Pickle Juice

Preparation time: 10 minutes;

Cooking time: 12 minutes; Serve: 4

Ingredients:

- 12 chicken offers (1 ¼ pounds in total)
- 1 ¼ cups pickled dill juice
- 1 large egg
- 1 large egg white
- ½ tsp kosher salt
- Freshly ground black pepper
- ½ cup seasoned breadcrumbs, regular or gluten free
- ½ cup seasoned breadcrumbs, regular or gluten free
- Olive oil spray

Direction:

1. Place the chicken in a shallow bowl and cover with the pickle juice (enough to cover completely). Cover and marine for 8 hours in the refrigerator.
2. Drain the chicken and dry it completely with a paper towel (discard the marinade). In a medium bowl, beat the whole egg, egg white, salt, and pepper. In a shallow arch, combine the breadcrumbs.
3. Dip the chicken in the egg mixture, piece by piece, then in the breadcrumbs, pressing lightly. Remove excess breadcrumbs and place it on a work surface. Spray generously both sides of the chicken with oil.
4. Preheat the fryer to 400°F.
5. Working in batches, place a single layer of chicken in the fryer basket. Cook 10 to 12 minutes, turning halfway through cooking, until cooked, crispy and golden brown. (For a toaster-style air fryer, the temperature stays the same; cook for about 10 minutes.)

Nutrition Value (Amount per Serving):

- Calories: 244kcal
- Carbohydrates 10g
- Protein: 37g
- Fat: 6g
- Cholesterol 150mg
- Sugar 1g

Chapter 5

Beef, Pork, Lamb Recipes

Perfect Garlic Butter Steak

Preparation: 20 min

Cooking time: 12 min.

Ingredients:

- 2 Ribeye steaks
- Salt
- Pepper
- Olive oil
- Garlic butter:
- ½ cup softened butter
- 2 tbsp chopped fresh parsley
- 2 garlic cloves, minced
- 1 tsp Worcestershire sauce
- ½ tsp salt (optional)

Direction:

1. Prepare the garlic butter by mixing all the ingredients together.
2. Place in parchment paper. Roll up and put in the fridge.
3. Let the steaks sit for 20 minutes at room temperature.
4. Brush with a little oil, salt, and pepper.
5. Preheat your hot air fryer to 400°F (200°C).
6. Cook for 12 minutes, turning halfway through cooking. Serve.
7. Place the garlic butter on the steaks and let sit for 5 minutes.
8. Enjoy!

Nutrition Value (Amount per Serving):

- Calories 250
- Fat 10g
- Carbohydrates 2g
- Sugars 1g
- Protein 36g
- Cholesterol 100mg

Crispy Pork Medallions

Preparation time: 20 minutes;

Cooking time: 5 minutes; Serve: 2

Ingredients:

- 1 pork loin, 330 g, cut into 6 or 7 slices of 4 cm
- 1 tsp Dijon mustard
- 1 tsp oil
- Salt, pepper and paprika
- Asian marinade
- 1 tsp salt reduced tamari sauce
- 1 tsp olive oil
- 1 clementine juice
- 1 pinch cayenne pepper
- 2 cloves garlic, pressed
- Crunchy coating
- 1/3 cup breadcrumbs
- ½ orange zest
- 2g freshly grated Parmesan cheese

Direction:

1. Prepare the marinade first. In a bowl, combine all the ingredients. Lightly salt the medallions, pepper, and sprinkle with paprika. Place these in the marinade and turn them several times to impregnate them completely. Cover with plastic wrap and marinate for 1 hour at room temperature.
2. Prepare the coating by combining the breadcrumbs, the orange zest, and the Parmesan cheese in a deep dish.
3. When the maceration time has elapsed, remove the marinade medallions, and dry them on absorbent paper. Spread with mustard, then move on to the crunchy layer. Brush lightly with oil.
4. Heat the air fryer to 350°F. Place the medallions in the fryer basket. Cook 5 minutes, stir, and then return to the fryer for another minute. Serve immediately.

Nutrition Value (Amount per Serving):

- Calories 222
- Carbohydrates 13g
- Fat 6g
- Protein 24g
- Sugars 0h
- Cholesterol 74mg

Nemos Beef with Dry Pepper Lactose Free

Preparation time: 30 minutes;

Cooking time: 20-25 minutes; Serve: 5

Ingredients:

- 250g of minced meat
- 1 handful of rice noodles
- 25 rice leaves
- 1 small onion
- 1 clove garlic
- 1 cube of chicken broth
- Roasted Sesame Oil
- 2 tsp dried pepper
- 1 tbsp soy sauce
- 1 tsp ground ginger

Direction:

1. Finely chop the onion and garlic and mix with the minced meat. Add half of the dried pepper, being careful to crush it beforehand. Add the ginger powder and soy sauce. Brown the preparation in roasted sesame oil, making sure you only have small pieces of minced meat.
2. Bring a pan of boiling water to which you will add chicken broth. Dip the rice noodles in it for only 3 minutes.
3. Add them to the ground beef preparation and then add the rest of the dried pepper.
4. Lightly moisten the rice leaves, place the filling in the middle and close them to create a perfect nem.
5. Place the spring rolls in the air fryer without oil previously heated at 150°C and cook for 10 to 15 minutes, according to taste.

Nutrition Value (Amount per Serving):

- Calories 203
- Carbohydrates 7g
- Fat 15g
- Protein 12g
- Sugars 5g
- Cholesterol 0mg

Pork and Parsni With Thai, Marinated with Honey and Soy

Preparation time: 20 minutes;

Cooking time: 30 minutes; Serve: 2

Ingredients:

- 2 pork ribs to choose from the tenderloin
- 1 large parsnip
- 1 coriander leaf
- 1 sprig fresh chopped parsley
- Salt
- For the marinade:
- 2 tbsp olive oil
- 2 tbsp soy sauce
- The juice of half a lemon
- 1 tbsp of honey, preferably flavored with orange blossom
- 1 tsp of specific spices for wok preparation
- 1 tsp of Asian spice mix
- Coriander powder

Direction:

1. Prepare the marinade by mixing all the ingredients in a large bowl. Mix to obtain a very homogeneous mixture.
2. Dip the pork chunks in the marinade, turning them over to make sure it covers the meat ribs perfectly. Prepare the parsnip by peeling and washing it, and then cut it into small dice.
3. Use a large plate to place the pieces of pork and parsnips covered with marinade. Pour the parsnips into the bowl and mix. Let stand for at least 1 hour before cooking.
4. Set the air fryer at 160°C without oil for 30 minutes and cook the parsnips.
5. At the end of the 10 minutes of cooking, add the pieces of pork or proceed to a traditional baking in the oven with 10 minutes on each side being careful to keep the cooking juices.

Nutrition Value (Amount per Serving):

- Calories 179
- Carbohydrates 11g
- Fat 13g
- Sugars 6g
- Protein 1g
- Cholesterol 0mg

Pork Fillet Mignon

Preparation time: 5 minutes;

Cooking time: 12 minutes; Serve: 3

Ingredients:

- 6 medallions of 100g to 150g cut in a pork loin
- Olive oil
- Salt and pepper

Direction:

1. Cut six pork medallions the same size as the pork loin you own.
2. Salt and pepper to your liking.
3. Use a cooking tool to spray a very small amount of olive oil.
4. Place your pork medallions on the air fryer previously preheated at 150°C and cook for 12 minutes.

Nutrition Value (Amount per Serving):

- Calories 125
- Fat 3.4g
- Carbohydrates 0g
- Sugars 0g
- Protein 22g
- Cholesterol 62mg

Lamb with Potatoes

Preparation time: 10-20 minutes;

Cooking time: 30 - 45 minutes; Serve: 2

Ingredients:

- 1 kg Lamb milk in pieces
- 600g Fresh potatoes
- 5 spoons Sunflower oil
- Salt and pepper
- 2 spoons Sage, rosemary, thyme
- ½ glass White wine

Direction:

1. Remove the mixing paddle from the tank.
2. Put the pieces of lamb, oil, sage, rosemary, and thyme in the cooking pot. Close the cover, set the thermostat to position 4, press the lower resistance power key and press the on / off key; brown for 4 min.
3. Add the wine and simmer for another 6 min.
4. Preheat the air fryer at 150°C for 5 minutes.
5. Finally pour the potatoes cut into pieces, salt, pepper and cook for 35 min. Extra by mixing the potatoes manually 2-3 times during cooking.

Nutrition Value (Amount per Serving):

- Calories 372.0
- Fat 12.3 g
- Carbohydrate 34.1 g
- Sugars 1.9
- Protein 31.5 g
- Cholesterol 86.7 mg

Veal Blanquette With Peas

Preparation time: 10-20;

Cooking time: 45-60; Serve: 2

Ingredients:

- 600g Veal meat
- 250g Frozen peas
- ½ Onions
- ½ glass White wine
- 1 tsp Oil
- 250 ml Broth

Direction:

1. Chop the onion and put it inside the tank with the oil. Close the lid
2. Brown for 5 min setting the air fryer at 150°C.
3. Add lightly floured meat, white wine, and simmer for 10 minutes.
4. Then add frozen peas, broth, salt, pepper, and simmer for 35 minutes. additional depending on the desired degree of cooking.

Nutrition Value (Amount per Serving):

- Calories 418
- Carbohydrates 24g
- Fat 14g
- Sugars 0g
- Protein 49g
- Cholesterol 357mg

Beef Stroganoff

Preparation time: 10-20;

Cooking time: 15 – 30; Serve: 6

Ingredients:

- 1000 g beef
- 500g onion
- Mushrooms 500g
- 150g sour cream
- 50 g butter
- 100 g of broth
- Salt, pepper to taste
- 2 tbsp paprika
- Flour

Direction:

1. Cut the onion into very thin slices, then clean the mushrooms well and cut them into slices, finally cut the meat into strips about 5 cm long.
2. Place the butter, onion, and mushrooms on the baking sheet.
3. Preheat the air fryer at 200C for 5 minutes. Simmer for 10 min.
4. Add the floured meat, paprika, broth, salt, pepper, and simmer for another 10 minutes.
5. Finally pour the cream and finish cooking for another 5 minutes or until ready.

Nutrition Value (Amount per Serving):

- Calories 391
- Fat 23g
- Carbohydrates 21g
- Sugars 3.2g
- Protein 25g
- Cholesterol 115mg

Meatballs with Tomatoes and Peas

Preparation time: 10 – 20;

Cooking time: 15 - 30, 6 people.

Ingredients:

- 425 g minced meat
- 1 egg
- 25 g grated cheese
- Salt to taste
- To taste breadcrumbs
- Parsley chopped to taste
- 150 g of frozen peas
- 400 g of tomatoes cut into large pieces
- 1 tsp oil
- 2 shallots

Direction:

1. Put the minced meat, the egg, the grated cheese, the salt, the parsley, the breadcrumbs in a bowl and mix until you get a consistent mixture. Form the meatballs (with these doses you will get 15-18 meatballs).
2. Chop the shallots and pour them into the basket greased with the oil. Close. Set the air fryer at 150°C and brown for 3 min.
3. Add the meatballs and simmer for an additional 7 minutes.
4. Then add the frozen peas, tomato, salt and pepper and simmer for another 18 minutes.

Nutrition Value (Amount per Serving):

- Calories 40
- Fat 2.9 g
- Carbohydrates 0.9 g
- Sugars 0.5 g
- Protein 2.7 g
- Cholesterol 15 mg

Cevapi

Preparation time: more than 30;

Cooking time: 15 – 30; Serve: 4

Ingredients:

- 150g of onion
- 350g ground beef
- 150g minced pork
- Leave at discretion
- Pepper at discretion
- Red paprika at discretion

Direction:

1. Mix all the ingredients in a bowl (the onion must be finely chopped) and knead well; form rolls 4 to 5 cm long and let stand in the refrigerator for at least 1 hour.

2. Place the cevapi in the basket of the air fryer. Set the temperature to 150°C.

3. Cook the cevapis (8 at a time) for about 13 to 15 minutes, turning them in the middle of cooking.

Nutrition Value (Amount per Serving):

- Calories 63
- Fat 4.84g
- Carbohydrates 0.25g
- Sugars 0.02g
- Protein 4.19g
- Cholesterol 17mg

Milanese Chop

Preparation time: 10 – 20;

Cooking time: 15 – 30; Serve: 2

Ingredients:

- 2 veal chops
- 1 egg
- 70 g of breadcrumbs
- Salt to taste
- 1 tsp oil

Direction:

1. Beat the egg in a bowl and prepare the breadcrumbs on a flat plate.
2. Pass each chop in the egg and then in breadcrumbs. Press the meat firmly into the pie. Put in the refrigerator for at least half an hour.
3. Pour the oil into the basket. Place the two chops.
4. Set the air fryer to 150^0 and cook the meat for 10 minutes and then turn the chop.
5. Cook for 5 minutes additional.
6. Serve the chops still hot, covering the bone with aluminum foil to facilitate tasting.

Nutrition Value (Amount per Serving):

- Calories 231
- Carbohydrates 8g
- Fat 9g
- Sugars 0g
- Protein 27g
- Cholesterol 97mg

Lemon Chops

Preparation time: 0-10;

Cooking time: 0-15; Serve: 2

Ingredients:

- 4 slices of pork
- 40g butter
- Flour to taste
- 1 lemon juice
- Salt to taste

Direction:

1. Preheat the air fryer at 180°C for 5 minutes.
2. Flour the pork slices. Place the butter in the basket and brown for 2 minutes.
3. Add the previously floured and salted pork slices, simmer for 3 another minutes. Turn them on themselves.
4. Add the lemon juice and simmer for 3another minutes.
5. Remove the slices and add a pinch of butter to the tank to thicken the juice. Mix the juice with a wooden spoon and pour the scallops over it.
6. Serve decorating the dish with lemon julienne.

Nutrition Value (Amount per Serving):

- Calories 242.4
- Fat 15.7 g
- Carbohydrate 0.7 g
- Sugars 0.0 g
- Protein 23.2 g
- Cholesterol 65.9 mg

Amatriciana

Preparation time: 0-10 minutes;

Cooking time: 15-30 minutes; Serve: 4

Ingredients:

- 200g Pork cheek
- 1 Medium onion
- 400g Peeled tomatoes
- 3 spoons Oil
- 1 Chile
- Salt

Direction:

1. Chop the onion and cut the pork cheek (removing the hard shell). Put everything in the basket, adding the oil.
2. Close the cover, set the air fryer to 3 minutes at 150°C to brown. Then pour the tomato, pepper, and salt.
3. Cook for an additional 17 minutes, or until desired cooking is achieved.

Nutrition Value (Amount per Serving):

- Calories 321
- Fat 9g
- Carbohydrate 49g
- Sugars 50g
- Protein 14g
- Cholesterol 20mg

Pork Chops with Chicory Treviso

Preparation time: 10-20;

Cooking time: 0-15; Serve: 2

Ingredients:

- 4 pork chops
- 40g butter
- Flour to taste
- 1 chicory stalk
- Salt to taste

Direction:

1. Cut the chicory into small pieces. Place the butter and chicory in pieces on the basket of the air fryer previously preheated at 180°C and brown for 2 min.
2. Add the previously floured and salted pork slices (directly over the chicory), simmer for 6 minutes turning them over after 3 minutes.
3. Remove the slices and place them on a serving plate, covering them with the rest of the red chicory juice collected at the bottom of the basket.

Nutrition Value (Amount per Serving):

- Calories 504
- Fat 33
- Carbohydrates 0g
- Sugars 0g
- Protein 42g
- Cholesterol 130mg

Venetian Liver

Preparation time: 10-20;

Cooking time: 15-30; Serve: 6

Ingredients:

- 500g veal liver
- 2 white onions
- 100g of water
- 2 tbsp vinegar
- Salt and pepper to taste

Direction:

1. Chop the onion and put it inside the pan with the water. Set the air fryer to 180°C and cook for 20 minutes.
2. Add the liver cut into small pieces and vinegar, close the lid, and cook for an additional 10 minutes.
3. Add salt and pepper.

Nutrition Value (Amount per Serving):

- Calories 131
- Fat 14.19 g
- Carbohydrates 16.40 g
- Sugars 5.15 g
- Protein 25.39 g
- Cholesterol 350.41 mg

Vegetable Cane

Preparation time: 10-20 minutes,

Cooking time: more than 60 minutes; Serve: 4

Ingredients:

- 2 calf legs
- 4 carrots
- 4 medium potatoes
- 1 clove garlic
- 300ml Broth
- Leave to taste
- Pepper to taste

Direction:

1. Place the ears, garlic, and half of the broth in the greased basket.
2. Set the temperature to 180°C.
3. Cook the stems for 40 minutes, turning them in the middle of cooking.
4. Add the vegetables in pieces, salt, pepper, pour the rest of the broth and cook for another 50 minutes (time may vary depending on the size of the hocks).
5. Mix the vegetables and the ears 2 to 3 times during cooking.

Nutrition Value (Amount per Serving):

- Calories 7.9
- Fat 0.49g
- Carbohydrate 0.77g
- Sugar 0.49g
- Protein 0.08mg
- Cholesterol 0mg

Milanese Veal Legs

Preparation time: 10-20 minutes,

Cooking time: more than 60 minutes;

Serve: 4

Ingredients:

- 1kg beef leg
- 1 onion
- 1 glass of white wine
- 150g hot broth
- Taste Flour
- Salt, pepper to taste
- 1 bunch of parsley
- ½ grated lemon
- 1 clove garlic

Direction:

1. Place the chopped onion in the basket. Brown for 4 minutes at 150^0C.
2. Add the lightly floured ears the white wine, season with salt and pepper and simmer for 6 minutes.
3. Turn the spikes, add the broth, and cook for another 50 minutes turning the meat 1-2 times.
4. At this point, add the chopped parsley, a grated peel of half a lemon and a clove of garlic and continue cooking for the remaining 10 minutes.
5. Serve hot with the juice that has formed in the cooking vessel.

Nutrition Value (Amount per Serving):

- Calories 499
- Fat 22.54g
- Carbohydrate 38.25g
- Sugars 2.27g
- Protein 34.23g
- Cholesterol 160mg

Veal, speck, and cheese paupiettes

Preparation time: 10-20 minutes,

Cooking time: 15-30 minutes;

Serve: 6

Ingredients:

- 12 slices of veal
- 6 speck slices
- 12 slices of provola
- Salt to taste
- Pepper to taste

Direction:

1. Place half a slice of stain and one of provola on each slice of veal; Roll each slice and close them with toothpicks.
2. Pour the oil and place the paupiettes in the basket, season with salt and pepper.
3. Set the air fryer to 180°C.
4. Cook the paupiettes for 15 minutes, turning them around after about 8 to 9 minutes.

Nutrition Value (Amount per Serving):

- Calories 261
- Carbohydrates 0g
- Fat 11g
- Sugar 0g
- Protein 30g
- Cholesterol 0mg

Fried Pork

Preparation time: 10 – 20 minutes,

Cooking time: 0 – 15 minutes;

Serve: 4

Ingredients:

- 300 g pork loin
- 2 egg yolks
- 4 tsp Worcestershire sauce:
- Salt to taste
- Taste Flour
- Gusto breadcrumbs

Direction:

1. Put the egg yolk, Worcestershire sauce and some flour (to thicken the sauce) in a bowl.
2. Cut the meat into pieces, lightly salt, and then pass it first in the sauce (previously prepared) and in breadcrumbs.
3. Grease the basket of the air fryer.
4. Preheat the air fryer for 1 minute at 200°C.
5. Add the pork and cook for 10 minutes, turning the meat halfway through cooking.

Nutrition Value (Amount per Serving):

- Calories 178
- Fat 11.89g
- Carbohydrates 0g
- Sugars 0g
- Protein 16.66g
- Cholesterol 51mg

Roast Pork with Vegetables

Preparation time: 10-20 minutes,

Cooking time: more than 60 minutes;

Serve: 8

Ingredients:

- 1 kg of pork loin
- 4 carrots
- 3 potatoes
- 1 onion
- 1 clove garlic
- 250 ml broth
- Salt and pepper to taste

Direction:

1. Place the tenderloin in the center of the tank, as well as the vegetables in small pieces, salt, pepper and pour a little broth.

2. Set the temperature to 160°C. Simmer for 1 hour and 30 minutes. Mix the vegetables occasionally and turn the loin halfway through cooking. Add some broth as necessary to keep the meat tender.

Nutrition Value (Amount per Serving):

- Calories 487.3
- Fat 16.7 g
- Carbohydrate 40.3 g
- Sugars 1.1 g
- Protein 44.9 g
- Cholesterol 95.3 mg

Saltimbocca Roman Veal

Preparation time: 10 – 20 minutes,

Cooking time: 0 – 15 minutes;

Serve: 4

Ingredients:

- 70-80 g See
- 16 slices of raw ham
- 16 sage leaves
- 20 g butter
- Salt to taste
- Pepper to taste

Address:

1. Place the meat slices on a sheet of parchment paper. Arrange the ham slices on the meat, put the washed sage leaf, roll, and close with a toothpick.
2. Place the butter in the basket at 150°C. Melt the butter for 2 min.
3. Add the meat and simmer for 6 minutes.

Nutrition Value (Amount per Serving):

- Calories 323
- Fat 18g
- Carbohydrates 1.7g
- Sugars 0.4g
- Protein 29g
- Cholesterol 124mg

Sautéed Meat with Potatoes

Preparation time: 10-20 minutes,

Cooking time: 30-45 minutes;

Serve: 6

Ingredients:

- 750g beef
- 350 g of potatoes
- 200 ml of hot broth
- 250 g of tomato coulis
- 1 onion
- Salt to taste
- Pepper to taste

Direction:

1. Chop the onion and put it in the basket previously greased.
2. Set the temperature to 150°C.
3. Brown the onion for 3 to 4 minutes and then add the pieces of meat, broth, salt, and pepper.
4. Cook the meat for 20 minutes and add the potatoes and the tomato coulis.
5. Cook for another 20 to 25 minutes, mixing the sautéed with a wooden spoon 3 to 4 times during cooking to prevent it from drying out too much.

Nutrition Value (Amount per Serving):

- Calories 317
- Carbohydrates 13g
- Fat 18g
- Sugars 1g
- Protein 24g
- Cholesterol 73mg

Sautéed Pork with Peppers

Preparation time: 10 – 20 minutes,

Cooking time: 15 – 30 minutes;

Serve: 6

Ingredients:

- 600 g pieces of pork taken from the loin or shoulder
- 200 g of peppers
- 1 shallot
- Salt to taste
- Pepper to taste

Direction:

1. Preheat the air fryer at 150°C for 5 minutes. Spray the basket.
2. Chop the shallot and cut the peppers into strips Place the shallot and oil in the basket then brown for 2 minutes.
3. Add the peppers and simmer for another 8 minutes.
4. Finally pour the pieces of pork, salt, pepper, and simmer for another 10 minutes.

Nutrition Value (Amount per Serving):

- Calories 334.2
- Fat 11.5 g
- Carbohydrate 31.8 g
- Sugars 2.0 g
- Protein 24.5 g
- Cholesterol 59.2 mg

Chapter 6

Vegan and Vegetarian Recipes

Frying Potatoes

Preparation time: 5 minutes;

Cooking time: 40 minutes;

Serve: 4

Ingredients:

- 5 to 6 medium potatoes
- Olive oil in a spray bottle if possible
- Mill salt
- Freshly ground pepper

Direction:

1. Wash the potatoes well and dry them.
2. Brush with a little oil on both sides if not with the oil
3. Crush some ground salt and pepper on top.
4. Place the potatoes in the fryer basket
5. Set the cooking at 190°C for 40 minutes, in the middle of cooking turn the potatoes for even cooking on both sides.
6. At the end of cooking, remove the potatoes from the basket, cut them in half and slightly scrape the melting potato inside and add only a little butter, and enjoy!

Nutrition Value (Amount per Serving):

- Calories 365
- Fat 17g
- Carbohydrates 48g
- Sugars 0.3g
- Protein 4g
- Cholesterol 0mg

Avocado Fries

Preparation time: 5 minutes

Cooking time: 10 minutes;

Serve: 1

Ingredients:

- 1 egg
- 1 ripe avocado
- ½ tsp salt
- ½ cup of panko breadcrumbs

Direction:

1. Preheat the air fryer to 400°F (200°C) for 5 minutes.
2. Remove the avocado pit and cut into fries. In a small bowl, whisk the egg with the salt.
3. Enter the breadcrumbs on a plate.
4. Dip the quarters in the egg mixture, then in the breadcrumbs.
5. Put them in the fryer. Cook for 8-10 minutes.
6. Turn halfway through cooking.

Nutrition Value (Amount per Serving):

- Calories 390
- Fat 32g
- Carbohydrates 24g
- Sugars 3g
- Protein 4g
- Cholesterol 0mg

Crispy French Fries

Preparation time: 5 minutes;

Cooking time: 10 minutes;

Serve: 2

Ingredients:

- 2 medium sweet potatoes
- 2 tsp olive oil
- ½ tsp salt
- ½ tsp garlic powder
- ¼ tsp paprika
- Black pepper

Direction:

1. Preheat the hot air fryer to 400°F (200°C)
2. Spray the basket with a little oil.
3. Cut the sweet potatoes into potato chips about 1 cm wide.
4. Add oil, salt, garlic powder, pepper and paprika.
5. Cook for 8 minutes, without overloading the basket.
6. Repeat 2 or 3 times, as necessary.

Nutrition Value (Amount per Serving):

- Calories 240
- Fat 9g
- Carbohydrates 36g
- Sugars 1g
- Protein 3g
- Cholesterol 0mg

Frying Potatoes with Butter

Preparation time: 5 minutes;

Cooking time: 10 minutes;

Serve: 2

Ingredients:

- 2 Russet potatoes
- Butter
- Fresh parsley (optional)

Direction:

1. Spray the basket with a little oil.
2. Open your potatoes along.
3. Make some holes with a fork.
4. Add the butter and parsley.
5. Transfer to the basket. If your air fryer to a temperature of 198°C (390°F).
6. Cook for 30 to 40 minutes.
7. Try about 30 minutes. Bon Appetite!

Nutrition Value (Amount per Serving):

- Calories 365
- Fat 17g
- Carbohydrates 48g
- Sugars 0.3g
- Protein 4g
- Cholesterol 0mg

Homemade French Fries

Preparation time: 5 minutes;

Cooking time: 10 minutes;

Serve: 2

Ingredients:

- 2.5 lb. sliced and sliced potato chips
- 1 tbsp olive oil
- Salt and pepper to taste
- 1 tsp salt to season or paprika

Direction:

1. Put the fries in a bowl with very cold water.
2. Let it soak for at least 30 minutes.
3. Drain completely. Add the oil. Shake
4. Put them in the fryer bowl. Cook for 15 to 25 minutes. Set to 380°F (193°C).
5. Set the time according to your preferences or the power of your fryer to 23 minutes.

Nutrition Value (Amount per Serving):

- Calories 118
- Fat 7g
- Carbohydrates 27
- Sugars 1g
- Protein 2
- Cholesterol 0mg

Mini pepper/tomato/shallot/goat cheese tartlets

Preparation time: 10 minutes;

Cooking time: 15 minutes;

Serve: 4-6

Ingredients:

- 1 pure butter puff pastry
- 3 peppers+ 2 tomatoes + 1 shallot + 1 degermed garlic clove
- 1 whole egg + 2 tbsp salad seeds (squash, sunflower, sesame ......)
- 3 tablespoons cheese in cubes + ½ goat cheese log + 50 g grated emmental cheese
- 6/8 mini silicone molds (round, square, heart ....)
- Salt + pepper 5 berries

Direction:

1. Put the grid / cubes in the 11 in 1 mandolin and cut all the vegetables (cleaned) into small pieces.
2. Beat the egg in an omelet and add the cut vegetables, the cubed cheese, the seeds, salt, and pepper.
3. Unroll the puff pastry and cut circles (squares of hearts ...) and darken the mini molds. Prick the bottom with a fork.
4. Garnish with the egg/vegetable preparation and add a little goat cheese and grated emmental cheese on top.
5. Place the molds on the fryer grid, close the hood, and program the "15-minute pie" function at 150°C.
6. When it is well cooked, remove the grid with the tongs. Serve hot or warm with a salad.

Nutrition Value (Amount per Serving):

- Calories 152g
- Fat 9g
- Carbohydrates 10g
- Sugars 10g
- Protein 4g
- Cholesterol 0mg

Almond Apples

Preparation time: 10 minutes;

Cooking time: 45 minutes;

Serve: 5-6

Ingredients:

- 600 g of peeled potatoes
- 2 egg yolks
- 2 eggs
- 60g of almond powder
- Salt,
- Pepper
- frying oil
- 30g of butter
- 50g of almond chips
- 50g of breadcrumbs
- 50g of flour

Direction:

1. Peel the potatoes (if you feel like it, instead of throwing the husks, baked shell chips, it's a delight).
2. Cut the potatoes into cubes and cook them in salted water (starting with cold water) approximately 15 minutes after boiling.
3. Drain and puree with a potato masher. Add salt and pepper.
4. Add the egg yolks, butter, and almond powder, mix well.
5. Place in the refrigerator for a quarter of an hour, then roll balls into the palm of your hand. Then, roll them rolling successively in flour, beaten eggs in an omelet, then in a mixture of breadcrumbs and flaked almonds.
6. Let cool for 15 minutes.
7. Put them in the air fryer at 180°C for 15 minutes. Then place the almond apples on a paper towel.

Nutrition Value (Amount per Serving):

- Calories 284.0
- Fat 19.1 g
- Carbohydrate 27.9 g
- Sugars 13.8 g
- Protein 5.0 g
- Cholesterol 0.0 mg

French fries without dry

Ingredients:

- 500g of French fries
- 1 tbsp oil

Preparation:

1. Peel and cut the potatoes, using a knife or a "fried cut".
2. Rinse with water and dry the fries.
3. Put them in a bowl and add the oil spoon, mix well.
4. Preheat the air fryer to 160°C. Put the fries in the basket for 15 minutes.
5. Pour the fries in the bowl, mix, and pass the fryer to more than 200°C.
6. Put the fries back in the basket and cook again for about 10 minutes. Look carefully because the overhead comes quickly!

Nutrition Value (Amount per Serving):

- Calories 118
- Fat 7g
- Carbohydrates 27
- Sugars 1g
- Protein 2
- Cholesterol 0mg

Bugnes Lyonnaises

Preparation: 30 minutes;

Rest: 2 hours;

Cook: 15 minutes

Ingredients:

- 250 g flour
- ½ packet of yeast
- 50g of powdered sugar
- 50g butter
- 2 eggs
- 1 tsp rum
- 1 pinch of salt
- Frying oil

Direction:

1. Soften the butter; beat the eggs with a fork.
2. Place the flour in a bowl; add the salt, the butter, the beaten eggs, the aroma.
3. Mix until you have a consistent paste. Form a ball and let stand at least 2 hours in the fridge.
4. Heat the fryer oil at 150°C for 15 minutes.
5. Stretch the dough to a thickness of 5 mm. Cut into strips of 10 cm by 4 cm and make an incision in the center of 5 cm.
6. Pass a corner of the strip in the incision to tie a knot or leave it as is.
7. Dip the bugnes in the fryer, flip them 1 time and drain once cooked on absorbent paper.
8. Sprinkle with icing sugar or icing sugar and serve hot.

Nutrition Value (Amount per Serving):

- Calories 140
- Carbohydrate 6 g
- Fat 13 g
- Protein 1 g
- Sodium 29 mg
- Sugar 1 g

Green salad with roasted pepper

Preparation time: 5 minutes;

Cooking time: 10 minutes;

Serve: 2

Ingredients:

- 1 red pepper
- 1 tbsp lemon juice
- 3 tbsp yogurt
- 2 tbsp olive oil
- Freshly ground black pepper
- 1 romaine lettuce, cut into large strips
- 50g arugula leaves

Direction:

1. Preheat the Air Fryer to 200°C.
2. Place the pepper in the basket and insert it into the Air Fryer. Set the timer for 10 minutes and roast the pepper until the skin is slightly burned.
3. Then cut the pepper into quarters and remove the seeds and skin. Cut the pepper into strips.
4. Prepare vinaigrette in a bowl with 2 tablespoons of pepper juice, lemon juice, yogurt, and olive oil. Add pepper and salt according to your taste.
5. Mix the lettuce and arugula leaves in the vinaigrette and garnish the salad with the pepper strips.

Nutrition Value (Amount per Serving):

- Calories 47.3
- Fat 0.4 g
- Carbohydrate 10.8 g
- Sugars 2.0 g
- Protein 1.8 g
- Cholesterol 0.0 mg

Fat Free Crispy Fries

Preparation time: about 15 minutes;

Cook time: 10 to 35 minutes;

Serve: 4

Ingredients:

- 500g of special fries
- 1 tbsp olive oil
- 1 freezer bag
- Salt + pepper

Direction:

1. Peel the potatoes, cut them with a potato chip cutter, rinse them with clean water and dry them well with a cloth.
2. It is important to cut all the potatoes evenly; otherwise you may have some overcooked and not enough fries.
3. Place the sliced fries in a freezer bag, add 1 tablespoon of oil, close the bag, and stir everything.
4. Place the French fries in the basket, close it, and close the lid of the fryer and set to 230°C to 35 minutes.
5. At the end of cooking, remove the basket with the tongs and remove the fries. Add salt and pepper.

Nutrition Value (Amount per Serving):

- Calories 118
- Fat 7g
- Carbohydrates 27
- Sugars 1g
- Protein 2
- Cholesterol 0mg

Marinated Potatoes with Chimichurri Sauce

Preparation time: 20 minutes;

Cooking time: 45 minutes;

Serve: 4

Ingredients:

- 1kg to 1.2kg of potatoes
- 2 tablespoons chimichurri sauce

Direction:

1. Depending on the taste, you can peel the potatoes, but the real potatoes are prepared with the skin.
2. Wash the potatoes before cutting them.
3. Cut them in quarters to get the shape of the potatoes and place them in a freezer bag.
4. Add the sauce and use the solid closure of the sachet to keep it closed.
5. Mix everything by handling the bag in all directions. Potatoes should be well impregnated with the preparation.
6. Pour all the preparation in the air fryer without oil.
7. Set the air fryer at 180°C for 45 minutes and serve immediately after the end of cooking.

Nutrition Value (Amount per Serving):

- Calories 367
- Sugars 2.0 g
- Fat 18.4 g
- Protein 5.7 g
- Carbohydrate 45 g
- Cholesterol 0mg

Homemade Gluten Free Spicy Chips

Preparation time: 25 minutes;

Cooking time: 30 minutes;

Serve: 1

Ingredients:

- 500g of potatoes to choose from among those with firm meat
- 1 tbsp vegetable oil
- 1 pinch of salt
- 1 mixture of texmex spices

Direction:

1. Peel the potatoes and cut them into slices approximately 2 millimeters thick. Preferably use a mandolin for a very fine and regular cut.
2. Rinse the potatoes to get rid of their starch and let them stand for 15 minutes in a bowl of cold water.
3. Drain the potatoes and dry them with a paper towel by simply sliding them. Avoid rubbing them as they could break.
4. Pour the potatoes in the fryer and cover them with the necessary tablespoon of oil.
5. Set the air fryer at 150°C for 30 minutes.
6. Be sure to stir the fries with a wooden utensil every ten minutes to make sure they cook perfectly.
7. Wait 5 minutes before the end of cooking to add salt and spices.

Nutrition Value (Amount per Serving):

- Calories 150
- Cal
- 17%
- Carbohydrates 15g
- Fat 32g
- Protein 1g
- Sugars 3g
- Cholesterol 0mg

Funghetto Eggplant (Golden Neapolitan)

Preparation time: 0-10 minutes;

Cooking time: 15-30 minutes;

Serve:

Ingredients:

- 600g Eggplant
- 100g Broth
- 1 Garlic clove
- Salt
- Pepper
- 3 spoons Olive oil
- Parsley

Direction:

1. Wash the eggplants, dry them, and cut them into 1.5 cm cubes.
2. Place the mixing blade in the tank
3. Pour oil and peeled garlic, close the lid.
4. Set the air fryer to 150°C to brown for about 2 min.
5. Add eggplant, broth, salt and pepper and simmer for another 23 min.
6. Finally, before serving, sprinkle with chopped fresh parsley.

Nutrition Value (Amount per Serving):

- Calories 142
- Fat 12.9g
- Carbohydrate 5.20g
- Protein 1.9g
- Sugars 0g
- Cholesterol 0.1mg

Fried Bananas

Preparation time: 0-10 minutes;

Cooking time: 0 – 15 minutes;

Serve: 3

Ingredients:

- 3 Bananas
- 2 Eggs
- Breadcrumbs
- Flour at discretion
- Salt
- 1 tsp Oil

Direction:

1. Peel the bananas and cut them into sections of approximately 2 to 3 cm.
2. Pass them first in the flour, then in the egg beaten with salt and then in the breadcrumbs.
3. Heat the air fryer at 180°C for 10 minutes. Then, place the breaded bananas.
4. Cook the bananas for 8 to 10 minutes, turning them 2 to 3 times during cooking to match the Dorado.
5. Serve warm.

Nutrition Value (Amount per Serving):

- Calories 262.4
- Fat 12.1 g
- Carbohydrate 33.9 g
- Sugars 20.7 g
- Protein 1.3 g
- Cholesterol 30.5 mg

Sautéed air mushrooms and parsley

Preparation time: 10 – 20 minutes;

Cooking time: 15 – 30 minutes;

Serve: 6

Ingredients:

- 600 g mushrooms
- 1 clove garlic
- 1 tsp olive oil
- Parsley
- Leave at discretion
- Black pepper at discretion

Direction:

1. Clean the mushrooms well and chop them.
2. Place the garlic and oil inside the basket close. Set the temperature to 150°C.
3. Brown for 2 minutes.
4. Add the mushrooms and cook for another 15 minutes.
5. Add (at discretion) salt and pepper, parsley, and finish cooking for another 3 minutes.

Nutrition Value (Amount per Serving):

- Calories 130
- Fat 7g
- Carbohydrates 17g
- Sugars 4g
- Protein 4g
- Cholesterol 0mg

Cauliflowers au gratin

Preparation time: 20-30 minutes;

Cooking time: 15-30 minutes;

Serve: 6

Ingredients:

- 800g cauliflower
- 4 slices of cheese
- ½ liter of Béchamel
- Parmesan to taste

Direction:

1. Separately, cook the cauliflowers in water. Meanwhile, prepare ½ liter of bechamel (dose: 500 ml of milk, 50 g of flour, 50 g of butter, salt, and nutmeg).

2. Pour some bechamel into the basket. Arrange the cauliflower flowers, covered with the slices of cheese and cover with the béchamel sauce. Sprinkle with Parmesan cheese.

3. Set the air fryer to 150°C. Simmer for about 20 minutes or according to the degree of gratin desired.

Nutrition Value (Amount per Serving):

- Calories 285
- Fat 19g
- Carbohydrates 17g
- Sugars 2.5g
- Protein 14g
- Cholesterol 55mg

Peach Clafoutis

Preparation time: 20 – 30 minutes;

Cooking time: 30 – 45 minutes;

Serve: 10

Ingredients:

- 300 g flour
- 150g butter
- 150g of sugar
- 4 eggs
- 1 sachet of baking powder
- 500g peaches in syrup
- 1 lemon
- 3-4 tbsp milk
- Icing sugar at discretion

Direction:

1. Melt the butter in the microwave; Work the butter, sugar, and eggs in a bowl.
2. Add flour, baking powder, grated lemon peel and milk. Work everything with an electric mixer until you get a smooth and homogeneous mixture.
3. Butter and flour the tank and pour the mixture inside, smearing well.
4. Place a whole peach in the center and place the others (cut into quarters) next to each other following the circumference of the mold.
5. Set the air fryer on the lower heating temperature.
6. Bake the cake for 45 minutes.
7. Let cool and remove it from the tank; sprinkle with icing sugar.

Nutrition Value (Amount per Serving):

- Calories 148
- Carbohydrates 14g
- Fat 8g
- Sugars 6 g
- Protein 4g
- Cholesterol 102mg

Zucchini thinly sliced

Preparation time: 0-10 minutes;

Cooking time: 15-30 minutes;

Serve: 6

Ingredients:

- 600g zucchini
- 1 clove garlic
- 100 ml of water
- 1 tsp olive oil
- Parsley Taste
- Salt to taste
- Pepper to taste

Direction:

1. Wash and turn the zucchini, then dry them and cut them into rings. Add the oil and peeled garlic to the basket.
2. Set the temperature to $150°C$.
3. Brown for about 2 minutes, then remove the garlic from the tank and pour the zucchini with the water, season with salt and pepper and close the lid.
4. Simmer for 23 minutes. At the end of cooking, add the chopped parsley, a drizzle of oil and serve.

Nutrition Value (Amount per Serving):

- Calories 21
- Fat 0.2g
- Carbohydrates 3.9g
- Sugars 3.1g
- Protein 1.5g
- Cholesterol 0mg

Couscous with Vegetables

Preparation time: 10-20 minutes;

Cooking time: 30-45 minutes; Serve: 8

Ingredients:

- 50g carrot
- Eggplant 250g
- 50g cherry tomatoes
- 1 shallot
- 150g broth
- 250g zucchini
- Salt to taste
- 1 clove garlic
- Chili pepper
- 375g couscous
- 400 ml of water
- Butter taste
- 1 ml of olive oil

Direction:

1. Peel the garlic, cut the chili into pieces, chop the shallot and place everything on the baking sheet, distributing it well through the bottom; add the oil. Before you start cooking, wash, and cut eggplants, zucchini, carrots, and small diced tomatoes (the latter should be reserved as they will be added to couscous when they are cold).

2. Set the air fryer to 150^0C and brown for 3 minutes. Add carrots, broth, and simmer for another 6 min. Finally pour the eggplant and zucchini, salt and pepper and simmer for another 25 minutes.

3. In addition to preparing the semolina by putting the water in a saucepan, boil, pour a small spoonful of salt. Add the couscous in the rain, oil, mix and stop the fire. Let swell for 3 min. Add a pinch of butter and cook again for another 3 min. mixing regularly with a fork to shell properly.

4. As soon as the vegetables have cooled, add the small tomatoes, and pour everything into a bowl with the couscous.

Nutrition Value (Amount per Serving):

- Calories 219.6
- Fat 4.0 g
- Carbohydrate 40.3 g
- Sugars 0.0 g
- Protein 6.5 g
- Cholesterol 0.0 mg

Rillette mushroom crusts

Preparation time: more than 30,

Cooking time: 15 - 30,

Calories: 273

Ingredients:

- 400g mushrooms
- 1 shallot
- 40g nuts without shell
- 150g of butter
- Parsley at discretion
- 1 tsp olive oil
- Bread slices

Direction:

1. Cut the shallot finely and pour it into the greased basket previously preheat at 150°C for 5 minutes.
2. Let brown for 2 minutes.
3. Add sliced mushrooms, salt, and cook for 20 minutes.
4. At the end of cooking, mix the mushrooms, soft butter and nuts until a homogeneous mixture is obtained.
5. Put everything in the fridge for 1 hour.
6. Remove the preparation paddle from the basket (be careful, it will be hot), place the slices of bread inside and toast them for 4 to 5 minutes or until golden brown.
7. Fill each crouton with the rillette.

Nutrition Value (Amount per Serving):

- Calories 190
- Fat 1.5g
- Carbohydrates 36g
- Sugars 3g
- Protein 7g
- Cholesterol 0mg

Mediterranean Bream

Preparation time: 10-20 minutes;

Cooking time: 15-30 minutes;

Serve: 2

Ingredients:

- 2 gold
- 200g cherry tomatoes
- 100g of black olives
- 1 clove garlic
- Thyme to taste
- Leaves to taste
- Pepper to taste
- 1 tsp peanut oil

Direction:

1. First, remove the golden scales. Clean them and gut them. Salt and pepper inside the belly, add a clove of garlic and two sprigs of thyme.
2. Grease the basket with the oil.
3. Cut the tomatoes in half and add them to the basket with the black olives and capers; salt everything
4. Set the temperature to 150°C and cook for 25 minutes.

Nutrition Value (Amount per Serving):

- Calories 248
- Carbohydrates 22g
- Fat 12g
- Sugars 3g
- Protein 8g
- Cholesterol 0mg

Draniki

Preparation time: 10-20 minutes;

Cooking time: 15-30 minutes;

Serve: 2

Ingredients:

- 4 medium potatoes
- ½ onion
- 1 carrot
- 1 egg
- 100g flour
- Leaves to taste
- 1 tsp oil

Direction:

1. Peel the potatoes, the onion and the carrot and wash them well.
2. Using a food processor cut all vegetables in julienne and place them in a large bowl.
3. Add the egg, salt, and flour (the doses of the latter may vary depending on the degree of moisture present in the vegetables) and mix well.
4. Cover the bottom of the basket with baking paper and pour a little of the mixture with a tablespoon and spread well.
5. Fill the useful space inside the tank (about 5 to 6 empanadas at a time).
6. Set the air fryer to 180^0C.
7. Cook for 10 to 12 minutes depending on the degree of browning desired.
8. After finishing the mixture, remove the baking paper, grease the bottom of the tank, and brown the previously cooked empanadas for another 2 minutes on each side.

Nutrition Value (Amount per Serving):

- Calories 84
- Carbohydrates 16g
- Fat 2g
- Sugars 0g
- Protein 3g
- Cholesterol 0mg

Chips

Preparation time: 10-20 minutes;

Cooking time: 30-45 minutes;

Serve: 8

Ingredients:

- 1500g of fresh potatoes
- Fine salt to taste
- 1 tsp peanut oil

Direction:

1. Peel the potatoes and cut them into sticks of approximately 1 cm per side.
2. Put the cut potatoes in water for a few minutes and rinse thoroughly.
3. Drain and clean well with a paper towel.
4. Pour the potatoes and the correct amount of oil in the pan.
5. Cook for 37/40 minutes at 180°C. Salt then serve.

Nutrition Value (Amount per Serving):

- Calories 365
- Fat 17g
- Carbohydrates 48g
- Sugars 0.3g
- Protein 4g
- Cholesterol 0mg

French Fries with Paprika

Preparation time: 10-20 minutes,

Cooking time: 15-30 minutes;

Serve: 8

Ingredients:

- 700g of carrots
- 1 tsp sweet paprika
- 1 tsp oil

Direction:

1. Peel the carrots and cut them into sticks.
2. Add carrots and paprika in the basket. Set the temperature to 180°C.
3. Cook the carrots for about 20 minutes (time may vary depending on the size of the carrots).

Nutrition Value (Amount per Serving):

- Calories 299
- Carbohydrates 33g
- Sugars 3g
- Fat 16g
- Protein 7g
- Cholesterol 163 mg

Frozen French Fries

Cooking time: 15-30 minutes;

Serve: 8

Ingredients:

- 1000g Standard French fries (10 X 10) mm frozen
- Fine salt to taste

Direction:

1. Preheat the air fryer at 150°C.
2. Let cook for 27 minutes: salt and serve.

Nutrition Value (Amount per Serving):

- Calories 150.0
- Fat 0.0 g
- Carbohydrate 20.0 g
- Sugars 0.0 g
- Protein 2.0 g
- Cholesterol 0.0 mg

Beans in sauce

Preparation time: 0-10 minutes,

Cooking time: 15-30 minutes;

Serve: 8

Ingredients:

- 500g canned beans
- 300g of tomato puree
- ½ carrot
- 1 onion
- ½ sprig of rosemary
- Salt and pepper to taste
- 1 tsp olive oil

Direction:

1. Prepare a chopped carrot and onion and place it inside the cooking tray with rosemary. Grease the basket with the oil.
2. Set the air fryer to 150°C and brown for 4 min.
3. Add the drained beans from your vegetable water and rinse thoroughly, simmer for another 3 min.
4. Add the tomato, ½ glass of water, salt and pepper and continue cooking for another 13 minutes.

Nutrition Value (Amount per Serving):

- Calories 270
- Fat 1g
- Carbohydrates 53g
- Sugars 14g
- Protein 14g
- Cholesterol 0mg

Spicy Potatoes

Preparation time: 10-20 minutes;

Cooking time: 30-45 minutes;

Serve: 8

Ingredients:

- 1250g of fresh potatoes
- 10g sweet paprika
- Tomato puree
- 2 tbsp vinegar
- Salt and pepper to taste

Direction:

1. Peel the potatoes and cut them into 1 cm cubes on each side. Put the potatoes in the water for a few minutes and rinse them well. Drain and clean with a paper towel.
2. Pour the potatoes, rosemary, and the exact amount of oil inside the tank, salt, and pepper.
3. Set the air fryer to 160°C and cook for 25 min.
4. Add the paprika, tomato puree and vinegar, then finish cooking and simmer for another 10 minutes.
5. Prepare the "tapas" by piercing the potatoes with toothpicks.

Nutrition Value (Amount per Serving):

- Calories 250
- Carbohydrates 33g
- Fat 11g
- Sugars 0g
- Protein 4g
- Cholesterol 0mg

Frozen Potatoes

Cooking time: 15-30 minutes;

Serve: 8

Ingredients:

- 1000 g of potatoes in frozen rooms
- Fine salt to taste

Direction:

1. Cook for 30 minutes at 160°C.
2. Salt and serve

Nutrition Value (Amount per Serving):

- Calories 18.2
- Fat 0.0g
- Carbohydrate 4.1g
- Protein 0.6g
- Cholesterol 0mg

Potatoes (Unpeeled) And Yogurt Sauce

Preparation time: 10 – 20 minutes,

Cooking time: 30 – 45 minutes;

Serve: 4

Ingredients:

- 750 g of fresh potatoes
- 1 pepper
- 1 onion
- Salt taste
- Basil at ease
- 50 g lean yogurt
- 50 g of mayonnaise
- 20 g tomato sauce
- 1 pinch sweet paprika

Direction:

1. Wash the potatoes and let them soak in cold water and baking soda for 15 minutes and then brush them well with water.
2. Cut them in quarters and put them in the basket previously greased.
3. Set the air fryer to 150°C.
4. Cook the potatoes for 15 minutes and then add the chopped pepper and sliced onion; Salt.
5. Cook for another 15 minutes and then add the fresh basil cut from the menu.
6. Cook for another 15 minutes.
7. If you want to accompany the potatoes with the yogurt sauce, simply mix all the ingredients until you get a creamy sauce.

Nutrition Value (Amount per Serving):

- Calories 49.1
- Fat 2.5 g
- Carbohydrate 2.4 g
- Sugars 1.7 g
- Protein 4.1 g
- Cholesterol 5.2 mg

Frozen New Potatoes

Cooking time: 30-45 minutes;

Serve: 8

Ingredients:

- 1200 g of frozen new potatoes
- Fine salt to taste

Direction:

1. Pour the potatoes in the basket.
2. Cook for 38 minutes at 180°C.
3. Salt and serve.

Nutrition Value (Amount per Serving):

- Calories 89
- Carbohydrates 19g
- Fat 0g
- Sugars 0g
- Protein 2g
- Cholesterol 0mg

Potatoes, Beets and Carrots

Preparation time: 10-20 minutes,

Cooking time: 30-45 minutes;

Serve: 6

Ingredients:

- 300g beet
- 300 g of carrots
- 300 g of potatoes
- 2 cloves of garlic
- Rosemary to taste
- Salt to taste
- Pepper to taste

Direction:

1. Clean, wash all vegetables (beets, carrots, and potatoes) and cut them into pieces of 2 to 3 cm.
2. Put the garlic clove, chopped vegetables, rosemary and spray the basket; Season with salt and pepper.
3. Cook for about 35 minutes at 150°C.

Nutrition Value (Amount per Serving):

- Calories 170.5
- Fat 7.1 g
- Carbohydrate 26.5 g
- Sugars 9.5 g
- Protein 3.4 g
- Cholesterol 0.0 mg

Frozen Onion Rings

Cooking time: 15-30 minutes;

Serve: 6

Ingredients:

- 15 pieces onion rings: 15 pieces
- Fine salt to taste

Direction:

3. Cook everything for 15 minutes at 180°C.

Nutrition Value (Amount per Serving):

- Calories 220
- Sugar 5g
- Fat 11g
- Protein 4g
- Carbohydrates 27g
- Cholesterol 0mg

Sautéed Potatoes and Pumpkin

Preparation time: 10 – 20 minutes,

Cooking time: 15 – 30 minutes;

Serve: 4

Ingredients:

- 450 g of potatoes
- 550 g pumpkin
- 20 g of breadcrumbs
- Coarse salt

Direction:

1. Preheat the air fryer to 180°C for 5 minutes.
2. Thoroughly clean the pumpkin and potatoes and cut them into large pieces. Pour all ingredients into the basket.
3. Cook for 30 minutes or until you get the crispy you want.

Nutrition Value (Amount per Serving):

- Calories 30
- Fat 0.1g
- Carbohydrates 8g
- Sugars 3.2g
- Protein 1.2g
- Cholesterol 0mg

Rice spaghetti with vegetables

Preparation time: 10 – 20 minutes;

Cooking time: 15 – 30 minutes;

Serve: 4

Ingredients:

- 100 g of celery
- 150 g of carrots
- 150g kale
- 2 scallions
- 2 tbsp soy sauce
- 100 g of bean sprouts
- 200 g of rice spaghetti

Direction:

1. Spray the basket of the air fryer. Cut all the vegetables in julienne and put the celery, chives, and carrots in the basket.
2. Set the air fryer to 150°C. Cook for 10 minutes.
3. Add the sprouts and soy sauce and cook for another 10 minutes.
4. Meanwhile, cook the rice spaghetti in salted water and boil and serve with the previously prepared sauce.

Nutrition Value (Amount per Serving):

- Calories 235.0
- Fat 10.9 g
- Carbohydrate 34.7 g
- Sugars 6.4 g
- Protein 13.9 g
- Cholesterol 0.5 mg

Strapatsada

Preparation time: 10-20 minutes;

Cooking time: 15-30 minutes;

Serve: 4

Ingredients:

- ½ onion
- 1 red pepper
- 100g mushrooms
- 300 g of tomatoes
- 6 eggs
- Fine salt to taste
- Black pepper to taste

Direction:

1. Cut the mushrooms (washed) and onions in julienne.
2. Distribute everything in the tank with the oil.
3. Set the temperature to 180°C and Cook for 12 minutes.
4. Add the tomatoes (skinless) cut into pieces, salt, and cook for another 8 minutes.
5. Remove the trowel (take care that it is hot!) And distribute the vegetables at the basket.
6. In a bowl, beat the eggs with salt and pepper and pour all over the vegetables. Cook another 7 to 8 minutes.

Nutrition Value (Amount per Serving):

- Calories 380
- Carbohydrates
- Fat 30g
- Sugars 6g
- Protein 19g
- Cholesterol 370g

Chicory Strudel

Preparation time: 10-20 minutes;

Cooking time: 30-45 minutes;

Serve: 6

Ingredients:

- 1 puff pastry
- Red chicory
- 100 g of stravecchio cheese
- 100 g of cow mozzarella
- 3 slices of Italian stuffed piglet

Direction:

1. Unroll the puff pastry, cover with a layer of cheese shavings, add the pieces of raw chicory and diced mozzarella.
2. Cover the whole with slices of stuffed piglet and close the puff pastry to form a stake.
3. Place the lining on the baking paper inside the basket.
4. Set the temperature to 160°C and cook for 35 minutes.
5. Very good with cheese sauce.

Nutrition Value (Amount per Serving):

- Calories 210
- Carbohydrates 30g
- Fat 5g
- Sugars 10g
- Protein 9g
- Cholesterol 0mg

Toast with Eggplant Caviar

Preparation time: 10-20 minutes,

Cooking time: 15-30 minutes;

Serve: 8

Ingredients:

- Eggplants 450g
- 1 tbsp concentrated tomatoes
- 100 g almonds
- 1 shallot
- 25 g of Parmesan
- 15 basil leaves
- Bread slices

Direction:

1. Cut the shallot finely and pour it into the basket previously greased with the spray.
2. Brown for 2 minutes at 160°C.
3. Add chopped eggplants, tomato puree diluted in 100 ml of water, salt and cook for 23 minutes.
4. Chill the eggplants after cooking. Place the almonds in the basket and roast them for 4 to 5 minutes.
5. Mix eggplant with almonds, parmesan, and basil separately until a homogeneous compound is obtained.
6. Remove the preparation paddle from the tank (be careful, it will be hot), place the slices of bread inside and roast them for 4 to 5 minutes or until golden brown.
7. Fill each crust with the previously prepared sauce.

Nutrition Value (Amount per Serving):

- Calories 91.8
- Fat 6.1 g
- Carbohydrate 9.2 g
- Sugars 0.0 g
- Protein 1.5 g
- Cholesterol 1.3 mg

Provencal Tomatoes

Preparation time: 10 – 20 minutes,

Cooking time: 15 – 30 minutes;

Serve: 4

Ingredients:

- 4 tomatoes
- 80 g of breadcrumbs
- 1 clove garlic
- 2 marjoram branches
- 1 rosemary branch
- Parsley chopped to taste
- Salt to taste
- Butter to taste

Direction:

1. Remove the top of the tomatoes and drain them. Separately, place all other ingredients (except butter) in a bowl and mix them; The mixture must be quite sandy.
2. Fill the tomatoes and then place them in the basket by adding the butter.
3. Set the temperature to 160°C and cook for 20 minutes depending on the size of the tomatoes.
4. It can be served both cold and hot.

Nutrition Value (Amount per Serving):

- Calories 69
- Carbohydrates 8g
- Fat 2g
- Sugars 2g
- Protein 3g
- Cholesterol 7g

Potato Omelet

Preparation time: 10 – 20 minutes,

Cooking time: 15 – 30 minutes;

Serve: 6

Ingredients:

- 600 g of potatoes
- ½ onion
- 6 eggs
- Salt, pepper to taste

Direction:

1. Peel the potatoes and cut them into squares of approximately 1 cm; Peel the onion and cut it into slices that are not very thin.
2. Pour the onion, oil and potatoes in the basket Cook for 25 minutes at 160°C.
3. Distribute potatoes and onion well in the bottom of the basket. Then pour the previously made egg, salt, and pepper mixture. Continue cooking for another 5 minutes.

Nutrition Value (Amount per Serving):

- Calories 193
- Carbohydrates 27g
- Fat 5g
- Sugars 1g
- Protein 10g
- Cholesterol 185 mg

Vol Au Vent with Mushrooms

Preparation time: 10 - 20 minutes,

Cooking time: 15 – 30 minutes;

Serve: 6

Ingredients:

- 1 roll of puff pastry
- Whole milk to taste
- 100 g of air sautéed mushrooms and parsley
- Brie to taste

Direction:

1. Unroll the puff pastry, prick the bottom with a fork and cut 18 discs about 7 cm in diameter. Place 6 discs in the bowl covered with baking paper.
2. Make a hole of approximately 3 cm in the other 12 discs and place them two at a time in the large discs. Brush with milk so that they adhere well to each other.
3. Set the temperature to 160°C
4. Cook for 15 to 17 minutes. Rotate the baking paper after 10 minutes for best results.
5. Fill the vol au vent with a preparation of mushrooms sautéed in air and parsley and cover with a piece of cheese.
6. Serve still hot

Nutrition Value (Amount per Serving):

- Calories 94
- Fat 6.4g
- Carbohydrates 6.7g
- Protein 1.7g

Spanish Potatoes

Preparation time: 10 minutes;

Cooking time: 57 minutes;

Serve: 2

Ingredients:

- 400 g potato
- Water
- 1 tbsp olive oil
- Salt

Direction:

1. Peel and cut the potato in julienne about 0.5 CM thick.
2. Prepare a bowl with very cold water, if necessary, add ice. Place the cut potatoes for at least 30 minutes to make them starch.
3. Dry each potato with an absorbent napkin and place in another dry bowl.
4. When they are all dry, sprinkle with oil or brush with olive oil and season with salt and whatever you like (sweet paprika, oregano, etc.).
5. In this case place in a fryer without oil at temperature 160°C for 17 minutes.
6. Set the fryer at 180°C another 10 minutes and that's it.

Nutrition Value (Amount per Serving):

- Calories 77
- Fat 0.09g
- Carbohydrate17.47g
- Sugars 0.78g
- Protein2.02g
- Cholesterol 0mg

Green Salad with Roasted Pepper

Preparation time: 15 minutes;

Cooking time: 10 minutes;

Serve: 4

Ingredients:

- 1 red pepper
- 1 tbsp lemon juice
- 3 tbsp yogurt
- 2 tbsp olive oil
- Freshly ground black pepper
- 1 romaine lettuce in wide strips
- 50 g arugula leaves

Direction:

1. Preheat the air fryer to 200°C.
2. Place the pepper in the basket and place it in the air fryer. Set the timer to 10 minutes and roast the pepper until the skin is slightly burned.
3. Place the pepper in a bowl and cover it with a lid or with transparent film. Let stand 10 to 15 minutes.
4. Next, cut the pepper into four parts and remove the seeds and skin. Cut the pepper into strips.
5. Mix a dressing in a bowl with 2 tablespoons of the pepper juice, lemon juice, yogurt, and olive oil. Add pepper and salt to taste.
6. Pour the lettuce and arugula leaves into the dressing and garnish the salad with the pepper strips.

Nutrition Value (Amount per Serving):

- Calories 77.9
- Fat 0.4 g
- Carbohydrate 19.3 g
- Sugars 4.6 g
- Protein 2.7 g
- Cholesterol 0.0 mg

Garlic Mushrooms

Preparation time: 10 minutes;

Cooking time: 10 minutes;

Serve: 2

Ingredients:

- 1 slice of white bread
- 1 crushed garlic clove
- 1 tbsp chopped parsley
- Freshly ground black pepper
- 1 tbsp olive oil
- 12 mushrooms

Direction:

1. Preheat the air fryer to 200°C.
2. Grate the slice of bread until it is thin in the kitchen robot and mix it with the garlic, parsley, and season to taste. Finally, pour the olive oil.
3. Remove the mushroom stems and fill the caps with the breadcrumbs.
4. Place the mushrooms in the basket and place it in the air fryer. Set the timer to 10 minutes. Bake until golden brown and crispy.
5. Serve them on a tray.

Nutrition Value (Amount per Serving):

- Calories 139
- Fat 11.6g
- Carbohydrates 6.1g
- Sugars 3.5g
- Protein 4.7g
- Cholesterol 30.4mg

Roasted Potatoes with Paprika and Greek Yogurt

Preparation time: 10 minutes;

Cooking time: 20 minutes;

Serve: 4

Ingredients:

- 800 g of white potatoes
- 2 tbsp olive oil
- 1 tbsp spicy paprika
- Freshly ground black pepper
- 150 ml Greek yogurt

Direction:

1. Preheat the air fryer to 180°C. Peel the potatoes and cut them into cubes of 3 cm. Dip the cubes in water for at least 30 minutes. Dry them well with paper towels.

2. In a medium-sized bowl, mix 1 tablespoon of olive oil with the paprika and add pepper to taste. Coat the potato dice with the spiced oil.

3. Place the potato dice in the fryer basket and place it in the air fryer. Set the timer to 20 minutes and fry the dice until golden brown and ready to take. Spin them occasionally.

4. In a small bowl, mix the Greek yogurt with the remaining tablespoon of olive oil and add salt and pepper to taste. Spread the paprika over the mixture. Serve the yogurt as a sauce with the potatoes.

5. Serve the potato dice on a tray and salt them. They will be delicious with ribs or kebabs.

Nutrition Value (Amount per Serving):

- Calories 225.1
- Fat 13.8 g
- Carbohydrate 24.2 g
- Sugars 9.7 g
- Protein 2.5 g
- Cholesterol 0.0 mg

Mini peppers with Goat Cheese

Preparation time: 10 minutes;

Cooking time: 8 minutes;

Serve: 4

Ingredients:

- 8 mini peppers
- ½ tbsp olive oil
- ½ tbsp dried Italian herbs
- 1 tsp freshly ground black pepper
- 100 g soft goat cheese in eight portions

Direction:

1. Preheat the air fryer to 200°C.
2. Cut the top of the mini peppers and remove the seeds and the membrane.
3. Mix the olive oil in a deep dish with the Italian herbs and pepper. Pour the portions of goat cheese in the oil.
4. Press a serving of goat cheese against each mini pepper and place the mini peppers in the basket next to each other. Insert the basket in the air fryer and set the timer to 8 minutes. Bake the mini peppers until the cheese is melted.
5. Serve mini peppers in small dishes such as snacks or snacks.

Nutrition Value (Amount per Serving):

- Calories 17
- Fat 1g
- Carbohydrates 1g
- Sugar 1g
- Protein 0g
- Cholesterol 60mg

Chapter 7

Desserts

Cake with cream and strawberries

Preparation time: 10 minutes;

Cooking time: 15 minutes;

Serve: 2

Ingredients:

- 1 pure butter puff pastry to stretch
- 500g strawberries (clean and without skin)
- 1 bowl of custard
- 3 tbsp icing sugar baked at 210°C in the air fryer

Direction:

1. Unroll the puff pastry and place it on the baking sheet. Prick the bottom with a fork and spread the custard. Arrange the strawberries in a circle and sprinkle with icing sugar.
2. Cook in a fryer setting a 210°C for 15 minutes.
3. Remove the cake from the fryer with the tongs and let cool.
4. When serving sprinkle with icing sugar
5. And why not, add some whipped cream.

Nutrition Value (Amount per Serving):

- Calories 212.6
- Fat 8.3 g
- Carbohydrate 31.9 g
- Sugars 17.4 g
- Protein 2.3 g
- Cholesterol 21.4 mg

Caramelized Pineapple and Vanilla Ice Cream

Preparation time: 0-10;

Cooking time: 15-30;

Serve: 4 people

Ingredients:

- 4 slices Pineapple
- 20g Butter
- 50g Cane sugar
- Ice cream/vanilla cream

Direction:

1. Heat the Air Fryer at 150°C for 5 minutes. Let it brown for 15-30 minutes. Then, take it out and top with the cream.

Nutrition Value (Amount per Serving):

- Calories 648
- Fat 36.4g
- Carbohydrates 73.2g
- Sugar 61.6g
- Protein 9.5g
- Cholesterol 94mg

Apple Pie

Preparation time: 20-30;

Cooking time: 45-60; Serve: 3

Ingredients:

- 600g Flour
- 350g Margarine
- 150g Sugar
- 2 Eggs
- 50g Breadcrumbs
- 3 Apples
- 75g Raisins
- 75g Sugar
- 1tsp Cinnamon

Direction:

2. Put the flour, sugar, eggs, and margarine nuts in the blender just outside the refrigerator.
3. Mix everything until you get a compact and quite flexible mixture. Let it rest in the refrigerator for at least 30 minutes.
4. Preheat the air fryer at 150°C for 5 minutes.
5. Spread 2/3 of the mass of broken dough in 3-4 mm thick covering the previously floured and floured tank and making the edges adhere well, which should be at least 2 cm.
6. Place the breadcrumbs, apple slices, sugar, raisins, and cinnamon in the bottom; cover everything with the remaining dough and make holes in the top to allow steam to escape.
7. Cook for 40 minutes and then turn off the lower resistance.
8. Cook for another 20 minutes only with the upper resistance on. Once it has cooled, put it on a plate and serve.

Nutrition Value (Amount per Serving):

- Calories 411
- Fat 19.38g
- Total Carbohydrate 57.5g
- Sugars 50g
- Protein 3.72g
- Cholesterol 0mg

Apple Rotation

Preparation time: 10 – 20 minutes,

Cooking time: 15 – 30 minutes;

Serve: 6

Ingredients:

- 1 roll of rectangular puff pastry
- 220g of apples
- 50g of sugar
- 100g raisins
- 50g pine nuts
- To taste breadcrumbs
- Cinnamon powder to taste

Direction:

1. Put the raisins in warm water for at least 30 min. Meanwhile, peel the apples, remove the kernel, and cut them into thin slices. Pour the apples into a large bowl and add the dried raisins.

2. Add the cinnamon, sugar, and pine nuts, gently mix the ingredients and let stand.

3. Meanwhile, spread the puff pastry on a work surface with parchment paper. Sprinkle with the breadcrumbs, leaving a 2-3 cm border around. Place the mixture in the center of the dough and close the coating along.

4. Be careful not to tear the dough, close the sides tightly so that the contents do not come out during cooking.

5. Place the liner on the air fryer and Cook over low temperature for about 25 min. When finished cooking, sprinkle the strudel with icing sugar and serve warm sliced.

Nutrition Value (Amount per Serving):

- Calories 411
- Fat 19.38g
- Total Carbohydrate 57.5g
- Sugars 50g
- Protein 3.72g
- Cholesterol 0mg

Stuffed brioche crown

Preparation time: more than 30 minutes;

Cooking time: 30 – 45 minutes;

Serve: 8

Ingredients:

- 250g Manitoba flour
- 250g flour 00
- 200 ml of warm milk
- 100 ml of warm water
- 50 ml of olive oil
- 25g baker's yeast
- 1 tbsp sugar
- 1 tsp fine salt
- 250g cooked ham
- 8 slices of emmental
- Poppy seeds
- 1 tbsp of water
- 1 tsp olive oil

Direction:

1. Prepare the brioche crown and let it grow in a lightly floured and closed container with food wrap for about an hour.
2. Once the survey is finished, spread the dough with a rolling pin, forming a narrow rectangle. First place the ham and then the cheese, leaving about 2 cm of free edge around.
3. Roll everything up to get a cylinder. Cut approximately 2 cm slices and place them in the basket covered with baking paper by placing them side by side to form a crown.
4. Let the preparation rise for another hour before cooking. In the end, brush with a mixture of warm water and oil over the entire surface of the crown and sprinkle with poppy seeds.
5. Preheat the air fryer at 180°C for 5 minutes. Cook for 40 minutes.

Nutrition Value (Amount per Serving):

- Calories 516
- Fat 32g
- Carbohydrates 39g
- Sugars 7g
- Protein 17g
- Cholesterol 0mg

Fried Cream

Preparation time: 10-20 minutes;

Cooking time: 15-30 minutes;

Serve: 8

Ingredients:

For the cream:

- 500 ml of whole milk
- 3 egg yolks
- 150 g of sugar
- 50 g flour
- 1 envelope Vanilla Sugar

Ingredients for the pie:

- 2 eggs
- Unlimited Breadcrumbs
- 1 tsp oil

Direction:

1. First prepare the custard; once cooked, pour the cream into a dish previously covered with a transparent film and level well. Let cool at room temperature for about 2 hours.
2. Grease the basket and distribute it all over.
3. When the cream is cold, place it on a cutting board and cut it into dice; Pass each piece of cream first in the breadcrumbs, covering the 4 sides well in the beaten egg and then in the pie.
4. Place each part inside the basket. Set the temperature to 150^0C.
5. Cook for 10 to 12 minutes, turning the pieces after 6 to 8 minutes.
6. The doses of this cream are enough to make 2 or even 3 kitchens in a row.

Nutrition Value (Amount per Serving):

- Calories 355
- Fat 18.37g
- Carbohydrates 44.94g
- Sugars 30.36g
- Protein 4.81g
- Cholesterol 45mg

Apple, cream, and hazelnut crumble

Preparation time: 10-20 minutes;

Cooking time: 15-30 minutes;

Serve: 6

Ingredients:

- 4 golden apples
- 100 ml of water
- 50g cane sugar
- 50g of sugar
- ½ tbsp cinnamon
- 200 ml of fresh cream
- Chopped hazelnuts to taste

Direction:

1. In a bowl, combine the peeled apples, cut into small cubes, cane sugar, sugar, and cinnamon.
2. Pour the apples inside the basket, add the water. Set the air fryer to 180°C and simmer for 15 minutes depending on the type of apple used and the size of the pieces.
3. At the end, divide the apples in the serving glasses, cover with previously whipped cream and sprinkle with chopped hazelnuts.

Nutrition Value (Amount per Serving):

- Calories 828.8
- Fat 44.8 g
- Carbohydrate 120.6 g
- Sugars 54.2 g
- Protein 4.4 g
- Cholesterol 29.5 mg

Fregolotta (Venetian puff pastry pie) with hazelnuts

Preparation time: 10-20,

Cooking time: 15-30, 8 people, Calories: 347

Ingredients:

- 200g of flour
- 150g of sugar
- 100 g melted butter
- 100g hazelnuts
- 1 egg
- ½ sachet of yeast

Direction:

1. Do not finely chop the hazelnuts. In a large bowl, pour all the ingredients (the butter once melted should be cooled before using), mix lightly, without the dough becoming too liquid.
2. Place parchment paper on the bottom of the basket and pour the mixture into it. Spread it evenly.
3. Set the air fryer to 180°C and simmer for 15 minutes and then turn the cake.
4. Cook for an additional 5 minutes.
5. Let cool and sprinkle the cake with icing sugar.

Nutrition Value (Amount per Serving):

- Calories 465
- Carbohydrates 37g
- Fat 25g
- Sugars 3g
- Protein 20g
- Cholesterol 0mg

Frozen Treats

Cooking time: 15-30 minutes;

Serve: 8

Ingredients:

- 14 frozen pieces

Direction:

1. Place the handles, placing them on the parchment paper and place them on the basket.
2. Set the temperature to 150°C.
3. Cook everything for 25 min.

Nutrition Value (Amount per serving):

- Calories 111
- Fat 20 g
- Carbohydrates 21 g
- Sugars 45g
- Protein 7g
- Cholesterol 0mg

Roscon Of Reyes (Spanish King's Cake)

Preparation time: 10-20 minutes;

Cooking time: 30-45 minutes;

Serve: 4

Ingredients:

- 2 puff pastries
- 100g almond flour
- 1 egg
- 75g of sugar
- 50g butter
- 1 vial of almond aroma
- 1 porcelain bean

Direction:

First, prepare the filling:

1. In a bowl mix the flour, egg, sugar, butter at room temperature and almond extract.
2. Stretch a puff pastry with the baking paper inside the basket. Prick with a fork and spread the filling well.
3. Place the bean inside, choosing an external position for the cake.
4. Cover with the second roll of puff pastry and weld the edges well. Brush the surface with an egg yolk diluted with milk and decorate with small incisions.
5. Set the temperature to 180^0C. Bake the pie for 25 minutes
6. Turn the baking paper half a turn and cook for another 10 minutes.
7. Tradition says that the person who finds the hidden bean becomes the "king" of the day.

Nutrition Value (Amount per Serving):

- Calories 1426
- Fat 10.54g
- Carbohydrates 56.54g
- Sugar 23.51g
- Protein 6.58g
- Cholesterol 29mg

Nut cake

Preparation time: 10-20 minutes,

Cooking time: 30-45 minutes;

Serve: 10

Ingredients:

- 250 g of walnuts
- 150g Maïzena
- 4 medium eggs
- 200g of butter (room temperature)
- 1 sachet of yeast
- 1 sachet of vanilla sugar
- 200g of sugar

Direction:

1. Chop the nuts with 50 g of sugar. Using a food processor, beat the butter with the remaining sugar until you get a shiny and foamy mixture.
2. Add the eggs one by one, making sure the mixture is still soft, then add the vanilla.
3. Add the chopped nuts with the sugar and then the cornstarch that will sift with the yeast.
4. Butter and flour the basket, then pour the mixture in the center.
5. Set the air fryer at 180°C.
6. Cook for 45 minutes (turn off the lower heating element 40 minutes later). Let cool before serving.

Nutrition Value (Amount per Serving):

- Calories 440
- Fat 20.48g
- Carbohydrate 62.22g
- Sugars 49.65g
- Protein 3.72g
- Cholesterol 53mg

Italian cake

Preparation time: 10-20 minutes;

Cooking time: 30-45 minutes;

Serve: 8

Ingredients:

- 250g of potato starch
- 150g of flour 00 (flour 55)
- 250g of sugar
- 6 eggs
- 50 g butter
- 1 sachet of yeast
- Powdered sugar

Direction:

1. Melt the butter in a small saucepan and let it cool.
2. Beat the eggs with the fine sugar until you get a light and frothy mixture. Add the flour, starch, sifted yeast, melted butter and mix until a homogeneous mixture is obtained.
3. Butter and flour the basket and pour the preparation into it.
4. Set the temperature to 180°C and cook the cake for 35 min.
5. Remove the cake from the bowl, let it cool and sprinkle with icing sugar.

Nutrition Value (Amount per Serving):

- Calories 440
- Carbohydrates 40g
- Fat 30g
- Sugars 28g
- Protein 4g
- Cholesterol 65mg

Marble cake

Preparation time: 10-20 minutes;

Cooking time: 45-60 minutes; Serve: 10

Ingredients:

- 190g Butter
- 1g bag of vanilla sugar
- 12g baking powder
- 375g Flour
- 22g cocoa powder
- 4g medium eggs
- 225g of sugar
- 165 ml of milk
- Salt (a pinch)

Direction:

1. Put the previously softened butter into small pieces in a bowl with the sugar, mount the ingredients until a white and foamy cream forms.
2. Add the eggs at room temperature, one by one, the salt and beat about 5 minutes until you get a mixture without lumps. Add the flour (except 30 g that will keep aside), the yeast and vanilla sugar sifted alternately with the milk.
3. Mix the ingredients well, then divide them evenly and add the remaining flour in a bowl and the sifted cocoa in another.
4. Butter and flour the basket and first place the transparent mixture divided into three separate parts. Do the same with the dark mixture by filling the remaining gaps between the light mixture.
5. To get the veined effect, rotate a fork from top to bottom through the two colors of the mixture.
6. Set the air fryer to 180°C and cook for 40 minutes and then turn off the lower resistance.
7. Cook for another 10 min. Control the baking of the cake with the tip of a knife.

Nutrition Value (Amount per Serving):

- Calories 195
- Fat 7.6g
- Carbohydrates 28g
- Sugars 14g
- Protein 3.5g
- Cholesterol 47mg

Genoves Cake

Preparation time: 10-20 minutes;

Cooking time: 30-45 minutes;

Serve: 10

Ingredients:

- 6 eggs
- 190g of sugar
- 150g of flour 00 (flour 55)
- 75g potato starch
- 2g vanilla sugar

Direction:

1. In a bowl, beat the eggs with the sugar until you get a light and smooth mixture. Add the sifted flour, starch and vanilla sugar and mix with a whisk until a homogeneous mixture is obtained.
2. Butter and flour the basket, then pour the mixture.
3. Set the air fryer to 180°C and simmer for 35 minutes.

Nutrition Value (Amount per Serving):

- Calories 74
- Fat 1.83g
- Carbohydrate 10.91g
- Sugars 5.08g
- Protein 3.83g
- Cholesterol 74mg

Frozen Sorrentino gnocchi

Cooking time: 0 – 15 minutes;

Serve: 2

Ingredients:

- 550 g Sorrentino gnocchi

Direction:

5. Pour the gnocchi in the basket and cook for 13 minutes at 150°C mixing once halfway through cooking.

Nutrition Value (Amount per Serving):

- Calories 170
- Carbohydrates 30g
- Fat 2g
- Sugars 11g
- Protein 6g
- Cholesterol 5mg

Khachapuri (Georgian bread)

Preparation time: more than 30 minutes;

Cooking time: 15 – 30 minutes;

Serve: 4

Ingredients:

- 500g of flour
- 450g whole yogurt
- ½ tsp baking soda
- ½ tsp salt
- 150 g ricotta
- 100g provokes smoked
- 150g Greek feta cheese
- 4 tbsp fine parsley

Direction:

1. Prepare the khachapuri dough by mixing all the ingredients until a smooth and homogeneous mixture is obtained. Divide the dough into 8 equal parts.
2. Form 8 balls cover them with a clean cloth. Let them rest in a warm place and away from drafts. After about 1 hour of lifting, start spreading the dough.
3. Meanwhile, prepare the filling by grating provokes smoked and the feta cheese and then mix with the ricotta and parsley.
4. Spread the 8 balls by hand in circles of 10 to 15 cm, fill 4 circles with the previously prepared filling and close with the other 4. Now roll the 4 khachapuri with a roller until you get a diameter of the size of the basket.
5. Grease the bottom of the basket and place 1 khachapuri. Also grease the surface and prick with a fork.
6. Set the air fryer to 180°C and cook each khachapuri for 15 minutes.

Nutrition Value (Amount per Serving):

- Calories 556
- Fat 33g
- Carbohydrates 37g
- Sugars 3.6g
- Protein 28g
- Cholesterol 181mg

Sweet and Sour Onions

Preparation time: 10-20 minutes,

Cooking time: 30-45 minutes;

Serve: 8

Ingredients:

- 600g of borretano onions
- 30g butter
- 30g of sugar
- 50g of Modena balsamic vinegar

Direction:

1. First peel and wash the onions.
2. Add the butter and set the air fryer to $160^{\circ}C$
3. Melt the butter for 2 minutes.
4. Add the sugar and vinegar and cook for another 3 minutes.
5. Then pour the onions and cook them for 30 minutes or to the desired cooking point (this may vary depending on the size of the onions).
6. They can be served as an appetizer or to accompany meat dishes.

Nutrition Value (Amount per Serving):

- Calories 80
- Carbohydrates 17g
- Fat 1g
- Sugars 12g
- Protein 1g
- Cholesterol 0mg

Frozen Paella

Cooking time: 15-30 minutes;

Serve: 2

Ingredients:

- 600 g of paella

Direction:

1. Pour the paella in the basket and set the temperature to 150°C.
2. Cook for 15 minutes, mixing once in the middle of cooking.

Nutrition Value (Amount per Serving):

- Calories 315
- Carbohydrates 0g
- Fat 9g
- Protein 0g
- Sugar 0g
- Cholesterol 0mg

Spice Bread

Preparation time: 10 – 20 minutes;

Cooking time: 0 – 15 minutes;

Serve: 10

Ingredients:

Ingredients for 30 - 35 cookies:

- 350g flour
- 160g of sugar
- 150g of butter
- 1 egg
- 1 pinch of salt
- 150g of honey
- 2 tsp cinnamon
- ¼ tsp nutmeg
- 2 tsp ginger
- ½ tsp of clove (powder)

Direction:

1. Put all the ingredients in a blender (the butter should be cold as soon as it comes out of the fridge).
2. Mix everything until you get a compact and sufficiently elastic mixture. Let it rest in the refrigerator for about 2 hours.
3. Then spread a 4 mm thick puff pastry with the rolling pin. Use templates to cut the dough in several ways.
4. Bake the cookies for 7 minutes at 180°C, and then rotate the baking paper.
5. Cook for additional 5 minutes, after cooling. Decorate to your liking.

Nutrition Value (Amount per Serving):

- Calories 100
- Fat 0g
- Carbohydrates 21g
- Sugar 6g
- Protein 3g
- Cholesterol 0mg

Rolls

Preparation time: 20 – 30 minutes;

Cooking time: 30 – 45 minutes;

Serve: 4

Ingredients:

- 20 ml of water
- 350 g flour
- 4 g of sugar
- 6 g of salt
- 10 g fresh yeast

Direction:

1. Put the flour in a large bowl (or on a pastry board), form a hole in the center and pour all the ingredients. Knead everything until you get a ball that you must knead for at least 10 minutes or until it becomes soft and elastic.
2. Cover with a slightly damp cloth and let it grow in a warm room without drafts for at least two hours. The mass should double in volume.
3. When the dough has risen, place it on a floured surface, cut several pieces (according to the size of the bread you want to obtain) and form the bread with your hands.
4. Place the rolls in the basket covered with parchment paper.
5. Set the temperature to 160°C and simmer for 30 minutes.

Nutrition Value (Amount per Serving):

- Calories 96
- Fat 1.7g
- Carbohydrates 18g
- Sugars 3.1g
- Protein 3.1g
- Cholesterol 0mg

Small Frozen Pizzas

Cooking time: 15-30 minutes;

Serve: 8

Ingredients:

- 14 pieces Small frozen pizzas

Direction:

1. Place the small pizzas, place them on the parchment paper, close the lid, place the thermostat in position 3, press the power key of the lower heating element and press the on / off key.
2. Cook everything for 20 minutes at 180°C.

Nutrition Value (Amount per Serving):

- Calories 350.0
- Fat 16.0 g
- Carbohydrate 38.0 g
- Sugars 3.0 g
- Protein 16.0 g
- Cholesterol 30.0 mg

Small Slippers With Flour

Preparation time: more than 30 minutes,

Cooking time: 15 – 30 minutes; Serve: 4

Ingredients:

- 200 ml of water
- 250 g flour
- 250 g Manitoba flour
- 12 g fresh beer yeast
- 10 g of salt
- 5 g of sugar
- 250 g mozzarella
- 150 g of tomato coulis
- Oregano to taste
- Salt to taste

Direction:

1. Pour the flours into a bowl, form a well and then add the other ingredients in the center.
2. Knead by hand until you get soft and flexible dough. Form a ball with this dough and then let it grow in a previously floured bowl.
3. Cover with a clean cloth, let stand in a warm place away from drafts. After about 1 hour of lifting, separate the small slipper by dividing the dough into 8 equal parts to obtain 8 circles.
4. Fill each slipper with the desired ingredients, close the dough to form a crescent and weld the ends well with a fork.
5. Grease the basket and place 4 small turnovers (brush each rotation with a little tomato sauce).
6. Set the air fryer to 150°C.
7. Cook for another 15 to 20 minutes and then put the other 4 empanadas for cooking.

Nutrition Value (Amount per Serving):

- Calories 455
- Fat 1.2g
- Carbohydrates 95.4g
- Sugars 0.3g
- Protein 12.9g

Peas with Bacon

Preparation time: 10 – 20 minutes,

Cooking time: 30 – 45 minutes;

Serve: 8

Ingredients:

- 750 g of frozen peas
- 100 g smoked bacon
- 2 shallots
- Salt and pepper to taste
- 200ml broth

Direction:

1. Preheat the air fryer to 160°C for 5 minutes.
2. Pour the chopped onion, bacon, oil in the basket
3. Brown for 5 min.
4. Add the peas, broth, salt, pepper, and simmer for additional 30 minutes.

Nutrition Value (Amount per Serving):

- Calories 129.6
- Fat 6.0 g
- Carbohydrate 13.6 g
- Sugars 3.3 g
- Protein 6.0 g
- Cholesterol 7.7 mg

Fresh Pizza

Preparation time: 10-20 minutes,

Cooking time: 30-45 minutes;

Serve: 1

Ingredients:

- 70ml of water
- 125 g flour
- 3g salt
- 7 g fresh yeast
- 100 g of tomato
- 100 g mozzarella
- Oregano to taste

Direction:

1. Pour the flour into a bowl, form a well, and then add the other ingredients in the center.
2. Knead with your hands until you get soft and flexible dough. Form a ball with this dough, and then let it grow in a previously floured bowl.
3. Cover with a clean cloth and let stand at room temperature, away from drafts. After about 1 hour of lifting, start spreading the dough
4. Preheat the air fryer to 150^0C for 5 minutes.
5. Grease the bottom and spread the pizza dough. Cover with tomato coulis. Add a pinch of salt and oregano.
6. After 15 minutes cook add the diced mozzarella
7. Approximately after 10 minutes, turn the pizza half a turn
8. Cook for an additional 7 minutes.

Nutrition Value (Amount per Serving):

- Calories 290
- Carbohydrates 36g
- Fat 11g
- Sugars 0g
- Protein 11g
- Cholesterol 15mg

Frozen Pizza

Cooking time: 15-30 minutes;

Serve: 1

Ingredients:

- 1 piece Frozen Pizza

Direction:

1. Cook for 20 minutes at 180°C turning after 15 minutes.

Nutrition Value (Amount per Serving):

- Calories 576
- Fat 26g
- Carbohydrates 62g
- Sugars 7.7g
- Protein 22g
- Cholesterol 30mg

Poivronnade

Preparation time: 10-20 minutes,

Cooking time: 45-60 minutes;

Serve: 8

Ingredients:

- 750g Peppers
- 220g onion
- 300 g of tomato puree
- Broth 175g
- Salt and pepper to taste

Direction:

2. First, prepare the ingredients: chop the onion and cut the peppers into strips.
3. Put the onion and oil inside the basket at 150°C and brown for 5 min.
4. Add peppers, broth, salt, pepper, and simmer for 20 minutes.
5. Then add the tomato and finish cooking for an additional 30 minutes.

Nutrition Value (Amount per Serving):

- Calories 118
- Carbohydrates 5g
- Fat 10g
- Sugars 0g
- Protein 1g
- Cholesterol 0mg

Stuffed Peppers

Preparation time: 10 – 20 minutes,

Cooking time: 30 – 45 minutes;

Serve: 4

Ingredients:

- 2 Peppers
- 150 g minced meat
- 75 g Sausage
- 40 g French toast
- 1 spoon chopped parsley
- 1 egg
- 50 g grated cheese
- 1 garlic clove
- Salt and pepper to taste
- Butter to taste

Direction:

Prepare the filling:

1. Place all the ingredients, except the peppers, in a food processor (the bread must be soaked in milk to soften it) and mix until a homogeneous and compact compound is obtained.
2. Cut the peppers in half lengthwise, remove the white filaments and seeds.
3. Place the four halves of peppers inside the tray and fill them with the previously prepared mixture. Put in each of them pieces of butter.
4. Set the air fryer to 150°C and cook for 45 minutes depending on the size of the peppers.

Nutrition Value (Amount per Serving):

- Calories 444
- Fat 24g
- Carbohydrates 30g
- Sugars 8.2g
- Protein 29g
- Cholesterol 121mg

Baked Apples with Cinnamon

Preparation time: 0-10 minutes;

Cooking time: 15-30 minutes;

Serve: 4

Ingredients:

- 4 golden apples
- 1 roll of rectangular puff pastry
- 100 g apricot jam
- Raisins (sufficient quantity)
- Cinnamon (sufficient quantity)
- Sugar taste

Direction:

1. Peel the apples and remove the core. Unwind the puff pastry and cut it transversely to obtain 4 mini rectangles. Put the apples in the center and fill the hole with jam and some raisins.

2. Sprinkle with cinnamon and sugar (optional) and close with the edges of the puff pastry, pressing well to seal the apple inside. Brush the surface with a little milk to make them color during cooking.

3. Cook for 30 minutes or until desired browning is obtained, at 180°C.

Nutrition Value (Amount per Serving):

- Calories 173
- Fat 3.2g
- Carbohydrates 39g
- Sugars 32g
- Protein 0.8g
- Cholesterol 7.8mg

Baked Potatoes

Preparation time: 0-10 minutes,

Cooking time: more than 60 minutes;

Serve: 4

Ingredients:

- 4 whole potatoes (230 g each)
- 4 slices of cheddar cheese
- 20 g butter
- 4 slices of bacon
- Salt to taste
- Pepper to taste

Direction:

1. Wash potatoes well, brushing them gently to remove all traces of dirt without damaging the skin.
2. Cover each potato with oil and cover with a handful of salt (this will make the skin crisp).
3. Place the potatoes in the basket of the pan on parchment paper.
4. Set the air fryer to 160°C. Simmer for 60 min. (the time varies according to the size of the potatoes used), therefore, it will be useful to verify from time to time that the cooking is perfect.
5. After cooking, cut the potatoes crosswise and dig a little inside. Cover each potato with a piece of butter, a slice of bacon and a slice of cheese.
6. Sprinkle with black pepper and always brown with the thermostat in position 4 for another 3 minutes.

Nutrition Value (Amount per Serving):

- Calories 160.9
- Fat 0.2g
- Carbohydrates 36.6g
- Sugar 2g
- Protein 4.3g
- Cholesterol 160mg

Potatoes with Small Bacon

Preparation time: 10-20 minutes,

Cooking time: 30-45 minutes;

Serve: 8

Ingredients:

- 1250 g of fresh potatoes(peeled)
- 100 g smoked bacon
- Salt and pepper to taste
- 1 sprig rosemary

Direction:

1. Peel the potatoes and cut them into quarters. Put the potatoes in the water for a few minutes and rinse them well. Drain and clean with a paper towel.
2. Pour the potatoes, rosemary in the basket previously greased, season with salt and pepper.
3. Set the temperature to 150°C and cook for 15 minutes.
4. Add the bacon and finish cooking, simmer for another 20 minutes.

Nutrition Value (Amount per Serving):

- Calories 180
- Fat 6g
- Carbohydrates 30g
- Sugars 5g
- Protein 3g
- Cholesterol 60mg

Butter and bread pudding (dessert)

Preparation time: 10-20 minutes,

Cooking time: 15-30 minutes;

Serve: 4

Ingredients:

- 5/6 slices of honey bread
- 30 g butter
- 20 g raisins
- 400 ml of milk
- 4 egg yolks
- 90 g of sugar
- Cinnamon to taste
- 1 vanilla pod

Direction:

1. Remove the crust from the slices of bread and spread the butter on each slice, place them in the container previously buttered.
2. Pour the raisins over the bread. Separately, beat the eggs and sugar with an electric mixer and then add the milk (previously heated with the vanilla pod) until a very homogeneous mixture is obtained.
3. Pour the mixture over the slices of bread, being careful to distribute it evenly. Sprinkle with sugar and cinnamon.
4. Cook at 160°C for 30 minutes or until desired browning is achieved.
5. Serve hot with whipped cream or jam.

Nutrition Value (Amount per Serving):

- Calories 313
- Fat 15g
- Carbohydrates 36g
- Sugars 13g
- Protein 8.6g
- Cholesterol 98mg

Risotto with Porcini Mushrooms

Preparation time: 0-10 minutes,

Cooking time: 15-30 minutes;

Serve: 6

Ingredients:

- 320 g of basmati rice
- 200 g of porcini mushrooms
- 1250ml of broth
- 1 clove garlic
- Parsley to taste
- Grated cheese to taste
- Butter to taste

Direction:

1. Grease the basket and add the garlic clove.
2. Set the temperature to 150°C and brown for 2 minutes.
3. Remove the garlic, add the porcini mushrooms and simmer for another 5 minutes.
4. Add the rice, half the amount of the broth and simmer for another 10 minutes.
5. Pour the rest of the broth and finish cooking for another 13 minutes. Mix 2-3 times with a ladle at the end of cooking.
6. At the end of cooking, add the chopped parsley and mix with butter and grated cheese, serve.

Nutrition Value (Amount per Serving):

- Calories 365.0
- Fat 19.3 g
- Carbohydrate 30.5 g
- Sugars 1.7 g
- Protein 17.5 g
- Cholesterol 50.8 mg

Speck and Cheese Roll

Preparation time: 10 – 20 minutes,

Cooking time: 0 – 15 minutes;

Serve: 6

Ingredients:

- 1 roll of puff pastry
- 6 speck slices
- 4 slices of provola (spun cheese)

Direction:

1. Unroll the puff pastry and spread the speck slices.
2. Place the cheese slices on the speck and roll the puff pastry until you get a roll. Weld well.
3. Cut the roll into slices and place it inside the mold lined with baking paper.
4. Set the temperature to 180°C.
5. Cook the rolls for 13 minutes or according to the desired degree of cooking.

Nutrition Value (Amount per Serving):

- Calories 96
- Carbohydrates 8g
- Fat 4g
- Sugars 1g
- Protein 4g
- Cholesterol 6mg

Pesto Rolled and Brie

Preparation time: 10 – 20 minutes,

Cooking time: 0 – 15 minutes;

Serve: 6

Ingredients:

- 1 roll of puff pastry
- 100 g Genovese pesto
- 100 g of brie

Direction:

1. Unroll the puff pastry and spread the pesto.
2. Cut the cheese into thin slices and cover the pesto. Roll the puff pastry until you get a roll. Weld well.
3. Cut the roll into slices and place it inside the mold lined with baking paper.
4. Set the temperature to 160°C.
5. Cook the rolls for 13 minutes or according to the desired degree of cooking.

Nutrition Value (Amount per Serving):

- Calories 483
- Carbohydrates 0g
- Fat 19g
- Sugars 0g
- Protein 35g
- Cholesterol 60mg

Santiago's Cake

Preparation time: 10-20 minutes;

Cooking time: 30-45 minutes;

Serve: 8

Ingredients:

- 250 g of almonds:
- 160 g of sugar
- 6 eggs
- Grated orange rind
- Grated lemon rind
- 5 drops of almond flavor

Direction:

1. In a food processor, chop the almonds until you get flour
2. With an electric mixer, beat the egg yolks with the sugar; add the grated lemon peel, the almond extract and the previously made flour.
3. Separately, beat the egg whites and fold them gently with the rest of the ingredients.
4. Remove the mixing paddle from the tank.
5. Butter and flour the tank and pour the mixture inside.
6. Set the temperature to 180°C.
7. Bake the cake for 35 minutes.
8. For the final touch, cut a cardboard Santiago cross, place it in the center of the cake and sprinkle with icing sugar. By removing the cross, you will get the design on the cake.

Nutrition Value (Amount per Serving):

- Calories 295.2
- Fat 16.5 g
- Carbohydrate 29.9 g
- Sugars 26.2 g
- Protein 10.1 g
- Cholesterol 142.5 mg

Cream and Pine Nuts Cake

Preparation time: more than 30 minutes,

Cooking time: 45-60 minutes; Serve: 10

Ingredients:

- 250 g flour
- 125 g butter
- 110 g of sugar
- 2 eggs (1 whole and egg yolk)
- Salt to taste
- 500ml pastry cream
- 120 g of pine nuts

Direction:

1. Remove the flour, sugar, eggs, butter nuts from the refrigerator and a pinch of salt in the blender.
2. Mix everything until you get a compact and quite flexible mixture. Let it rest in the refrigerator for at least 30 minutes.
3. Butter and flour the basket. Spread the mass of broken dough with a thickness of ¾ cm and place it at the bottom of the basket, carefully cutting the edge.
4. Prick with a fork and spread the custard with a spoon.
5. Finish the cake by covering it completely with pine nuts.
6. Set the air fryer to 180°C.
7. Cook for 40 minutes and then turn off the lower resistance.
8. Cook another 15 minutes. Cool the cake well before turning it over to turn it off.

Nutrition Value (Amount per Serving):

- Calories 191
- Fat 19g
- Carbohydrates 3.7g
- Sugars 1g
- Protein 3.9g

Ricotta Cake

Preparation time: 10 minutes;

Cooking time: 40 minutes;

Serve: 10

Ingredients:

- 250 g flour
- 200 g of sugar
- Eggs
- 350 g ricotta
- 120 g melted butter
- 1 sachet of yeast
- 50 g of chocolate chips

Direction:

1. Add ricotta with sugar, add eggs and melted butter. Add the sifted flour with the yeast and finally the chocolate chips.
2. Butter and flour the basket and pour the mixture inside, smearing well.
3. Set the temperature to 180°C and bake the cake for 40 minutes.
4. Let cool and remove it from the basket; sprinkle with icing sugar.

Nutrition Value (Amount per Serving):

- Calories 269
- Fat 9.9g
- Carbohydrates 39g
- Sugars 21g
- Protein 6g
- Cholesterol 64mg

Ricotta Cake and Chocolate Chips

Preparation time: 10-20 minutes, Cooking time: 45-60 minutes; Serve: 10

Ingredients:

For the dough:

- 380g flour
- 165 g of sugar
- 185 g of butter
- 2 eggs
- 1 egg yolk
- 1 pinch of salt

Ingredients for filling:

- 600 g ricotta
- 1 lemon zest
- 100 g of chocolate chips

Direction:

1. Put the flour, sugar, eggs, butter in pieces just outside the refrigerator and a pinch of salt in a blender. Mix everything until you get a compact and sufficiently elastic mixture. Let it rest in the fridge for at least half an hour.

2. Grease and flour the basket. Unroll the mass of broken dough to a thickness of 3-4 mm and cover the bottom and walls. In a bowl, beat the ricotta with the eggs, the sugar, and the lemon zest until you get a smooth and smooth mixture. Finally, add the chocolate chips.

3. Pour everything inside the baking sheet covered with broken dough and slightly bend the edges inwards.

4. Set the temperature to 180^0C.

5. Cook for 40 minutes and then turn off the lowest resistance. Cook for another 10 minutes. Cool well before removing from the baking sheet.

Nutrition Value (Amount per Serving):

- Calories 143.7
- Fat 7.8 g
- Carbohydrate 17.3 g
- Sugars 11.5 g
- Protein 3.0 g
- Cholesterol 28.7 mg

Amandine Pistachio Cake

Preparation time: more than 30 minutes,

Cooking time: 30 – 45 minutes; Serve: 8

Ingredients:

For the broken dough:

- 250 g flour
- 110 g of sugar
- 125 g butter
- 2 eggs
- Salt to taste

Direction:

Broken dough:

1. Remove flour, sugar, eggs, butter nuts from the refrigerator and a pinch of salt in the blender.
2. Mix everything until you get a compact and quite flexible mixture. Let it rest in the refrigerator for at least 30 minutes.

Almond cream:

3. Put the chopped almonds, sugar in a blender, and mix everything, then add the flour, eggs and mix well. Separately, cut the pistachios and cut them into large pieces.
4. Butter and flour the bottom of the basket. Unroll the broken dough leaving an edge that may contain almond cream. Prick with a fork and spread the jam.
5. Spread the almond cream and distribute the chopped pine nuts and pistachios.
6. Cook for 45 minutes at 180°C
7. Let cool and sprinkle with icing sugar.

Nutrition Value (Amount per Serving):

- Calories 242
- Carbohydrates 35g
- Fat 9g
- Sugars 21g
- Protein 3g
- Cholesterol 61mg

Asparagus and Sheep Cheesecake

Preparation time: 10-20 minutes,

Cooking time: 15-30 minutes;

Serve: 6

Ingredients:

- 250g asparagus
- 6 medium eggs
- ½ white onion
- 30 g grated Roman sheep cheese
- Breadcrumbs to taste
- Salt to taste
- Pepper to taste

Direction:

1. Peel the asparagus tail with a peeler. Cut the tip and boil them in salted water for about 5 to 7 minutes.
2. Cut 3 asparagus, the slightly larger ones in length and set them aside. Cut all others into pieces.
3. Beat the eggs in a bowl with salt and pepper. Add the pecorino and the chopped onion and mix well. Then add the asparagus into pieces and mix gently.
4. Butter the basket and cover with breadcrumbs
5. Pour the egg mixture into the basket. Arrange the asparagus cut lengthwise to beautify the cake.
6. Cook for 15 minutes at 180°C.

Nutrition Value (Amount per Serving):

- Calories: 548.5
- Fat 41.7 g
- Carbohydrate 22.9 g
- Sugars 4 g
- Protein 21.5 g
- Cholesterol 252.2 mg

Cherry tomato and mozzarella cake

Preparation time: 10 – 20 minutes,

Cooking time: 15 – 30 minutes;

Serve: 4

Ingredients:

- 1 roll of puff pastry
- ½ yellow pepper
- 100 g mozzarella
- 5 cherry tomatoes
- 2 eggs
- 20 g Parmesan
- 50 ml of milk
- Salt and pepper to taste

Direction:

1. Beat the eggs, milk, Parmesan in a bowl with a little salt and pepper.
2. Unroll the puff pastry (leaving the baking paper) and then prick the bottom with a fork.
3. Arrange the chopped mozzarella, pepper, and sliced tomatoes; pour the prepared preparation.
4. Fold the edges of the dough in and cut the excess baking paper with scissors (keep the ends cut so you can easily rotate and extract the cake).
5. Set the temperature to 160°C and cook another 15 minutes.
6. Turn to 180°C and cook for another 12 minutes (using the baking paper).

Nutrition Value (Amount per Serving):

- Calories 277.8
- Fat 23.5 g
- Carbohydrate 5.1 g
- Sugars 0.6 g
- Protein 13.3 g
- Cholesterol 44.8 mg

Tasty Chicory and Mota Cake

Preparation time: 10-20 minutes,

Cooking time: 15-30 minutes;

Serve: 6

Ingredients:

- 1 roll of puff pastry
- 200 g of cooked chicory
- 120 g speck in pieces
- 100 ml of fresh cream
- 2 eggs
- 20 g grated cheese:
- 50 ml of milk:
- Salt to taste
- Pepper to taste

Direction:

1. Beat the eggs, cream, grated cheese, and milk in a bowl with a little salt and pepper.
2. Unroll the puff pastry with parchment paper and prick the bottom with the teeth of a fork.
3. Put the speck in pieces and cooked chicory (see recipe "Treviso chicory sauce") in the tank. Add the previously prepared liquid mixture.
4. Fold the edges of the dough and with scissors cut the excess baking paper (keeping some points that will be used to rotate the quiche easily)
5. Cook the cake for 15 minutes at 180° (using parchment paper). Turn and cook for an additional 8 minutes.

Nutrition Value (Amount per Serving):

- Calories 6.7
- Fat 0.1g
- Carbohydrate 1.4g
- Sugars 2g
- Protein 0.5g
- Cholesterol 0.0mg

Frozen Salty Cake

Cooking time: 30-45 minutes;

Serve: 6

Ingredients:

- 1 piece of frozen salted cake

Direction:

1. Preheat the air fryer at 160°C for 5 minutes. Place the savory cake in the basket.

2. Cook everything for 45 minutes, turning it to 180°C (using parchment paper) after about 30 minutes.

Nutrition Value (Amount per Serving):

- Calories 250
- Fat 13g
- Carbohydrate 32g
- Sugars 22g
- Protein 2g
- Cholesterol 20mg

Toad in the hole

Preparation time: 10-20 minutes,

Cooking time: 30-45 minutes;

Serve: 4

Ingredients:

- 8 sausages
- 8 slices of bacon
- 100 g onion
- Thyme to taste

Ingredients for donut dough:

- 130 g flour
- 2 g baking powder
- 1 whole egg
- 1 egg-yolk
- 200 ml of milk
- 100 ml of water
- Salt to taste
- Pepper to taste

Direction:

1. Prepare the donut dough. Beat all the ingredients together until you get a homogeneous mixture without lumps. Cover with the film and let stand for about 10 minutes.
2. Chop the onion and pour it into the tank with the oil; Wrap each sausage with a slice of bacon and place on the onions with a few sprigs of fresh thyme. Pour 100 ml of water.
3. Cook for 15 minutes at 160^0C.
4. Turn the sausages and cook for 10 minutes. At the end of cooking, pour the donut dough over the sausages, turn off the bottom element and close.
5. Cook for 15 to 20 minutes depending on the degree of cooking desired.
6. Serve the toad in the still hot hole with a side sauce

Nutrition Value (Amount per Serving):

- Calories 366
- Fat 23.8g
- Carbohydrates 20.4g
- Fiber 3.4g
- Protein 11.9g
- Cholesterol 160 mg

Asparagus, Cheese and Speck Pie

Preparation time: 10-20 minutes,

Cooking time: 30-45 minutes;

Serve: 6

Ingredients:

- 150 g of green asparagus
- 150 g of water:
- 1 roll of broken dough
- 100 g of diced mota
- 100 g of Italian cow's milk cheese
- 3 eggs
- 100 ml of milk
- Salt to taste
- Pepper to taste

Direction:

1. Clean the asparagus. Cut them into small pieces and place them in the basket with the water.
2. Set the air fryer to 150°C.
3. Cook for about 15 minutes.
4. Remove the asparagus from the tank once cooked and wait for them to cool
5. Unroll the broken dough (leaving the baking paper) and then prick the bottom with a fork.
6. Arrange the diced speck and cheese and asparagus, then pour the prepared preparation.
7. Fold the edges of the dough in and cut the excess baking paper with scissors (keep the ends cut so you can easily rotate and extract the cake).
8. Cook another 25 minutes.

Nutrition Value (Amount per Serving):

- Calories 260
- Fat 17g
- Carbohydrates 18g
- Protein 7g

Mushroom, Egg and Mozzarella Cake

Preparation time: 10 minutes;

Cooking time: 50 minutes;

Serve: 6

Ingredients:

- 2 rolls of puff pastry: 2
- 300 g mushrooms
- 1 onion
- Parsley to taste
- 150 g mozzarella
- 3 eggs

Direction:

1. Clean the mushrooms well and chop them.
2. Spray the basket of the air fryer. Pour the chopped onion in the basket
3. Brown for 2 minutes at 160^0C.
4. Add the mushrooms and cook for another 15 minutes. Add (at discretion) salt and pepper, parsley, and finish cooking for another 3 minutes. Meanwhile, prepare hard boiled eggs.
5. In a bowl, mix the mushrooms with the crushed eggs and the chopped mozzarella, salt, and pepper.
6. Unroll the broken dough (leaving the baking paper) and then prick the bottom with a fork.
7. Arrange the egg and mushroom mixture and close with the other dough roll. Weld the edges well.
8. Brush the surface of the dough with egg yolk and prick the steam out.
9. Bake the cake for 30 minutes.

Nutrition Value (Amount per Serving):

- Calories 345.0
- Fat 28.6 g
- Carbohydrate 2.0 g
- Sugars 1.1 g
- Protein 20.4 g
- Cholesterol 464.1 mg

Roasted pears

Preparation time: 5 minutes;

Cooking time: 20 minutes;

Serve: 2

Ingredients:

4 portions

- 4 pears with rind well washed
- 50 g Raisins
- 2 tbsp jam without sugar
- 1 tsp honey
- 1 pinch cinnamon powder

Direction:

1. Pears are washed, hollowed out by extracting the heart.
2. Separate the pulp
3. Mix the jam chosen with the pulp of pears, honey and raisins and cinnamon
4. Fill the pears with that mixture
5. Place the pears in the fryer
6. In the bowl place a glass of water
7. Cook for 20 minutes at $180^\circ C$
8. Serve them alone or accompanied with a scoop of vanilla ice cream.

Nutrition Value (Amount per Serving):

- Calories 101
- Fat 0.3g
- Carbohydrates 27g
- Fiber 5.5g
- Sugars 17g
- Protein 0.6g

Gluten-Free Yogurt Cake

Preparation time: 10 minutes;

Cooking time: 40 minutes;

Serve: 2

Ingredients:

- 1 Greek yogurt
- 3 eggs
- 150 g sugar
- 100 g cream
- 50 g sunflower oil
- 50 g butter
- 200 g gluten free flour
- Salt
- 1 on yeast

Direction:

1. Put the eggs, yogurt, and sugar in the basket. Mix well. Add the rest of the ingredients and mix.
2. Put the dough in the sponge cake container, previously brushed with oil. Preheat the fryer and put the mold with the dough for 40 minutes at 170°C.
3. When it cools, unmold, and decorate to taste.

Nutrition Value (Amount per Serving):

- Calories 361.2
- Fat 10.9 g
- Carbohydrate 59.2 g
- Sugars 31.2 g
- Protein 9.6 g
- Cholesterol 53.1 mg

Rösti (Swiss Potatoes)

Preparation time: 10 minutes;

Cooking time: 15 minutes;

Serve: 4

Ingredients:

- 250 g peeled white potatoes
- 1 tbsp chopped chives
- Freshly ground black pepper
- 1 tbsp olive oil
- 2 tbsp sour cream
- 100 g smoked salmon

Direction:

1. Preheat the air fryer to 180°C. Grate the thick potatoes in a bowl and add three quarters of the scallions and salt and pepper to taste. Mix it well.

2. Grease the pizza tray with olive oil and distribute the potato mixture evenly throughout the pan. Press the grated potatoes against the pan and spread the top of the potato pie with olive oil.

3. Place the pizza tray in the fryer basket and place it in the air fryer. Set the timer to 15 minutes and fry the rösti until it has a pretty brown color on the outside and is soft and well done inside.

4. Cut the rösti into 4 quarters and place each quarter on a plate. Garnish with a tablespoon of sour cream and place the slices of salmon on the plate next to the rösti. Spread the rest of the scallions on sour cream and add a touch of ground pepper.

Nutrition Value (Amount per Serving):

- Calories 123.3
- Fat 6.9 g
- Carbohydrate 7.2 g
- Sugars 0.3 g
- Protein 7.5 g
- Cholesterol 27.4 mg

Thai Fish Cake with Mango Sauce

Preparation time: 20 minutes;

Cooking time: 14 minutes;

Serve: 4

Ingredients:

- 1 ripe mango
- 1 tsp and a half of red chili paste
- 3 tbsp fresh cilantro or parsley
- 1 lime juice and zest
- 500 g of white fish fillets
- 1 egg
- 1 chopped chive
- 50 g ground coconut

Direction:

1. Peel the mango and cut it into small dice. Mix the mango dice in a bowl with ½ teaspoon of red chili paste, 1 tablespoon of cilantro and the juice and zest of a lime.
2. Beat the fish in the kitchen robot and mix it with 1 egg, 1 teaspoon of salt and the rest of the lime zest, red chili paste and lime juice. Mix everything with the rest of the cilantro, chives and 2 tablespoons of coconut.
3. Place the rest of the coconut on a deep plate. Divide the fish mixture into 12 portions, shape them in round cakes and coat them with the coconut.
4. Place six fish cakes in the basket and place it in the air fryer at 180°C. Set the timer to 7 minutes and fry the cakes until golden brown and ready to drink. Fry in the same way the rest of the fish cakes.
5. Serve with mango sauce.

Nutrition Value (Amount per Serving):

- Calories 361
- Fat 22.8g
- Carbohydrate 13.8g
- Sugars 8.7g
- Protein 25.8g
- Cholesterol 93.9mg

Conclusion

Throughout this book, we have learned a lot about owning and using an air fryer. We can confidently say that the air fryer is one of the best inventions of kitchen appliances.

Healthy food should not be a fad or an impossibility to choose; it should be part of everyone's life. Of course, this does not mean that you must give up enjoying the kitchen; neither of the many dishes that can be prepared healthy. To get it there are certain appliances that can help you and a lot: for example, an air fryer.

In our earlier chapters, you could see that with an air fryer, you will cook different foods in a similar way as a traditional one would. But thanks to its special operation, you can do it without using a single drop of oil. In this way, you can prepare exquisite dishes without added fats and with a considerably lower caloric intake.

Now you know some of the many functions and recipes of an air fryer. We hope that this eBook has helped you discover some interesting features.

Having an air fryer is a great option. You can enjoy a healthier meal and save a good part of the oil expense, all without giving up enjoyable, fried foods

Please enjoy the different recipes that we have listed for you in this cookbook.

CPSIA information can be obtained
at www.ICGtesting.com
Printed in the USA
LVHW060348161020
668889LV00016B/479